Praise for

Stress Test: The Israel-Hamas War and Christian-Jewish Relations

Aptly titled *Stress Test*, these essays are the reflections of twelve Catholics and Protestants engaged for decades in Jewish-Christian dialogue and scholarship. The horrific terrorist attack on Israel on October 7, 2023, and the Israeli response escalated into a war that has wrought further Israeli deaths, the deaths of thousands of innocent Palestinians, and widespread destruction, displacement, and political destabilization. Inevitably, these events have altered the conversations between Jews and Christians, even among long-standing dialogue partners and friends. The essays in this book do not offer answers, either to the ongoing conflict or to the tensions in interreligious relations. They do offer thoughtful historical insights into this conflict, courageous and critical questions, and real compassion for all Israelis and Palestinians—a potential starting point for a different kind of conversation.

Victoria Barnett
Scholar, Author, Teacher

The women and men presented in *Stress Test: The Israel-Hamas War and Christian-Jewish Relations* are Christian veterans of the historic Jewish-Christian dialogue. No one in this volume rides a moral high horse. The scholars gathered here have spent their careers—their lives—preparing honestly and compassionately for this fraught moment.

James Carroll
Author, *Constantine's Sword: The Church and the Jews, A History*
and *Jerusalem, Jerusalem: How the Ancient City Ignited Our Modern World*

Stress Test: The Israel-Hamas War and Christian-Jewish Relations is a brilliant title for this beckoning book which invites readers into an imperative dialogue which must not be politely postponed until some more comfortable moment.

Joseph Cornelius Donnelly
Permanent Delegate Emeritus
Caritas Internationalis, United Nations, New York

Stress Test collects earnest, careful, and often agonized essays responding to 10/7 and the Israel-Hamas/Gaza war. It raises questions about what kind of conversation is needed and who needs to be in it. Reading this book is a valuable and illuminating exercise.

David P. Gushee
Distinguished University Professor of Christian Ethics
Mercer University

This timely and confronting book edited by Carol Rittner and John K. Roth propels the reader to move beyond thirty-second media grabs and binary formulations of parallel monologues to wrestle with profound questions central to issues arising from the Israel-Hamas war and its effect on Christian-Jewish dialogue.

Peta Goldburg, R.S.M.
Professor and Chair of Religious Education
Australian Catholic University

The Israeli-Palestinian conflict has long represented a fissure in the foundation of Jewish-Christian relations. At times, this fissure has remained hidden; at other times, its subterranean vibrations have been felt on the surface. In the wake of the Israel-Gaza war, this fissure threatens to become an abyss that swallows the entire structure. Can the building survive? One thing is certain: all attempts to negotiate and repair the breach will begin with this book, which is both fearless in its acknowledgment of realities on the ground and wise in its reliance on the hard-won lessons of the Holocaust and Jewish-Christian dialogue. *Stress Test: The Israel-Hamas War and Christian-Jewish Relations* is essential reading for anyone wishing to assess the implications of the ongoing conflict.

Stephen R. Haynes
A.B. Curry Professor of Religious Studies
Rhodes College

Jews, Christians, and Muslims who have been working to turn the page in a centuries-old story of conflict between religious traditions now find themselves, in the thick of the Israel-Hamas war, challenged to recognize the friend they thought they knew. Conscious of the sense of abandonment and betrayal of trust experienced by their colleagues, the contributors to *Stress Test* pose the necessary, even if uncomfortable, questions to be addressed if erstwhile companions in dialogue are to find their way back to one another.

Russell McDougall, C.S.C.
Executive Director, Secretariat of Ecumenical and Interreligious Affairs
US Conference of Catholic Bishops, Washington, DC

Stress Test

Stress Test

The Israel-Hamas War and Christian-Jewish Relations

Edited and Introduced

by

Carol Rittner and John K. Roth

iPub Cloud International

Poughkeepsie, New York

Published in the United States by
iPub Cloud International
Poughkeepsie, New York 12603
www.ipubcloud.org

Copyright © 2025 by Carol Rittner and John K. Roth

All rights reserved. No part of this book may be reproduced, stored in a retrieval system, or transmitted, in any form or by any means, electronic, mechanical, photocopying, recording, or otherwise, without the express written permission of the publisher.

Unless otherwise noted, Scripture quotations are taken from the New Revised Standard Version Bible, copyright © 1989 National Council of the Churches of Christ in the United States of America. Used with permission. All rights reserved worldwide.

Library of Congress Control Number: 2024925551

ISBN: 978-1-948575-79-9 (paperback)
ISBN: 978-1-948575-82-9 (hardback)
ISBN: 978-1-948575-80-5 (ebook)

To

CCJR

The Council of Centers on Jewish-Christian Relations

You are not obligated to finish the work. Neither are you free to desist from it.

—Pirkei Avot 2:21

Putting away falsehood, let all of us speak the truth to our neighbors, for we are members of one another.

—Ephesians 4:25

Contents

Acknowledgments263	xi
Prologue: Rights and Wrongs	
Carol Rittner and John K. Roth	1
A Timeline 1945–2024	
Carol Rittner and John K. Roth	15
PART ONE: FRANK DIALOGUE	50
1 Conflicted, Not Confused	
Carol Rittner	55
2 The Impact of the Israel-Hamas War on Christian-Jewish Relations: The Historical and Ethical Context	
John T. Pawlikowski	69
3 Reflections on Catholic-Jewish Relations in Light of the Israel-Hamas War	
Philip A. Cunningham	85
4 A Dream Betrayed	
Christopher M. Leighton	99
PART TWO: WHAT WE OWE EACH OTHER	115
5 Protesting the Israel-Hamas War: Implications for Relations Between Christians and Jews	
Mary C. Boys	119
6 Catholic-Jewish Relations and Their Discontents: The Israel-Hamas War, the Holocaust, and a Globalized World	
Massimo Faggioli	133
7 Learning and Lamenting: At the Corner of Union and Division	
Elena Procario-Foley	145

8 The Israel-Hamas War: Challenges and Opportunities for Interreligious Dialogue

    James G. Paharik   **161**

PART THREE: I WILL NOT BE SILENT   173

9 Admitting the Sins of Christian-Jewish Relations

    Michael G. Azar   177

10 Stresses of the Israel-Hamas War: Interfaith and Intrafaith

    Peter A. Pettit   193

11 Holocaust Remembrance, Theodicy, and Christian Zionism

    Sarah K. Pinnock   209

12 Making the Best of What We Have

    John K. Roth   225

Epilogue: An Enormous Effort

    Carol Rittner and John K. Roth   243

Selected Bibliography   253

Editors and Contributors   259

Index   263

Acknowledgments

On December 13, 2023, with the death toll in the two-month-old Israel-Hamas war approaching 20,000, we (Carol Rittner and John K. Roth) sent invitations to American Christian friends who have long been leaders in advancing Christian-Jewish relations. We asked them to join us in writing a book that assesses how that war affects those important interactions.

About a month later, as the writing circle formed and explorations with book publishers advanced, we learned that another friend, Rabbi James Rudin, had coauthored a book called *Why (Not) Me? Searching for God When We Suffer*. Its publisher, iPub Cloud International, was new to us but not for long.

Website visits underscored iPub's commitment to interreligious dialogue. To find out more, we contacted Jim Rudin, whose enthusiasm included encouragement for us to explore working with Sandy Mayer, iPub's publishing director, and her partners. Our thanks go to Jim for his guidance because the fit proved right. We are deeply grateful for the conscientious expertise, energy, and efficiency that Sandy and her colleagues—especially Jessica DiDonato, Elyse Draper, Janine Phillips, Zizi Subiyarta, Esther Elizabeth Suson, Carolyn Wooddall, and Jennifer Wyman—devoted to ensuring the deft and punctual publication of this timely book.

Some books can be written only by a single author. Others depend on more. We have published more than a dozen books together. None of them could have been created by either of us alone. As editors, moreover, we are profoundly indebted to the many scholars and teachers who have joined us to produce significant works like this one, which could not exist without teamwork.

Stress Test illustrates that creating a writing team, and getting it to function well, can be difficult. Not everyone we contacted was willing to engage in an unavoidably fraught and contentious challenge, one that required American Christians to address the atrocities, carnage, and suffering of the Israel-Hamas war. Those who accepted had to make tough choices about how to handle demanding questions that we insisted the book must address lest it become little more than "polite diplomacy," a phrase that Jim Rudin uses—not in complimentary ways—to describe

Acknowledgments

much of what passes for Christian-Jewish dialogue. *Stress Test* writers rose to the occasion. With candor and clarity, conviction and compassion, they created compelling narratives and telling assessments. We know, furthermore, that they join us in expressing thanks to readers who accept the invitation to advance the interchanges that this book opens but must not close.

Books are usually dedicated to people. *Stress Test*, however, is dedicated to an organization: The Council of Centers for Jewish-Christian Relations (CCJR). Established in 2001, CCJR (https://ccjr.us/) is an association of centers and institutes in the United States and Canada devoted to enhancing mutual understanding between Christians and Jews. Most of this book's contributors are affiliated with CCJR. Especially in stressful times, we express heartfelt appreciation for this organization's salutary work and ongoing encouragement. Special gratitude goes to Stress Test contributor Philip A. Cunningham for the archive of documents about the impact of the Israel-Hamas war on Christian-Jewish relations that he has compiled and sustained for CCJR (https://ccjr.us/dialogika-resources/themes-in-today-s-dialogue/israel-hamas). We also thank Daniel Myers, president of Misericordia University, for permission to use assets from the Sister Carol Rittner, R.S.M. Holocaust Fund to support the publication of this book.

Carol Rittner and John K. Roth

Prologue
Rights and Wrongs

Carol Rittner and John K. Roth

This book promotes dialogue. It does so by raising questions and focusing challenges that need to be confronted by American Christians who are committed to advancing good Christian-Jewish relations amid the current Israel-Hamas war and its aftermath. Those relations comprise not only organizations and communities—including churches, synagogues, and temples—but also personal relationships, many of them deeply bonded friendships. Interactions between Christians and Jews have a long and often troubling history, but since World War II, the connections have grown closer while embracing pluralism that respects diversity and difference. The Israel-Hamas war threatens to derail Christian-Jewish relations. To avoid that unfortunate outcome, Christians and Jews must engage clearly and candidly, critically and compassionately, about the war and its aftermath. *Stress Test*—this book's title—warns that the task is difficult.

One reason for the difficulty is that *Stress Test* entered the publication process in October 2024, one year after the Israel-Hamas war began. The war, a decisive crisis in the decades-long and often violent Israeli-Palestinian conflict, was ongoing at that time. Much about it will remain unresolved when the book appears in 2025 and thereafter. Time's passage means that the book cannot deal with events that took place after the writing ended, but that fact does not outdate the questions and responses highlighted in the chapters that follow. To the contrary, with the war's resolution in suspense, the work of twelve Christians from the United States grows in importance as they probe what they and their traditions need to say and do to keep Christian-Jewish relations on the right track. They do not speak with one voice. At times, they strongly disagree, but they concur that the Israel-Hamas war creates a stress test for Christian-Jewish relations that must be confronted and surmounted.

Applicable in a variety of human activities—health, finance, and engineering, for example—the concept of a stress test fits this volume's investigations in three ways: (1) Stress testing assesses heart health. (2) It looks for breaking points and strategies for managing them. (3) Stress testing concentrates on risk and resilience. The Israel-Hamas war stress tests Christian-Jewish relations in all those ways.

At the heart of good Christian-Jewish relations is a determination to stand together through thick and thin, to resist paralyzing seizures and forestall fatal attacks. Good Christian-Jewish relations recognize that the ability to withstand breaking points must not be taken for granted. Unfortunately, the stress is often too great. Thus, failure can never be ruled out. But, if the right steps are taken, a permanently fractured outcome need not take place. Good Christian-Jewish relations do not ignore or walk away from the risks of disagreement that live within them. Far from blocking and undermining those relationships, the risks can foster resilience to keep working through them together. The Israel-Hamas war will change Christian-Jewish relations. How those war-affected relations can change for the better—that is what this book is about. So, *Stress Test* begins where the pressure is acute: the Gaza Strip, a Palestinian enclave twenty-five miles long and six miles wide.

Nowhere Safe to Go

Before October 7, 2023, most Americans knew little and cared less about the Gaza Strip, a 140-square-mile territory on the eastern coast of the Mediterranean Sea, bordered by Egypt to the south and the State of Israel to the north and east. The ignorance and indifference changed early that 10/7 morning when Hamas—provoked by Israel's long-standing siege of Gaza and the expansion of Jewish settlements in the West Bank—launched a gruesome surprise attack against Israel.[1]

Supported by Iran, Hamas's attack, the deadliest single-day assault on Jews since the Holocaust and among the saddest days in Israeli history, killed more than 1,200 Israelis and foreign nationals, including at least thirty-five American citizens living in Israel.[2] Hamas took more than 250 hostages—children, women, and elderly people among them. In addition, the United Nations found that "there are reasonable grounds to believe that conflict-related sexual violence—including rape and gang-rape—occurred across multiple locations of Israel and the Gaza periphery during the attacks."[3] The Hamas attack traumatized Israel and put Jews on anxious alert worldwide.

The sources of Hamas terror and Israeli trauma are often burrowed deep and emerge from underground. After Hamas gained control of Gaza in 2007, it vastly expanded a network of militarized tunnels, now estimated to be between 350 and 450 miles long.[4] The Israeli army calls it the "Gaza metro." Hamas has long used the tunnels—housing cities beneath cities—to advance its struggle against Israel. They have enabled Hamas to smuggle goods into Gaza, to move armed militants from place to place within Gaza, to manufacture weapons and store food, to terrorize Israelis living on the border with Gaza, to provide military headquarters for planning how to fight the Israeli army, and to imprison hostages taken by Hamas on October 7, 2023.

The Hamas tunnel network winds under schools and hospitals, mosques and community centers, as well as under homes and apartment complexes in Gaza, making it difficult for the Israel Defense Forces (IDF) to neutralize, if not defeat, Hamas without destroying the tunnel system and the structures above it, often populated by civilians. As carried out by the Israeli military, that strategy—including massive tunnel-busting bombardments—has displaced millions of defenseless, non-Hamas Palestinians and killed thousands more, with Israeli warnings about the need to evacuate making too little difference. With cynical calculation, Hamas knows that its tunnel-facilitated violence does a great deal to put Gaza's Palestinian population at risk. The decimation of Palestinian civilians has produced international sympathy for them and considerable hostility toward the State of Israel.

With Hamas and its lethal tunnel system bearing significant responsibility for the carnage in a hideous war, Israel's counteroffensive after 10/7 has made Gaza uninhabitable. Facing constant exhaustion, hunger, and fear, more than two million defenseless Palestinians have become refugees with nowhere safe to go in a homeland that has been called "the world's biggest open-air prison."[5] Aryeh Neier, a Holocaust survivor and the cofounder of Human Rights Watch, has been so concerned about what he calls Israel's "sustained policy of obstructing the movement of humanitarian assistance into the territory" that he claimed "Israel is engaged in genocide against Palestinians in Gaza."[6] No issue about the Israel-Hamas war has been more hotly and divisively debated than that one.[7]

Adding fuel to the fire, battles between Iran-backed and Lebanon-based Hezbollah and the Israeli military have worsened and displaced more than 60,000 Israelis from their northern Israel homes.[8] In another region, the West Bank, a 2,000-square-mile area occupied by Israel since the June 1967 Six-Day War, tensions have increased between almost three million Palestinians, many of them refugees, and half a million Israelis, portending violence that will make hopes for a two-state solution increasingly forlorn.[9] Not only that is discouraging. According to

Benjamin Netanyahu, Israel's prime minister, Iran must be checked because it is fighting Israel on "a seven-front war." Beyond Hamas in Gaza and Hezbollah in Lebanon, that dire situation includes Houthis in Yemen, Iran-backed militias in Iraq and Syria as well as in the West Bank, and Iran itself, which directly attacked Israel in April and September 2024. Unless a good resolution is found, the Israel-Hamas war could be the prelude to much more Gaza-level violence and prolonged devastation.[10] The IDF's 2024 killings of Hezbollah leader Hassan Nasrallah (September 27) and Hamas's Yahya Sinwar (October 16), who masterminded the 10/7 attack on Israel, raised some hopes that "the day after" the current warfare might be at hand, but that optimism is hollow.

In the United States, as controversy and upheaval ignited by the Israel-Hamas war grind on, some two dozen Holocaust museums continue to teach about the Nazi genocide against the European Jews during World War II.[11] Visitors usually learn that many Holocaust survivors immigrated to Palestine and to the new State of Israel in 1948 and thereafter. Often, the museum visitors are young people. Many are Jewish; most are not. But they all have questions, and those questions sometimes illustrate that for younger Americans, the humanitarian crisis in Gaza is more present and pressing than the Holocaust, an event that recedes increasingly into the past. American Holocaust museums have new challenges during the Israel-Hamas war. How can they best teach about the Holocaust when the eyes of their younger visitors may be on Gaza and on Palestinians who have nowhere safe to go?

Israel and the Israelis

In March 2024, the journalist Nicholas Kristof raised an important question: "Does the West have a double standard when it comes to Israel, pouncing on everything it does with undue harshness?"[12] What would the United States have done in response to an attack like the one Hamas launched against Israel on October 7, 2023? Outrage explodes about Israel's military intervention in Gaza, including the civilian casualties resulting from cruel urban warfare, but Americans usually have no qualms about justifying the far worse destruction caused by the bombing of German and Japanese cities—including the atomic bombing of Hiroshima and Nagasaki—during World War II.

"It is undeniably true," Kristof continued, "that the world applies more scrutiny to Israel's oppression of Palestinians than to many other horrors." Nevertheless, he insisted, "there is a reason to focus on Gaza today, for it is not just one more place of pain among many contenders." Gaza, Kristof contended, has been "the world's most dangerous place to be a child." Most Americans, including most American Christians, support

Israel in its war against Hamas. Unfortunately, that means complicity in making Gaza an especially unhopeful and lethal place to be a child. Crucially needed are commitments, including those found in good Christian-Jewish relations, that change those desperate circumstances for the better.

October 7, 2023, must not be forgotten, overlooked, or minimized. On that day, Hamas militants stormed across the Gaza border. They attacked Israeli kibbutzim, destroying homes, killing Jews and foreign workers, raping women, and kidnapping men, women, and children. Those events triggered the current Israel-Hamas war, bringing with it an upsurge of antisemitism that unjustly adds to the war's harm and misery.

After months of war, Israel's superior military might has not achieved the clear-cut victory it seeks. Israel has crippled but not destroyed Hamas. Nor has Israel eliminated the possibility that a terrorist organization, embedded among civilians and using its own Palestinian people as human shields, will still exert political influence, if not control, in the postwar politics of Gaza. Unable or unwilling to uphold traditional values relative to protecting civilians in a war zone, Benjamin Netanyahu and his war cabinet have dragged Israel into the grievous zone of war crimes and crimes against humanity, if not genocide.

Displacement compounds the misery of Palestinians in Gaza. The numbers are hugely different, but thousands of Israelis were also displaced by the 10/7 Hamas invasion, and many more in the north have been dislocated by Hezbollah's drone and missile attacks on towns and villages in Galilee and along the border with Lebanon. "It is time for this war to stop," writes Ron Kronish, an Israeli rabbi, adding that "most people in Israel agree with this by now, as do most leaders in the international community."[13] Eventually, the war will stop, but irretrievable losses will continue to mount before it does. That means something ominous about the war-related statistics that inform *Stress Test*'s assessment of the Israel-Hamas war's impact on Christian-Jewish relations: most of the statistics are undercounts; as long as the conflict continues, the statistics will usually have to be revised upward.

By early autumn 2024, more than 40,000 Palestinians, mostly civilians, had been killed—another 92,000 wounded—in the Israel-Hamas war.[14] Millions more Palestinians have escaped death only to be displaced, devastated, and traumatized for life. What about Israel and the Israelis? Taking 10/7 to be an existential threat to the nation's future, Israel exercised its right to defend itself. The cost has been high, including 704 soldiers and sixty-three police officers killed in the Israel-Hamas war.[15] In fact, the costs are incalculable. Not only have hundreds of Israeli soldiers and civilians lost their lives during the Israel-Hamas war, but also 10/7 and its aftermath leave Israeli families bereft. Parents, sons, and daughters have been killed and injured, taken hostage, killed in captivity. Women have been raped, mutilated, and traumatized for life. As a result of 10/7 and the ensuing war, Israelis are suffering and will continue to suffer. True, far more Palestinians than Israelis have been killed or injured, but every life is precious.

What is the Israel-Hamas war doing, what has the war done, to the State of Israel as well as to Israelis? Maybe nothing good, nothing positive, but the answer to that question hangs in suspense. So much depends on the choices that Israel and Israelis will make, especially regarding Palestinian statehood.

Demanding Questions

Old Christian friends—one a Roman Catholic, the other a Protestant—Carol Rittner and John K. Roth have spent decades learning, teaching, and writing about the Holocaust and Christianity's complicity in that genocide. Our commitments continue to make us deeply concerned about Christian-Jewish relations. Like other Christians with a profile like ours—Holocaust scholars who came of age in the 1960s and 1970s—we hold views that are friendly and favorable toward the State of Israel, but by no means are those loyalties uncritical, let alone naïve or gullible. To the contrary, our Holocaust insight focuses attention not only on antisemitism but also on Islamophobia. It requires defense of human rights wherever they are abused and strengthens determination to protest war crimes and crimes against humanity wherever they take place.

The Israel-Hamas war deepens those concerns. It led us to develop *Stress Test: The Israel-Hamas War and Christian-Jewish Relations*, a book that explores how Christian-Jewish relations are faring and what they need to be during anguished times and agonizing circumstances in Israel, Gaza, and the West Bank. Both of us participate in the work of the Council of Centers for Jewish-Christian Relations (CCJR). The CCJR is primarily an association of centers and institutes in the United States and Canada devoted to enhancing mutual understanding between Christians and Jews, but individuals committed to the CCJR's goals can belong as well.[16] Most of the contributors to this book are affiliated with the Council, which means that they have long been committed to improving interfaith relationships and to sustaining that aim even when, indeed especially when, those relationships are veering off track and can be derailed.

As this book's timeline details, the decades-long Israeli-Palestinian conflict has often been violent but never more extremely so than in the current Israel-Hamas war. We saw that the situation required Christians like us to wrestle with tough, demanding questions—not so much to answer them, least of all to answer them with finality and closure, but to self-interrogate so that we would be better prepared, more honestly positioned, to engage with Jewish (and Christian) friends and colleagues in dialogue that is bound to be painful if it breaks through polite diplomacy—as it must—and finds new ways to move through the scarred terrain of a devastating war and its problematic aftermath.

Our invitation to Christian colleagues to contribute to *Stress Test* included guidance from the team at iPub Cloud International, our publisher, who urged us to develop a book that speaks clearly, honestly, and courageously about the carnage unleashed by the Hamas attack on October 7, 2023, the State of Israel's devastating response, and the impacts and implications of these tragic events on Christian-Jewish relations. They urged that *Stress Test* should recognize the anger, frustration, and grief that grip people, especially young people, as they confront the violence and the immense humanitarian crisis in Gaza. No deflection or "watering down," they implored. Instead, they insisted on straightforward engagement with demanding questions.

Fortified and encouraged by our publisher's expectations, we realized that the book's coherence required unifying themes. We challenged the contributors to address, in ways of their own choosing, two fundamental questions and a variety of subtopics under both. Write, we said, about what is foremost on your mind—as a Christian with American perspectives—concerning the Israel-Hamas war and Christian-Jewish relations, emphasizing that the chapters and the book as a whole should address as many of the following questions as possible.

First, how has the current Israel-Hamas war affected your understanding of—and outlook for—Christian-Jewish relations? That question suggests others: (1) How do you understand the place—the importance—of the State of Israel in Christian-Jewish relations? Is the State of Israel essential for the identity and security of the Jewish people? (2) How does the plight and future of Palestinians affect the way you think about and respond to the impact of the Israel-Hamas war on Christian-Jewish relations? (3) How do your American perspectives affect your thinking on such questions? (4) Do you think of yourself as a Zionist? Are you pro-Palestinian? (5) If you stand in solidarity with the State of Israel and/or the Palestinian people, what does that mean? (5) How do you distinguish between (a) the State of Israel and its policies, especially Benjamin Netanyahu's, and (b) the people of Israel? (6) How does your commitment to Christian-Jewish relations include—or exclude—commitment to the well-being of and statehood for Palestinians? (7) To what extent is religion a factor in the Israel-Hamas war and its outcome, and what difference might your response make for Christian-Jewish relations? (8) Are the biblical land promises part of what has been called the irrevocability of God's covenant with Israel?

Second, as a Christian with American perspectives, what do you identify as the most important ethical issues and political consequences of the current Israel-Hamas war? What are their implications for Christian-Jewish relations? Again, those questions suggest others: (1) Do you think that Hamas and/or Israel have committed war crimes, crimes against humanity, or even genocide? (2) To what extent does Israel have a right to defend itself? Does that right include destroying Hamas? (3) Do Palestinians have a right to a state of their own? If so, what do you think they should do—and not do—to achieve it? (4) What is your position on American policy regarding Israel and the Israel-Hamas war and its aftermath? (5) What should happen when the war ends? Do you favor a two-state solution? If so, what solution do you support? If not, what outcome to the war do you favor? How might or should your responses to these questions affect Christian-Jewish relations?

True Dialogue

Such stress-testing questions are complicated, even controversial, but if work for beneficial Christian-Jewish relations is to be honest and credible, responsible and loyal to what is right and good, they cannot be evaded. Christians committed to that cause need to reflect and speak about them, not to state "last words" that close discussion but to provide opening words intended to promote dialogue. Those words can be pro-Israeli, pro-Palestinian, and both. They also need to be, as Nicholas Kristof argues, "anti-massacre, anti-starvation and anti-rape."[17]

More verb than noun, *dialogue* refers not only to what has been said and recorded but also to the ongoing action of sharing, discussing, and changing what a person or community affirms and rejects, explores and probes, reconsiders and questions. At its best, dialogue changes and even transforms the people who pursue it. Intensive and open listening, thoughtful and considerate speaking, receptive and respectful sharing of silence—when dialogue changes people deep down, all these elements are more important than arguing and debating, although those actions also have a place in seeking clarity and in honestly expressing the convictions that sound dialogue tests and revises.

True dialogue embraces questioning, responding, and questioning some more. Such inquiry weighs the strengths and weaknesses of different views. It aims at a more balanced and complete perspective than one's starting points or even one's conclusions provide. Sound dialogue pursues truth but stays humble about possessing it. Errors and mistakes are common; there is always more to find out. Disagreements arise, but wise dialogue says, Let the discussion unfold. Listen better. Keep evaluating what is said. Follow where questioning and evidence lead. Do not give up.

Dialogue underscores that people differ, and communities are diverse. Pluralism is a fact, a fundamental aspect of reality. In a crowded human world, moreover, pluralism means that people and communities need to understand and mediate their differences to minimize destructive conflict and to maximize constructive interaction.

When done well, dialogue among people and communities opens new inquiries and expands outlooks. The results are not known or even knowable in advance. By focusing on the ways in which the Israel-Hamas war stress-tests Christian-Jewish relations, this book explores how those challenges, upsetting to conventional wisdom and tradition though they are, can help to transform human relations.

Commencement

In 1948, the year in which the State of Israel was established, Brandeis University, grounded in Jewish values and experiences, was founded in Waltham, Massachusetts, in response to antisemitism and discrimination against Jews at American universities. Named after Louis Brandeis, the first Jewish justice on the Supreme Court of the United States, the university strives for inclusivity as it seeks to expand the legacy of Brandeis, who affirmed that "the most important political office is that of the private citizen." Championing freedom of inquiry and speech, Brandeis also held that "repression breeds hate; that hate menaces stable government; that the path of safety lies in the opportunity to discuss freely supposed grievances and proposed remedies; and that the fitting remedy for evil counsels is good ones."[18]

On November 7, 2023, Brandeis University—about 35 percent of its undergraduates identify as Jews—became the first private American university to ban a local chapter of National Students for Justice in Palestine (SJP), doing so, the university said, because that group "openly supports Hamas, a terrorist organization," a position "not protected by Brandeis' principles of free speech."[19] Within the university and outside it as well, debate churned about this decision and the reasoning that drove it. As winter came and went, Brandeis remained deeply concerned about upheaval on American campuses from the Israel-Hamas war, including antisemitic hostility against Jewish undergraduates. On April 22, 2024, an open letter to the Brandeis community from President Ron Liebowitz announced that the university would extend its transfer application deadline by several weeks to "welcome all—Jews and students from every background—who seek an excellent undergraduate education and an environment striving to be free of harassment and Jew-hatred."[20]

Meanwhile, the acclaimed American filmmaker, Ken Burns, delivered the 2024 commencement address at Brandeis on Sunday morning, May 19. Observing that he has been in "the business of history" for a long time, Burns stressed that history's stories have taught him important lessons worth remembering and passing along from one generation to another.[21]

"I've been struggling for most of my life," Burns said, "to try to tell good, complex, sometimes contradictory stories, appreciating nuance and subtlety and undertow, sharing the confusion and consternation of unreconciled opposites." And then he spoke about what worries him:

> Everything is either right or wrong, red state or blue state, young or old, gay or straight, rich or poor, Palestinian or Israeli, my way or the highway. Everywhere we are trapped by these old, tired, binary reactions, assumptions, and certainties.... That preoccupation is imprisoning.... We forget the inconvenient complexities of history and of human nature. That, for example, three great religions, their believers, all children of Abraham, each professing at the heart of their teaching a respect for all human life, each with a central connection to and legitimate claim to the same holy ground, violate their own dictates of conduct and make this perpetually contested land a shameful graveyard.

Burns concluded this part of his commencement address by recalling how "a very wise person with years of experience with the Middle East" had recently challenged him: "Could you hold the idea that there could be two wrongs and two rights?"

Far from being only a graduation ceremony, a conclusion or an ending, *commencement* signifies a beginning, the pioneering of something new and needed. Holding the challenge that there could be two wrongs and two rights commences the work that the chapters in this book— individually and collectively—try to do. Pursuing that work is an ongoing stress test for Christians who seek to sustain good Christian-Jewish relations amid the Israel-Hamas war. In that work, what Burns calls "complex, sometimes contradictory stories" will be found. The chapters that follow appreciate "nuance and subtlety and undertow" as they share "the confusion and consternation of unreconciled opposites." In those struggles, which are embedded not only within individual chapters but also in the encounters and even collisions among them, important lessons that are worth remembering and passing along from one generation to another await discovery by the readers of *Stress Test*.

Contextualizing those lessons, this book's significant timeline directs attention to key moments and particularities necessary for confronting the decades-long Israeli-Palestinian conflict and the Israel-Hamas war. A page-turn away, the timeline is a not-to-be-missed prequel to the chapters after it.

Notes

1. For a reliable snapshot of Hamas, see Kali Robinson, "What Is Hamas?" Council on Foreign Relations, April 18, 2024, https://bit.ly/4h6VZoZ.

2. According to CSIS, "The October 7 attack was the deadliest terrorist attack against Israel since the state's establishment in 1948, and the scale of the death toll was unprecedented in Israeli history." For significant details about the comparative magnitude of the Hamas attack, see Daniel Byman et al., "Hamas's October 7 Attack: Visualizing the Data," Center for Strategic and International Studies (CSIS), December 19, 2023, https://bit.ly/4hq4zPh.

3. "Reasonable Grounds to Believe Conflict-related Sexual Violence Occurred in Israel During 7 October Attacks, Senior UN Official Tells Security Council," United Nations Security Council, March 11, 2024, https://bit.ly/42tAt9b. On the fraught issue of the extent of Hamas's sexualized violence and alleged use of rape as a weapon of war, see Tia Goldenberg and Julia Frankel, "How 2 Debunked Accounts of Sexual Violence on Oct. 7 Fueled a Global Dispute over Israel-Hamas War," ABC News, May 21, 2024, https://bit.ly/4h53mNJ. See also https://www.oct7factcheck.com/.

4. For further graphic information about the Hamas tunnel network, see Adolfo Arranz et al., "Inside the Tunnels of Gaza: The Scale, and the Sophistication, of Hamas's Tunnel Network," Reuters, December 31, 2023, https://bit.ly/3PM5RbH. See also Joby Warrick and Loveday Morris, "Hamas Built an Underground War Machine to Ensure Its Own Survival," *Washington Post*, October 5, 2024, https://bit.ly/4jwkb5B.

5. For a helpful thumbnail sketch of Gaza, see Fatima Al-Kassab, "What Is the Gaza Strip? Here's What to Know," NPR (National Public Radio), October 10, 2023, https://bit.ly/3E8WHU1. For the "open-air prison" description, see Scott Simon and Hadeel Al-Shalchi, "Gaza Is Called an Open-air Prison. How Did It Get to This?" NPR (National Public Radio), November 4, 2023, https://bit.ly/3E6TtQJ.

6. Aryeh Neier, "Is Israel Committing Genocide" *New York Review*, June 6, 2024, 9–13, https://bit.ly/3CiMzHL. See also Neier's follow up, "Counting the Dead in Gaza," *New York Review*, June 20, 2024, https://bit.ly/3CpK2vo.

Prologue

7. For helpful commentary on this point, see Linda Kinstler, "The Bitter Fight Over the Meaning of 'Genocide,'" *New York Times Magazine*, August 20, 2024, https://bit.ly/3CpK2vo.

8. See Isabel Kershner, "In Hezbollah's Sights, a Stretch of Northern Israel Becomes a No-Go Zone," *New York Times*, March 28, 2024, https://bit.ly/4h2SKia. A few months after Kershner's report, the number of displaced Israelis in the north had risen to 75,000. For helpful background about Hezbollah, see Kali Robinson, "What Is Hezbollah?" Council on Foreign Relations, October 4, 2024, https://bit.ly/4hv7QwQ.

9. See "Israel/OPT: Palestinians Face Drastic Escalation in Unlawful Killings, Displacement as Israel Launches West Bank Military Operation," Amnesty International, August 28, 2024, https://bit.ly/4jyb0BU.

10. On these points, see Elliot Abrams et al., "One Year After the October 7 Attacks: The Impact on Four Fronts," Council on Foreign Relations, October 2, 2024, https://bit.ly/3WwQZ4C; Fawaz A. Gerges, "The Rising Risk of a New Forever War," *New York Times*, September 30, 2024, https://bit.ly/40Kj8HX; and Amy Mackinnon and Jack Detsch, "What War Is Israel Fighting?" *Foreign Policy*, September 12, 2024, https://bit.ly/42upvk4. See also Kim Hjelmgaard, "Spiking West Bank Violence Adds to Israel's Growing Collection of Conflicts, *USA Today*, September 12, 2024, https://bit.ly/3Wzncbr. See further, Tom O'Connor, "Israel's War with Iran on Seven Fronts," *Newsweek*, July 3, 2024, https://bit.ly/4husuNr. For helpful background about the Houthis, see Kali Robinson, "Iran's Support of the Houthis: What to Know," Council on Foreign Relations, March 1, 2024, https://bit.ly/40tcdSe.

11. On this topic, see Dana Goldstein and Marc Tracy, "Holocaust Museums Debate What to Say about the Israel-Hamas War," *New York Times*, June 3, 2024, https://bit.ly/40L05Nw.

12. Nicholas Kristof, "Israel, Gaza, and Double Standards, Including Our Own," *New York Times*, March 2, 2024, https://bit.ly/3PQ8WYb.

13. Ron Kronish, "Raise Your Voice Now for Ending the War and Seeking Peace," *Times of Israel*, June 6, 2024, https://bit.ly/40KQPcd.

14. This book frequently cites statistics about the Israel-Hamas war. They come from reliable sources, but the "fog of war" entails that the numbers often lack verifiable precision, need revision, and may be contested. On such points, see "Gaza Death Toll: How Many Palestinians Has Israel's Campaign Killed?" Reuters, August 15, 2024, https://bit.ly/4gbM5kz. This article includes discussion about the debates that swirl around the casualty and fatality statistics from the Israel-Hamas war. Particularly on the Palestinian side, the statistics typically come from the Gaza Health Ministry (GHM), whose counts do not distinguish between civilians and combatants. The State of Israel often contests the GHM numbers, finding them too high, but the United Nations, the World Health Organization, and Human Rights Watch tend to consider the GHM's data reliable.

15. See Emanuel Fabian, "Authorities Name 704 Soldiers, 63 Police Officers Killed in Gaza War," *Times of Israel*, August 28, 2024, https://bit.ly/4hoPLQM.

16. For more information, see the CCJR website: https://ccjr.us/. This website includes an extensive archive of writings and documents about the Israel-Hamas war, carefully curated by Philip A. Cunningham, one of the contributors to *Stress Test*, who is professor of theology and director of the Institute for Jewish-Catholic Relations at Saint Joseph's University, Philadelphia. See https://bit.ly/3PP6OzR.

17. Nicholas Kristof, "How to Think Through the Moral Tangle in Gaza," *New York Times*, June 1, 2024, https://bit.ly/4ayUgWI.

18. See Brandeis's concurring opinion in *Whitney v. California* (1927), https://bit.ly/3WzpSpv.

19. See Jericho Tran, "Brandeis University Bans Pro-Palestinian Student Group," NBC Boston, November 7, 2023, https://bit.ly/4g88u21.

20. Ron Leibowitz, "Extending Transfer Application Deadline," April 22, 2024, https://bit.ly/4jrxgNB. Five months later, on September 25, 2024, Leibowitz resigned his presidency after a close vote of no confidence from the Brandeis faculty. The allegations against him included "excessive responses to student protests."

21. The text of Burn's Brandeis University commencement address is accessible at: https://bit.ly/4asWZ49.

A Timeline
1945–2024

Carol Rittner and John K. Roth

On January 14, 2025, Israel and Hamas agreed to a phased ceasefire that may end the devastating war in Gaza, which started when Hamas attacked Israel on October 7, 2023. This timeline identifies major events in the Israeli-Palestinian conflict from 1945 to 2024. Sources include the Associated Press, the Council on Foreign Relations, the *New York Times*, the United Nations, the United States Holocaust Memorial Museum, and the *Washington Post*.

1945

May 7–8   V-E Day: Nazi Germany surrenders. World War II in Europe ends. The perpetrators of Nazi Germany's genocidal "Final Solution" have murdered two-thirds of Europe's Jews, approximately six million persons.

1945–1946

David Ben-Gurion, the leader of the Jewish community in British-controlled Palestine, visits postwar DP (displaced persons) camps, where more than 250,000 Jewish survivors await opportunities to relocate. Ben-Gurion's visits encourage immigration to Palestine. By 1952, despite British restrictions, approximately 136,000 Jewish survivors reach Palestine and the new State of Israel.

1947

November 29   The post-World War I mandate from the League of Nations (1922) that confirmed British military and administrative control of Palestine honored language from the so-called Balfour Declaration (1917), which proclaimed support for a Jewish national home. On November 29, 1947, the General Assembly of the United Nations (UN) passes

Resolution 181. (As a "permanent observer" at the United Nations, the Holy See does not participate in the vote.) Resolution 181 calls for a two-state partition of Palestine. The Arab-Palestinian state, with an estimated population of almost 800,000, including 10,000 Jews, occupies 42 percent of the divided territory. The Jewish state, with an estimated population of almost 900,000, including more than 400,000 Arab Palestinians, occupies 56 percent of the territory, with the remaining area—Jerusalem and Bethlehem—internationalized. The Jewish community accepts the partition. The Arab community does not.

1948

February 11 — The Holy See creates the office of Apostolic Delegate to Jerusalem and pre-State of Israel Palestine to maintain relations with Palestine, which the Vatican calls the Holy Land.

May 14 — Appealing not only to UN Resolution 181 but also to "the natural right of the Jewish people to be masters of their own fate, like all other nations, in their own sovereign State," the Declaration of the Establishment of the State of Israel, issued at Tel Aviv, is read publicly by David Ben-Gurion, head of the Jewish Agency for Palestine and soon to be Israel's first prime minister. Within minutes of the state's establishment, US president Harry Truman becomes the first world leader to recognize Israel. Israel's declaration of independence ignites the first Arab-Israeli war, which continues until 1949.

May 26 — David Ben-Gurion orders the establishment of the Israel Defense Forces (IDF). It becomes the State of Israel's military, including ground forces, air force, and navy. With some exceptions, Israeli Law requires that most Israeli citizens begin serving in the Israeli military at the age of 18.

December 11 — During Israel's victory in the first Arab-Israeli war, at least 700,000 Palestinians flee their homes in what becomes known as the Nakba (Arabic for *catastrophe*). Palestinian displacement leads the UN General Assembly to pass Resolution 194. It states that "refugees wishing to return to their homes and live at peace with their neighbors should be permitted to do so at the earliest practicable date," a provision that bolsters ongoing Palestinian claims to a "right of return." Israeli policy rejects such claims.

1956

October 29 — After Egypt's Gamal Abdel Nasser nationalizes the Suez Canal, Israel, acting with approval from Britain and France, invades the Sinai Peninsula, occupying it until a negotiated withdrawal in March 1957.

1964

January 4–6 — Pope Paul VI visits the Holy Land (Jordan, Israel, Bethlehem) meeting with both Israeli and Jordanian political authorities. He avoids mention of the State of Israel or the Palestinians.

June 2 — With Ahmad Shukeiri as its first chairman, the Palestine Liberation Organization (PLO) is established. Officially representing the Palestinian people, the PLO, led by Yasser Arafat from 1969 until his death in 2004, advances Palestinian nationalism and hopes for a Palestinian state.

1965

October 28 — The Second Vatican Council adopts the "Declaration on the Relation of the Church to Non-Christian Religions," called *Nostra Aetate* (In our time). Although it makes no specific mention of the State of Israel, the declaration affirms the deep connection between Christianity and Judaism and rejects antisemitism.

1967

June 5–10 — In the Six-Day War (Arabs call it the June War), Israel responds to Egyptian provocations with preemptive attacks that cripple Arab armies—Syrian and Jordanian as well as Egyptian—and enable Israel to control not only the West Bank and the Gaza Strip but also East Jerusalem, the Golan Heights, and the Sinai Peninsula. Some 300,000 Palestinians—largely in the West Bank and Gaza—flee their homes during the war.

November 22 — In response to the Six-Day War, the UN Security Council passes Resolution 242. Lacking explicit references to

Palestinians, it calls for Israeli withdrawal from "territories occupied in the recent conflict." The resolution also affirms "the sovereignty, territorial integrity and political independence of every State in the area and their right to live in peace within secure and recognized boundaries free from threats or acts of force." Resolution 242 affirms the principle of a "just and lasting peace in the Middle East" and contains a "land for peace" implication that continues to be at play.

1973

October 6–26   Israel is acutely unprepared on the Jewish holy day of Yom Kippur when Egypt and Syria attack Israeli forces in the Sinai Peninsula and the Golan Heights. Despite initial setbacks, Israel—with significant support from the United States—prevails. But fifty years later, echoes of the Yom Kippur War, which sapped Israel's sense of security, reverberate in Israel because the 2023 Israel-Hamas war also caught Israelis badly off guard.

October 22   The UN Security Council passes Resolution 338, which calls for a ceasefire in the Yom Kippur War and negotiations "aimed at establishing a just and durable peace in the Middle East."

1974

October 22   Pope Paul VI establishes the Vatican Commission for Religious Relations with the Jews (CRRJ) to foster religious dialogue with Jews and Judaism.

December 1   The CRRJ publishes its first official document, "Guidelines and Suggestions for Implementing the Conciliar Declaration *Nostra Aetate,* No. 4." The document deplores that "such relations as there have been between Jew and Christian have scarcely ever risen above the level of monologue" and stresses that "from now on, real dialogue must be established."

1975

November 10   The UN General Assembly adopts Resolution 3379, which holds that Zionism "is a form of racism and racial discrimination." The United States joins Israel in voting against the resolution.

December 23 — In his Christmas message delivered to members of the College of Cardinals at the Vatican, Pope Paul VI appeals to the Israeli people to "recognize the rights and legitimate aspirations of Palestinians." He is the first pope to affirm explicitly the Palestinians as a people rather than simply as a group of refugees.

1978

September 17 — Brokered by US president Jimmy Carter with Israeli prime minister Menachem Begin and Egyptian president Anwar Sadat at Camp David, Maryland, agreements known as the Camp David Accords are signed. The Accords prepare the way for a 1979 peace treaty between Egypt and Israel, the first between Israel and any of its Arab neighbors.

1979

March 26 — Egypt and Israel agree on a peace treaty. It is signed in Washington, DC, by Anwar Sadat, president of Egypt, and Menachem Begin, prime minister of Israel, and witnessed by Jimmy Carter, president of the United States. Incorporating a "land for peace" principle, the treaty's terms include Israel's withdrawal from a demilitarized Sinai, the establishment of normal diplomatic relations between the two countries, and Egypt's opening of the Suez Canal to Israeli shipping.

1980

September 30 — An initiative of the global Christian Zionist movement, the International Christian Embassy in Jerusalem is dedicated at a ceremony attended by 1,000 Christians from thirty-two nations.

1982

April 26 — Egypt regains control of the Sinai Peninsula when Israel withdraws the last of its troops from the region. President Hosni Mubarak of Egypt and Prime Minister Menachem Begin of Israel pledge to keep their countries at peace. Ariel

A Timeline 1945-2024

Sharon, Israel's defense minister, promises expanded Jewish settlements in Gaza and the West Bank.

June 6 — In response to PLO attacks on northern Israel, Ariel Sharon and the Israel Defense Forces (IDF) invade southern Lebanon in Operation Peace for Galilee. Israeli power forces Yasser Arafat and other PLO leaders to leave Beirut. During the conflict, Hezbollah, an Iran-backed Shiite Muslim political party and militant group, gains traction in Lebanon.

September 15 — Pope John Paul II meets privately at the Vatican with Yasser Arafat, head of the PLO, provoking criticism from Israel and Jewish groups.

Sept 16–18 — Israel's invasion of southern Lebanon goes badly wrong when the IDF allows its Lebanese Christian allies to massacre as many as 2,750 Palestinians—mostly women, children, and the elderly—at the Sabra and Shatila refugee camps. International outrage against the atrocities focuses on Israel and Ariel Sharon in particular.

1985

June 24 — The Pontifical Commission for Religious Relations with Jews and Judaism issues "Notes on the Correct Way to Present the Jews and Judaism in Preaching and Catechesis in the Roman Catholic Church," the first post-Vatican II text to fully engage the existence of the modern State of Israel. This document states that "the existence of the State of Israel and its political options should be envisaged not in a perspective which is in itself religious, but in their reference to the common principles of international law."

1987

December 1 — As Israel increases land expropriation and settler construction in the West Bank and Gaza, Palestinians launch the first *intifada* (uprising), which lasts until September 1993. Of the nearly 2,000 dead, more than 1,500 are Palestinians. During the first month of the intifada, the Palestinian cleric Sheikh Ahmed Yassin founds Hamas, an acronym for *Harakat al-Muqawama al-Islamiya* ("Islamic Resistance Movement").

1988

August 18 — The Hamas charter calls for the destruction of Israel and the establishment of an Islamic society in historic Palestine.

November 15 — In Algiers, PLO chairman Yasser Arafat announces: "In the name of God and in the name of the Palestinian Arab people, the National Council declares the creation of the State of Palestine on our Palestinian land with noble Jerusalem as its capital."

December 13 — Addressing the UN General Assembly, Arafat says that "the PLO will work for the achievement of a comprehensive settlement among the parties concerned in the Arab-Israeli conflict, including the State of Palestine, Israel and the other neighboring States, within the framework of the International Peace Conference on the Middle East, on the basis of Security Council resolutions 242 (1967) and 338 (1973), so as to guarantee equality and the balance of interests, especially our people's rights to freedom and national independence, and respect for the right of all the parties to the conflict to exist in peace and security."

December 15 — UN General Assembly Resolution 43/177 "acknowledges the proclamation of the State of Palestine by the Palestine National Council on 15 November 1988; affirms the need to enable the Palestinian people to exercise their sovereignty over their territory occupied since 1967; decides that effective as of 15 December 1988, the designation 'Palestine' should be used in place of the designation 'Palestine Liberation Organization' in the United Nations system." Israel and the United States are the only countries that vote against the resolution.

1991

October 30 — During an international conference in Madrid, Spain, Israel permits Palestinian participation only as part of a joint delegation with Jordan and refuses to allow involvement from any PLO members, but official, face-to-face peace talks between Israelis and Palestinians take place for the first time.

December 17   Responding to a US appeal "to consign one of the last relics of the Cold War to the dustbin of history," the UN General Assembly rescinds the 1974 Resolution 3379, which determined that Zionism is "a form of racism and racial discrimination."

1992

July 29   A Bilateral Permanent Working Commission is established between the Holy See and the State of Israel "to study and define issues of common interest and in view of normalizing their relations."

1993

September 13   Following secret negotiations in Oslo, Norway, Israeli Prime Minister Yitzhak Rabin and PLO negotiator Mahmoud Abbas sign (at the White House in Washington, DC) a Declaration of Principles on Interim Self-Government Arrangements, commonly called the Oslo Accords. Prior to the signing, an exchange of letters between Rabin and PLO leader Yasser Arafat affirms Israel's acceptance of the PLO as the "representative of the Palestinian people" and Israel's negotiating partner and also the PLO's renunciation of terrorism and its recognition of "the right of the State of Israel to exist in peace and security." Israel, however, does not acknowledge a Palestinian right to statehood.

December 30   The Holy See and the State of Israel sign a diplomatic treaty. They exchange ambassadors a few months later.

1994

May 4   In Cairo, Egypt, Yasser Arafat and Yitzhak Rabin sign the Gaza-Jericho Agreement, which augments the Oslo Accords by establishing the Palestinian Authority to provide limited self-rule for Palestinians in the Gaza Strip and the West Bank. Israel agrees to a partial withdrawal from Gaza and parts of the West Bank.

October 25   The Holy See and the PLO begin "working contacts of a permanent and official character."

October 26	Israel and Jordan sign a peace treaty, which, after the peace agreement with Egypt, is the second between Israel and a neighboring Arab state.
December 10	In Oslo, Norway, Yasser Arafat, Palestinian leader, Shimon Peres, Israel's minister of foreign affairs, and Yitzhak Rabin, Israel's prime minister, share the Nobel Peace Prize for "their efforts to create peace in the Middle East."

1995

September 28	At the White House in Washington, DC, Arafat, Peres, and Rabin build on the Gaza-Jericho Agreement by signing the Israeli-Palestinian Interim Agreement on the West Bank and Gaza Strip (often called Oslo II). The agreement gives Palestinians more, but still limited, control of the West Bank. The Oslo Accords disappoint because they neither give Israelis the security they want nor provide Palestinians the freedom they seek.
November 4	Israeli Prime Minister Yitzhak Rabin is assassinated in Tel Aviv by an extremist Jew, Yigal Amir, who opposed the Oslo Accords, especially increased Palestinian control in parts of the West Bank.

1996

May 29	Israel elects right-wing Benjamin Netanyahu prime minister in a close race that unseats Shimon Peres and his hopes to advance the peace process. Netanyahu pledges to slow the peace process, build new Jewish settlements in the West Bank, block a Palestinian state, and secure the Golan Heights, captured from Syria.

1997

October 8	The US identifies Hamas as a foreign terrorist organization.

1998

March 16	The Vatican Commission for Religious Relations with the Jews (CRRJ) issues "We Remember: A Reflection on the Shoah," which apologizes for the Catholic Church's failure to do more for the Jewish people during the Holocaust.

October 23	Yasser Arafat and Benjamin Netanyahu sign the Wye River Memorandum at the White House in Washington, DC. The Palestinians agree to suppress terrorism. The Israelis expand areas in the West Bank that will be under the Palestinian Authority's jurisdiction.

1999

May 17	Labor Party leader Ehud Barak is elected prime minister of Israel after Benjamin Netanyahu's concessions on Israeli control in the West Bank weaken his support among his right-wing base and coalition partners.

2000

February 15	Mgr. Celestino Migliore, for the Holy See, and Dr. Emile Jarjoui, for the Palestine Organization, sign the "Basic Agreement Between the Holy See and the Palestine Liberation Organization," which is intended to "provide a solid and lasting foundation for the continued development of their present and future relations." Pope John Paul II receives Yasser Arafat at the signing of the "Basic Agreement."
March 20–26	Pope John Paul II makes a groundbreaking visit to the Holy Land. The pope meets with Israeli and Palestinian leaders, visits Christian, Jewish, and Muslim shrines, commemorates the Shoah (Holocaust) at Yad Vashem, the Israeli memorial to the six million Jews murdered during the Holocaust, and visits the Aida refugee camp, where Palestinians have languished since 1950.
July 11–25	During two weeks of intensive discussion, US president Bill Clinton hosts Israeli prime minister Ehud Barak and Palestinian leader Yasser Arafat at Camp David, Maryland. Hopes for a peaceful resolution of the Israeli-Palestinian conflict are raised when Barak proposes a Palestinian state in 91 percent of the West Bank, all of Gaza, and parts of East Jerusalem. But with both sides unable to reach an agreement on key issues, the talks break down without a settlement.
September 28	Accompanied by Israeli police, right-wing political leader Ariel Sharon makes a provocative visit to Jerusalem's

Temple Mount, where the Al-Aqsa Mosque and Dome of the Rock, among Islam's holiest sites, are also located. Following Sharon's visit to the Temple Mount, Palestinian protests erupt, escalating into what becomes the Second Intifada, a four-year cycle of violence that takes the lives of about 1,000 Israelis and 3,200 Palestinians.

2002

March 22 — The deadliest attack against Israeli civilians in the Second Intifada takes place during a Passover observance at the Park Hotel in Netanya. A Hamas-directed Palestinian suicide bombing—one of more than 150 during the Second Intifada—kills thirty Israelis and injures 140 more. In response to the "Passover massacre," as the disaster comes to be known, Israel reoccupies parts of the West Bank, including Ramallah, headquarters for Yasser Arafat and the Palestinian Authority.

June 23 — Seeking to deter Palestinian attacks, Israel constructs security barriers in the West Bank. The barriers, some of them cutting through Palestinian villages, restrict Palestinian movement and business. Bethlehem, which Christians believe is the birthplace of Jesus, is among the towns affected by the Israeli restrictions.

2003

April 30 — A so-called Roadmap for Peace, developed by the United States, in cooperation with Russia, the European Union, and the United Nations (the Quartet), is presented to Israel and the Palestinian Authority. It outlines steps to ensure Israel's security, its withdrawal from Palestinian territory occupied since September 2000, a freeze on Israeli settlements in the West Bank, and a two-state solution to the conflict. Implementation of the plan fails.

July 31 — The passage of Israel's law on citizenship and entry into Israel prevents inhabitants of the West Bank and Gaza Strip from obtaining residency permits and citizenship by marriage to an Israeli citizen.

November 16 — Pope John Paul II appeals for peace in the Holy Land, which, he says, "does not need walls but bridges."

2005

August 15 — Under the leadership of the Israeli prime minister, Ariel Sharon, Israel begins a unilateral withdrawal of troops and settlers from the Gaza Strip. Sharon sees this step as a demographic necessity. By reducing the number of Palestinians under Israeli control, Sharon thinks the chances are improved for Israel's future as a Jewish and democratic state. Many Palestinians, especially those affiliated with Hamas, contend that "armed struggle" has been vindicated because, they argue, it forced Israel out of Gaza. After Israel's withdrawal, Hamas and other militant Palestinian groups launch periodic rocket attacks on Israel from Gaza.

2006

January 26 — In Palestinian elections, Hamas defeats Fatah, the more secular and moderate Palestinian party. When a power-sharing deal fails, Hamas takes control of the Gaza Strip in 2007. In response, most Western governments boycott the Hamas regime. Israel declares Gaza a "hostile entity" and begins an ongoing blockade.

July 12 — Following Hezbollah rocket attacks on northern Israel, the IDF invades southern Lebanon. Hostilities continue until August 14.

2007

June 15 — Hamas takes complete control of the Gaza Strip. Its militarized tunnel network expands.

2008

December 27 — In response to extensive rocket assaults in November and December, Israel attacks Hamas in Gaza. Israel withdraws in January. The fatalities number more than 1,400 Palestinians and thirteen Israelis.

2009

March 31 — Benjamin Netanyahu again becomes prime minister of the State of Israel, holding the office until 2021.

2011

April 7 — Becoming operational in March, Israel's Iron Dome defense system first intercepts a Gaza Strip rocket, which targeted the Israeli city of Ashkelon.

2012

November 29 — The UN General Assembly grants Palestine Non-Member Observer State status in the United Nations. Israel and the United States vote against the resolution. The Holy See, which is also an observer member, supports it.

2014

April 23 — Hamas and the PLO agree to form a unity government, but factional tensions defeat that goal. The PLO-controlled West Bank and Hamas-controlled Gaza remain disconnected.

May 24–26 — Pope Francis visits the Holy Land. In Bethlehem, he makes headlines when he refers to his host country as "the State of Palestine" rather than simply referring to the Palestinian people. The pope invites Mahmoud Abbas, president of the Palestinian Authority, and Shimon Peres, president of Israel, to come to Rome and pray with him for peace. The meeting takes place on June 8.

June 12 — In the West Bank, three Jewish teenagers are kidnapped and murdered. Holding Hamas responsible, Israeli prime minister Benjamin Netanyahu vows that "Hamas will pay."

July 8–Aug 26 — Israel launches Operation Protective Edge, an aerial and ground attack on Gaza. During the 50-day war, Hamas fires more than 4,500 rockets and mortars into Israel, aiming much of the attack against major Israeli cities, but Israeli forces degrade Hamas's military power. More than 2,250 Palestinians are killed, most of them civilians. Israeli fatalities include sixty-six soldiers and six civilians.

2015

May 13 The Holy See issues an official statement recognizing the territories controlled by the Palestinian Authority as an independent state. Three days later, President Mahmoud Abbas visits Pope Francis and is received as a head of state.

June 26 The Holy See signs a treaty with the Palestinian Authority. Covering the life and activity of the Catholic Church in Palestine, the treaty is called the "Comprehensive Agreement Between the Holy See and the State of Palestine." It makes clear that the Holy See officially recognizes the State of Palestine, rather than the Palestine Liberation Organization, as the entity that represents Palestinians.

2017

December 6 Undoing long-standing American policy, US president Donald Trump officially recognizes Jerusalem as Israel's capital and announces plans to move the American embassy from Tel Aviv to Jerusalem. The change draws international criticism and sparks protest and violence in East Jerusalem, Gaza, and the West Bank.

2018

May 14 The American embassy in Israel moves from Tel Aviv to Jerusalem.

July 19 Israel's Knesset passes the "Basic Law: Israel as the Nation-State of the Jewish People." With constitutional status, the law affirms three principles: (1) "The land of Israel is the historical homeland of the Jewish people, in which the State of Israel was established." (2) "The State of Israel is the national home of the Jewish people, in which it fulfills its natural, cultural, religious and historical right to self-determination." (3) "The right to exercise national self-determination in the State of Israel is unique to the Jewish people." The law also asserts that Jewish settlement—without specifying where—is a national value and promises to encourage and advance settlement efforts. Critics assail the law as undemocratic, expansionist, and discriminatory against minorities in Israel and territories under Israeli control.

2019

March 25 — Israeli prime minister Benjamin Netanyahu applauds at the White House in Washington, DC, as President Donald Trump recognizes Israel's sovereignty over the Golan Heights territory annexed from Syria in 1981, making the United States the first country other than Israel to do so.

2020

January 28 — Flanked by Benjamin Netanyahu at the White House, US president Donald Trump unveils "Peace to Prosperity," his Middle East plan. The plan includes no Palestinian input, but Trump touts it as "a win-win opportunity for both sides." Palestinian leadership rejects the plan immediately. The plan's two-state solution favors Israeli interests because it provides for a Palestinian state with limited independence and recognizes Israeli sovereignty over West Bank settlements. Netanyahu announces plans to annex parts of the West Bank.

September 15 — Mediated by the Trump administration, the Abraham Accords produce agreement from Bahrain and the United Arab Emirates to normalize diplomatic relations with Israel. The two Arab countries are the first to do so since 1994. In return, Israel announces the suspension of its plans to annex territory in the West Bank. By year's end, Morocco and Sudan also normalize relations with Israel.

2021

April 27 — Human Rights Watch issues "A Threshold Crossed: Israeli Authorities and the Crimes of Apartheid and Persecution." The report holds Israel accountable for the crimes of apartheid and persecution against Palestinians not only in occupied Palestinian territory (the West Bank, including East Jerusalem, and the Gaza Strip) but also in the State of Israel itself.

May 6 — Israel plans to evict some Palestinian families from East Jerusalem. Clashes at the Al-Aqsa Mosque spark conflict between Israel and Hamas. Before the violence ends two weeks later, more than 250 Palestinians and at least thirteen Israelis are killed.

2022

August 5–7   West Bank conflicts between Israelis and Palestinians, including a raid on Jenin—long a stronghold of Palestinian resistance—in which Israeli forces arrest Bassam al-Saadi, a leader of the Palestinian Islamic Jihad, also ignite violence between Israel and Gaza. Israeli forces unleash air strikes, and Palestinian militants target Israel with more than 1,000 rockets.

2023

January 26   Israeli forces raid the Jenin refugee camp in the West Bank, justifying the action as prevention against terrorism. Hamas calls the attack a "massacre" committed by "the occupation" and vows that an armed response will follow. Further Israeli attacks on Jenin take place in July and September.

March 5   As it has done multiple times, the Israeli Knesset renews the so-called Citizenship Law—passed originally in 2003—that restricts Palestinians who marry Israelis from obtaining permanent residency and citizenship.

October 7   On the Jewish Sabbath and on the date of Simchat Torah, which celebrates the completion and beginning of the annual reading of the Torah, Hamas—provoked by Israel's long-standing siege of Gaza and the expansion of Jewish settlements in the West Bank—launch a gruesome surprise attack against Israel from Gaza. Israeli citizens, including foreign nationals, are raped, murdered, and taken hostage. Supported by Iran, the deadliest single-day attack on Jews since the Holocaust kills more than 1,200 Israelis and foreign nationals, including at least thirty-five US citizens living in Israel. Hamas takes more than 250 hostages—including children, women, and elderly people, as well as men and soldiers.

The next day, Hezbollah launches rockets toward northern Israel. Israel officially declares the Swords of Iron War against Hamas. Prime Minister Benjamin Netanyahu vows that Israel will "take mighty vengeance." Controversy swirls because the Hamas attack caught Israel off guard. First responders were slow to arrive. Israeli leaders ignored accurate intelligence reports regarding an imminent attack from Hamas.

October 9   Israel puts Gaza under siege. Israeli defense minister Yoav Gallant says that "no electricity, no food, no fuel" will be allowed entry.

October 13   As its military response begins, the IDF tells Palestinians in Gaza City—about one million of Gaza's 2.3 million people—to evacuate and move south. Aimed at destroying Hamas and its tunnel network, Israeli bombardments and ground attacks displace nearly all the Palestinian population of Gaza. Increasingly impoverished, hungry, and helpless, Palestinian civilians have no safe havens. A massive humanitarian disaster is underway. Hezbollah official Naim Qassem announces that Hezbollah is "fully ready" to support Hamas in the fighting.

October 18   US president Joe Biden visits Israel, the first American president to do so in wartime. At Israel's Ben Gurion Airport, he embraces Israeli prime minister Benjamin Netanyahu and assures Israelis that "as long as the United States stands—and we will stand forever—we will not ever let you be alone."

October 29   During the Sunday Angelus prayer service, Pope Francis calls for a ceasefire, saying, "Stop, brothers and sisters: war is always a defeat—always, always!"

November 6   More than 10,000 persons are killed in Gaza during the war's first month, most of them women and children.

November 12   More than 400 rabbis and scholars involved in interreligious dialogue sign an open letter urging Pope Francis to "extend a hand in solidarity to the Jewish community" by distinguishing between "Hamas's terrorist massacre aimed at killing as many civilians as possible" and "the civilian casualties of Israel's war of self-defense."

November 13   The executive committee of the World Council of Churches (WCC) issues a "Statement on the War in Palestine and Israel," which calls for "the immediate unconditional release and safe return of all hostages" as well as "an immediate ceasefire and the opening of humanitarian corridors."

November 22 Pope Francis meets separately with relatives of Palestinians killed in Gaza and with families of Israelis taken hostage by Hamas. Earlier in the day, the pope ignites a firestorm when he says that the conflict has "gone beyond war. This is terrorism." Although officially unconfirmed by the Holy See, some Palestinians report that the pope used the term *genocide* in their meeting with him.

November 24 During a seven-day pause in the fighting, Hamas releases more than 100 Israeli hostages. Some of them report witnessing sexual assaults on their fellow hostages. Israel frees 240 Palestinian prisoners.

December 4 After previously telling Palestinians to move south in Gaza for safety, Israeli forces move in that same direction, heading for the city of Khan Younis. Again, Israel tells civilians to move south, but increasingly there is no safe place in Gaza for Palestinians.

December 22 Gaza's health ministry, which does not distinguish between civilians and combatants, reports that the Gaza death toll passes 20,000.

2024

January 11 At the International Court of Justice, South Africa accuses Israel of committing genocide against Palestinians. Lior Haiat, Israel's foreign ministry secretary, calls the charges "baseless and false." Finding the South African allegations "unfounded," US national security spokesman John Kirby adds that the word *genocide* should not "be thrown around lightly, and we certainly don't believe that it applies here."

February 13 The Holy See's secretary of state, Cardinal Pietro Parolin, condemns the 10/7 Hamas attack against Israel, but he questions Israel's claim to be acting in self-defense when it inflicts "carnage" on Gaza. "Israel's right of self-defense," he says, "must be proportional, and with thirty thousand dead it certainly isn't."

February 19	World Council of Churches (WCC) general secretary Jerry Pillay meets with Palestinian president Mahmoud Abbas in Ramallah, West Bank, urging an end to the "seemingly endless cycle of violence and suffering." The next day, Pillay meets with Israeli president Isaac Herzog and calls for a ceasefire, freedom of religion, and humanitarian care for prisoners and hostages.
February 23	Israeli prime minister Benjamin Netanyahu issues postwar plans for Gaza. Israel will retain indefinite military control while allowing Gazans without links to Hamas to have civilian control. The plan hobbles prospects for a Palestinian state that would include Gaza and the West Bank.
February 29	The death toll in Gaza exceeds 30,000, with 70,000 injured.
March 5	Former US president Donald Trump declares that Israel must "finish the problem" in its war against Hamas. At the same time, the Progressive Israel Network, which represents liberal American Jews, writes to US president Joe Biden and calls for "a bilateral ceasefire that brings a stop to fighting, a release of all hostages, and a surge in humanitarian assistance."
March 10	As the Muslim holy month of Ramadan begins at sundown, Israeli retaliation for the atrocities committed by Hamas on October 7, 2023, has displaced 80 percent of the Palestinian people in Gaza.
March 14	Speaking on the floor of the US Senate, majority leader Chuck Schumer, the highest-ranking Jewish elected official in the US at the time, affirms support for Israel, urges Palestinians to reject Hamas, argues that Israeli prime minister Benjamin Netanyahu has "lost his way," calls for new elections in Israel, and says it would be a "grave mistake" for Israel to reject a two-state solution to the Israeli-Palestinian conflict.
March 18	Reliable reports based on the respected Integrated Food Security Phase Classification (IPC) show that 1.1 million Palestinians in Gaza, half of the region's population, face imminent famine. Also on this date, Donald Trump, the eventual Republican presidential nominee, claims that "any

A Timeline 1945-2024

Jewish person that votes for Democrats hates their religion. They hate everything about Israel, and they should be ashamed of themselves because Israel will be destroyed," if he is not reelected.

March 19　Representing more than 1,000 rabbis of all denominations, the Zionist Rabbinic Coalition "opposes calls for a ceasefire until all of the remaining hostages have been released and Hamas is no longer able to pose a threat to Israel." Maintaining that "Israel has taken unprecedented, unparalleled, unheard-of efforts to minimize the loss of lives of non-combatants," the Coalition insists that "Israel must not stop its military operations until Hamas is defeated."

March 22　In the single largest Israeli seizure of Palestinian territory since the 1993 Oslo Accords, Israel takes control of 3.8 square miles of West Bank land, complicating hopes for a two-state solution.

March 25　The UN Security Council approves a resolution calling for a ceasefire in Gaza during the remaining weeks of Ramadan. After vetoing three previous measures to halt the war, the United States abstains, allowing the measure to pass. Israeli prime minister Benjamin Netanyahu decries the American abstention, contending that it "harms both the war effort and the effort to release the hostages."

March 31　In Tel Aviv and Jerusalem, tens of thousands of Israelis call for new elections, demand the release of Hamas-held hostages, and protest Benjamin Netanyahu's leadership.

April 1　Israel bombs Iran's consulate in Damascus, Syria, killing two Iranian generals and five other officials. Iran vows revenge "at the same magnitude and harshness."

April 2　Israeli air strikes demolish a World Central Kitchen food aid convoy in the Gaza Strip, killing seven relief workers. Israel calls the event "a mistake that followed a misidentification." Benjamin Netanyahu says such tragedy "happens in war." International outrage ensues. On the same day, the Biden administration approves the transfer of thousands of American bombs to Israel. Since October 7, 2023, more than 200 humanitarian aid workers have lost their lives in Gaza.

April 4	American president Joe Biden tells Benjamin Netanyahu that "an immediate ceasefire is essential" and that future US support for Israel's war in Gaza depends on swift steps to protect civilians and aid workers.
April 7	Six months into the Israel-Hamas war, most of the hostages held by Hamas are still unreleased (many are dead). More than 33,000 Palestinians in Gaza have been killed and 75,000 injured. Israeli attacks have reduced much of Gaza to uninhabitable rubble. As humanitarian organizations warn of an impending famine, Israel withdraws most of its ground troops from Gaza, but plans to attack Rafah, home to 1.4 million displaced Palestinians, remain at play.
April 13	In response to Israel's bombing of Iran's consulate in Damascus, Iran launches hundreds of drones and missiles in its first-ever attack on the Israeli homeland. Israeli defense systems thwart 99 percent of them. Israel vows to respond.
April 18	The US vetoes a UN Security Council resolution to pave the way for full UN membership for the State of Palestine.
April 19	In retaliation for Iran's missile and drone attack on the Israeli homeland, Israel launches limited strikes against Iran's central city of Isfahan and northwest city of Tabriz.
April 25	Student protests against the Israel-Hamas war erupt at colleges and universities across the United States. The demonstrators call for a ceasefire in Gaza, a halt to US military aid for Israel, and an end to investments that support Israel.
May 1	The US House of Representatives overwhelmingly passes the bipartisan Antisemitism Awareness Act, which defines antisemitism to include: "Denying the Jewish people their right to self-determination, e.g., by claiming that the existence of a State of Israel is a racist endeavor" and "holding Jews collectively responsible for actions of the State of Israel."
May 6	Israeli forces begin a ground attack on Rafah, Gaza's southernmost city. Refugees from fighting elsewhere in Gaza have swollen the city's prewar population of 275,000 to 1.4 million. Two months later, the Israeli military claims victory over Hamas in Rafah. The city is a wasteland. Most

of its civilian residents have taken refuge in impoverished, vulnerable tent camps nearby.

May 7 — Speaking in the US Capitol at the US Holocaust Memorial Museum's annual Days of Remembrance ceremony, US president Joe Biden asserts that "there is no place on any campus in America—any place in America—for antisemitism or hate speech or threats of violence of any kind—whether against Jews or anyone else." He adds that "my commitment to the safety of the Jewish people, the security of Israel, and its right to exist as an independent Jewish state is ironclad, even when we disagree." Biden makes no mention of Israel's conduct of the war in Gaza, but earlier in the month he paused a US arms shipment to Israel, withholding 1,800 two-thousand-pound bombs and 1,700 five-hundred-pound bombs that might otherwise be dropped on Rafah, where more than one million Gazans are taking refuge.

May 10 — The United Nations General Assembly resolves that Palestine qualifies for full member status at the UN. Israel and the United States vote against the resolution.

May 14 — As Israel celebrates its 76th Independence Day, the first after Hamas's October 7 attack, the IDF's pressure on Rafah in southern Gaza has displaced half a million Palestinians in that city.

May 15 — Palestinians mark the 76th anniversary of the Nakba, the displacement of some 700,000 Palestinians from their homes during the 1948 Arab-Israeli war that followed Israel's declaration of independence and the establishment of the State of Israel.

May 20 — Karim Khan, the International Criminal Court's chief prosecutor, seeks arrest warrants for Israeli leaders Benjamin Netanyahu and Yoav Gallant and for Hamas heads Yahya Sinwar, Mohammed Deif, and Ismail Haniyeh, who are accused of war crimes and crimes against humanity in the Gaza Strip and in Israel, respectively. Calling the court's actions against Netanyahu and Gallant "outrageous," US president Joe Biden insists "there's no equivalence between Israel and Hamas" and asserts that Israel's military assault in Gaza "is not genocide."

May 22	Ireland, Norway, and Spain announce that they will formally recognize a Palestinian state. Israel recalls its ambassadors to those countries and reprimands the three countries' representatives in Israel.
May 24	The International Court of Justice rules that "in conformity with obligations under the Genocide Convention, Israel must immediately halt its military offensive, and any other action in the Rafah governorate, which may inflict on the Palestinian group in Gaza conditions of life that could bring about its physical destruction in whole or in part." Rejecting the ruling, Itamar Ben-Gvir, Israel's national security minister, asserts that "there ought to be one response: the conquest of Rafah, the escalation of military pressure, and the utter shattering of Hamas until the achievement of total victory."
May 26	Israeli air strikes ignite a deadly fire and kill at least forty-five people, including children, in a so-called safe zone near Rafah. Netanyahu says a "tragic mistake" took place. International outrage rises. US president Joe Biden says the event does not cross his red line about large-scale Israeli military operations in Rafah.
May 31	As the prelude to a permanent "cessation of hostilities" and a major rebuilding plan for Gaza, US president Joe Biden endorses a three-part peace proposal that includes a six-week ceasefire and withdrawal of Israeli forces from populated areas in Gaza, increased humanitarian aid for Palestinians, and release of Palestinian prisoners in exchange for Hamas-held hostages. In addition, Israeli prime minister Benjamin Netanyahu receives an official bipartisan congressional invitation to address the US Congress, which he accepts.
June 8	In Nuseirat, a town in central Gaza, Israeli forces rescue four Hamas hostages: Noa Argamani, age twenty-six; Almog Meir Jan, age twenty-two; Andrey Kozlov, age twenty-seven; and Shlomi Ziv, age forty-one, who were held captive by Hamas since October 7, 2023. During the rescue operations, more than 200 Palestinians are killed.

June 9	Protesting Benjamin Netanyahu's handling of the Israel-Hamas war, centrist Israeli politician Benny Gantz, a key member of the country's war cabinet, resigns from the government.
June 10	After 247 days of war in Gaza, the United Nations Security Council votes 14-0 (Russia abstaining) in favor of a US-backed, three-phase peace plan. Calling for an immediate temporary ceasefire, the plan calls for the release of hostages and works toward ending the Israel-Hamas war and rebuilding Gaza.
June 12	In response to an Israeli attack that kills Hezbollah commander Taleb Abdallah, the Iran-backed militant group fires more than 200 rockets toward northern Israel, inflaming fears that the Israel-Hamas war will expand beyond Gaza. Also on this date, the UN releases a report finding that war crimes have been committed by Hamas and Israel and that Israel has also committed crimes against humanity.
June 17	Israeli prime minister Benjamin Netanyahu dissolves his war cabinet after two members, Benny Gantz and Gadi Eisenkot, quit over disagreements about the direction of Israel-Hamas war.
June 25	In a decision that threatens to undo Benjamin Netanyahu's coalition government, the Israeli supreme court rules that Israel's military must draft previously deferred ultra-Orthodox Jewish (Haredi) men. Also on this date, the Integrated Food Security Phase Classification (IPC) reports that a catastrophic lack of food puts almost half a million Palestinians in Gaza at risk of starvation.
July 2	Israel orders new evacuations of Palestinians from the city of Khan Younis and its surroundings in southern Gaza.
July 9	An Israeli air strike kills more than thirty Palestinians and wounds more than fifty others, most of them women and children, at a school/shelter on the outskirts of Khan Younis, in southern Gaza.

July 10	The IDF tells all Palestinians remaining in Gaza City to leave and head south ahead of ramped up military action in the area. A day earlier, the UN reports that up to 1.9 million people (or nine in ten people) across the Gaza Strip are internally displaced, many of them numerous times.
July 11	A *Times of Israel* poll shows that 96 percent of Jews residing in thirteen European Union countries experience antisemitism in daily life. The United States announces that it will resume sending 500-pound bombs, 1,700 of them, to Israel.
July 16	Israel announces that half of Hamas's military leadership has been killed since 10/7. Roughly 14,000 Hamas fighters have been killed or apprehended to date during the Israel-Hamas war. Gaza's health ministry reports that more than 39,000 Palestinians have been killed in the war, and another 89,000 wounded. The latter reports do not distinguish between civilians and combatants.
July 17	The Israeli Knesset votes overwhelmingly to reject the establishment of a Palestinian state, even as part of a negotiated settlement with Israel.
July 19	In The Hague, Netherlands, the International Court of Justice (ICJ) finds that Israel should end its occupation of Palestinian territory in the West Bank and East Jerusalem, evacuate existing settlements, stop building new ones, and pay reparations to Palestinians who have lost land and property.
July 20	The day after Iran-backed Houthi militants in Yemen launch a drone attack on Tel Aviv, Israeli air strikes target Hodeida, a strategic Yemini port city.
July 21	American president Joe Biden announces that he will not run for reelection against former president Donald Trump in November 2024. Soon thereafter, Kamala Harris, the US vice president, becomes the Democratic Party's nominee.
July 23	In Beijing, rival Palestinian factions Hamas and Fatah sign an agreement "ending division and strengthening Palestinian unity." The unity agreement aims to advance Palestinian control in postwar Gaza.

A Timeline 1945-2024

July 24   With thousands of protesters near the US Capitol and some eighty Democrats boycotting the event, Israeli prime minister Benjamin Netanyahu delivers his fourth speech to the US Congress. He vows "nothing less" than total victory over Hamas and calls charges that Israel has committed war crimes in Gaza "utter nonsense."

July 27   At least twelve Druze children are killed and dozens more people are wounded in the Israel-controlled Golan Heights when a Hezbollah rocket fired from Lebanon hits a soccer field in the northern Druze town of Majdal Shams. Israel's prime minister, Benjamin Netanyahu, vows heavy retaliation as fears increase about a widening war in the Middle East.

July 30   Israeli fighter jets strike Harat Hriek, a southern suburb of Beirut, Lebanon, targeting and killing Fuad Shukr, a senior Hezbollah commander.

July 31   Hamas leader Ismail Haniyeh is assassinated in Tehran, Iran. Hamas and Iran blame Israel for Haniyeh's death and vow retaliation. Fears escalate further about a widened regional war in the Middle East.

August 4   Interviewed in Jerusalem by *Time* magazine, Israeli prime minister Benjamin Netanyahu expresses regret that 10/7 happened on his watch, dodges questions about accountability, insists that Israel "has gone out of our way to enable humanitarian assistance" in Gaza, contends that the IDF has made an "exemplary effort of avoiding civilian casualties or minimizing them," and envisions "a long-term arrangement, with the Palestinians [in which] they should have all the powers to govern themselves but none of the powers to threaten us."

August 6   Hamas announces a new leader, Yahya Sinwar, its top official in Gaza and the mastermind of the 10/7 attack on Israel.

August 8   Claiming the structures are used by Hamas terrorists, Israel bombs two schools in Gaza City, killing more than a dozen displaced Palestinian civilians and wounding many more.

August 10	In another Israeli attack, at least ninety-three Palestinian civilians are killed in an Israeli air strike on the al-Taba'een school-turned-shelter in Gaza City.
August 12	As Israel awaits retribution from Iran for the assassination of Hamas leader Ismail Haniyeh, the Israeli defense minister, Yaov Gallant, criticizes Benjamin Netanyahu's goal of "total victory" over Hamas, calling it "nonsense." The rift deepens when Netanyahu accuses Gallant of advancing an "anti-Israel narrative."
August 13	The US State Department clears the way to provide Israel with military equipment—including tank shells, combat vehicles, and fighter jets—valued at more than $20 billion.
August 15	With ceasefire talks in play, the Israel-Hamas war continues into its tenth month. The Palestinian death toll exceeds 40,000. Owing to the number of people unaccounted for, trapped or dead under rubble, UN Secretary-General António Guterres takes the 40,000 figure to be an undercount.
August 20	The Israel Defense Forces announce recovery of the bodies of six Hamas hostages, found in tunnels in the Khan Younis area of southern Gaza: Yagev Buchshtab, age thirty-five; Alexander Dancyg, age seventy-six; Avraham Munder, age seventy-nine; Yoram Metzger, age eighty; Nadav Popplewell, age fifty-one; and Chaim Peri, age eighty. Also on this date, an Israeli air strike on a school-turned-shelter kills at least ten Palestinians in Gaza City.
August 25	Israel and Hezbollah in Lebanon launch the biggest cross-border strikes since the beginning of the Israel-Hamas war.
August 27	Abducted on 10/7, Qaid Farhan al-Qadi, age fifty-two, a Bedouin Israeli, is rescued from a Hamas tunnel in Gaza by the IDF. Israel estimates that al-Qadi is one of more than 100 hostages remaining in Gaza, at least thirty-four presumed dead. On this same date, Israel begins its deadliest post-10/7 operation in the West Bank, the most extensive in twenty years. Since the start of the Israel-Hamas war, more than 650 Palestinians have been killed in the Occupied Palestinian Territory.

A Timeline 1945-2024

August 29   Israel announces that it will stagger military operations—not to be confused with a ceasefire—to permit vaccination of Palestinian children to stanch a polio outbreak in Gaza.

August 31   The Israeli military announces recovery of the bodies of six hostages found in a Hamas tunnel underneath the city of Rafah in the Gaza Strip. The recently murdered are Ori Danino, age twenty-five, Alex Lobanov, age thirty-three, Almog Sarusi, age twenty-seven, Carmel Gat, age forty, Eden Yerushalmi, age twenty-four, and Hersh Goldberg-Polin, age twenty-three, a California-born Israeli American, whose parents, Rachel Goldberg and Jon Polin, pleaded for his life at the Democratic National Convention in Chicago on August 21. Across Israel, the largest demonstrations in months protest Prime Minister Benjamin Netanyahu and his government for failing to obtain a ceasefire with Hamas, including the release of hostages.

September 2   Despite the largest anti-government protests since the start of the Israel-Hamas war, Benjamin Netanyahu remains defiant, asserting that Israel must "stand together as one against a cruel enemy that wants to destroy us all, each and every one."

September 3   The US Department of Justice indicts Yahya Sinwar and five other senior leaders of Hamas for orchestrating the terrorist organization's decades-long campaign of mass violence and terror, including the 10/7 kidnapping and eventual murder of Hersh Goldberg-Polin, a 23-year-old Israeli American.

September 7   In one of the largest protests in Israel's history, some 750,000 Israelis in Tel Aviv and other cities call for a ceasefire in Gaza and a hostage deal with Hamas.

September 10   In Muwasi, a designated humanitarian zone along the Gaza coast, the Israeli military strikes against a Hamas command-and-control center in the area, killing three senior Hamas militants directly involved in the 10/7 attack. Israel continues to hold that precautions are taken to prevent civilian casualties, but the Gaza Health Ministry reports at least nineteen Palestinians killed and sixty wounded in the attack. Israel disputes those numbers.

Sept 17–18   In Lebanon, Hezbollah pagers and walkie-talkies explode, killing at least thirty-seven people, including children, and wounding thousands more. Israel neither confirms nor denies responsibility for the complex attack, but Hezbollah calls it an "act of war" and promises retaliation. Amid stalled negotiations for a Gaza ceasefire and hostage release, Israeli defense minister Yoav Gallant indicates that Israel's military focus is shifting toward Lebanon. Fears rise that the low-grade war between Hezbollah and Israel since 10/7 will escalate into regional conflict.

September 20   Following Hezbollah's retaliation against Israel after the widespread detonation of communication devices a few days earlier, Israel launches the deadliest attack on Beirut in nearly two decades. Israeli air strikes kill Ibrahim Aqil and other top Hezbollah leaders. Linked to the 1983 deadly bombing of US Marines in Lebanon, Aqil had a $7 million bounty on his head from the United States.

September 23   In retaliation against repeated Hezbollah rocket attacks on northern Israel, IDF air strikes in Lebanon kill more than 490 people and injure an additional 1,600 during the deadliest barrage since the 2006 Israel-Hezbollah War.

September 24   As Hezbollah and the IDF continue to clash, the American president Joe Biden delivers his final address to the UN General Assembly, calling for the Israeli-Palestinian conflict to end in a two-state solution, "where Israel enjoys security and peace and full recognition and normalized relations with all its neighbors, where Palestinians live in security, dignity, and self-determination in a state of their own."

September 25   As the IDF prepares for a possible invasion of Lebanon, Benjamin Netanyahu vows that Israel will strike Hezbollah with "full force," dimming hopes for a ceasefire in the north.

September 26	Reports from the Gaza Health Ministry, which does not distinguish between civilians and combatants, state that 41,534 people in the Gaza Strip have been killed in the Israel-Hamas war and that 96,092 have been injured. Many of the dead are Palestinian women, children, and elderly persons.
September 27	In an address to the United Nations, which he calls a "swamp of antisemitic bile," Israeli prime minister Benjamin Netanyahu insists that "Hamas has got to go," that Israel will "continue degrading Hezbollah until all our objectives are met," and that Israel must defend itself "against Iran in [a] seven-front war."
September 28	As Israeli air strikes hit targets in the Beirut area, Hezbollah confirms that its longtime leader, Hassan Nasrallah, was killed the night before in an Israeli air raid. Affirming that "the United States fully supports Israel's right to defend itself against Hezbollah, Hamas, the Houthis, and any other Iranian-supported terrorist groups," US president Joe Biden emphasizes that "Hassan Nasrallah and the terrorist group he led, Hezbollah, were responsible for killing hundreds of Americans over a four-decade reign of terror. His death from an Israeli air strike is a measure of justice for his many victims, including thousands of Americans, Israelis, and Lebanese civilians."
September 29	The Israel-Hamas war spreads. Two weeks after a series of Israeli air strikes on Hezbollah, more than 1,000 persons are dead in Lebanon and hundreds of thousands are displaced. Israel also targets Houthi militants in Yemen.
September 30	For the first time since 2006, IDF ground troops invade southern Lebanon, targeting Hezbollah.
October 1	Retaliating for the killing of Hamas and Hezbollah leaders and Israel's ground incursion in Lebanon, Iran launches 180 ballistic missiles at Israel. Most are intercepted by Israel's Iron Dome and the US Navy. On a light rail train in the Jaffa neighborhood of Tel Aviv, at least six people are killed, twelve more wounded, in what Israeli police call an act of terrorism.

October 4	Israel's ongoing air and ground attacks on Hezbollah in Lebanon have displaced more than a million Lebanese. The day before, an Israeli air strike kills eighteen in the West Bank, the deadliest attack there since 10/7. In Tehran, Ayatollah Ali Khamenei, Iran's supreme leader, calls Israel "bloodthirsty," praises Hamas's 10/7 attack as "just," and says that "any strike on the Zionist regime is a service to humanity." The Israel-Hamas war has become the long-feared regional war.
October 7	As somber Israeli commemorations mark the first anniversary of Hamas's attack on Israel from Gaza, the deadliest in the country's history, Hamas fires missiles at Tel Aviv, and Hezbollah rockets target northern Israel. The IDF counters with air strikes on southern Lebanon, and Israel announces a "new phase of war" in Gaza. With war expanding and no end in sight, the conflict's statistics are grim: 42,000 Palestinians killed in Gaza, 95,000 injured, and 1.9 million out of 2.2 million persons displaced; more than 1,000 dead in Lebanon, and more than a million people displaced in that country; more than 700 Israeli soldiers dead, another 4,500 injured, and 75,000 Israelis displaced from northern Israel.
October 8	As Hezbollah continues its rocket barrage against the Israeli port city of Haifa, Israel expands its ground war in Lebanon, and Benjamin Netanyahu urges the Lebanese to reject Hezbollah and avoid "destruction and suffering like we see in Gaza."
October 11–12	As Israeli Jews observe Yom Kippur, Hezbollah fires more than 300 missiles into northern Israel, the IDF continues its attacks on targets in Lebanon, including Beirut, and Israel renews strikes on northern Gaza as attempts to destroy Hamas continue.
October 12	Documents recovered by the IDF from Hamas command centers show that Hamas's Gaza leader Yahya Sinwar urged Iran to provide support to ensure the complete destruction of Israel within two years.

October 13	On the same day that the US announces it will send Israel a Terminal High Altitude Area Defense (THAAD) battery and the troops to operate this specialized anti-missile system, the US also tells Israel that military aid could be suspended if Israel does not increase the flow of humanitarian aid to Palestinians in Gaza within a month.
October 16	At an emergency meeting of the UN Security Council, Riyad Mansour, the Palestinian UN ambassador, accuses Israel of besieging, bombing, and starving 400,000 Palestinians in northern Gaza during all-out war against the Palestinian people. "These are crimes," he says. "This is genocide." Danny Danon, Israel's UN ambassador, counters that Israel's humanitarian efforts remain "as comprehensive as ever," and he criticizes the Security Council's focus on the humanitarian situation in Gaza while Israeli civilians "are being targeted daily by those who seek our destruction."
October 17	The IDF announces that Yahya Sinwar, the Hamas leader who orchestrated the 10/7 attack on Israel, was killed in southern Gaza on October 16. Benjamin Netanyahu says that while Sinwar's death "is not the end of the war in Gaza, it's the beginning of the end." Sinwar's longtime deputy, Khalil al-Hayya, insists that Hamas's "banner will not fall."
October 26	Israeli air strikes respond to Iran's October 1 missile attacks by targeting Iranian missile factories and other military sites but avoiding Iran's nuclear and oil facilities. While the US urges de-escalation, Iran says it is "entitled and obligated" to defend itself.
October 29	Following the previous day's Israeli legislation that bans UNRWA, the United Nations agency aiding Palestinians, from operating in the Gaza Strip, IDF strikes in northern Gaza kill at least ninety-three Palestinians, including twenty-five children. According to Gaza Health Ministry reports, more than 43,000 Palestinians have been killed in Gaza during the war and more than 100,000 injured.

November 5   Donald Trump is elected president of the United States. Israeli air strikes on northern Gaza kill at least thirty Palestinians. Citing a "crisis of trust," Benjamin Netanyahu fires the Israeli defense minister, Yoav Gallant. Israel's attacks against Hezbollah strike targets in Syria.

November 7   Inflamed by the Israel-Hamas war, antisemitic violence erupts in Amsterdam ahead of the commemoration of Kristallnacht, the massively destructive 1938 pogrom against Jews in Nazi Germany.

November 10 As Israeli air strikes continue in northern Gaza and Lebanon, Benjamin Netanyahu confirms that he and president-elect Donald Trump "see eye-to-eye regarding the Iranian threat and all of its components."

November 13 US president-elect Donald Trump nominates former Arkansas governor Mike Huckabee to serve as the American ambassador to Israel. A Christian Zionist, Huckabee has claimed that there is "no such thing as a Palestinian."

November 17 Interview excerpts published from a new book indicate that Pope Francis calls for careful investigation to determine if Israel's attacks in Gaza constitute genocide.

November 20 In an unprecedented debate in the US Senate, a significant number of senators vote to send a clear message of disapproval regarding the Israeli government's conduct of the war in Gaza and its dismissal of President Joe Biden's requests and concerns over many months.

November 21 The International Criminal Court in The Hague, Netherlands, issues arrest warrants for Israeli prime minister Benjamin Netanyahu and his former defense minister, Yoav Gallant, as well as for Muhammad Deif, Hamas's military chief. The arrest warrants are for war crimes and crimes against humanity in the Israel-Hamas war.

November 26 According to the *Washington Post*, the fate of the 251 hostages taken by Hamas on 10/7 is as follows: sixty-three remain captive, 117 have been freed or rescued, seventy-one have been confirmed killed.

A Timeline 1945-2024

November 27	A ceasefire, calling for a sixty-day truce between Israel and the Lebanese militant group Hezbollah, goes into effect.
November 30	*Vatican News* reports that the death toll in Gaza exceeds 44,000, including 13,000 children. More than 1,700 Israelis and foreign nationals are also among the dead.
December 1	Former Israeli defense minister, Moshe Ya'alon, accuses Israel of committing war crimes and ethnic cleansing in the Gaza Strip.
December 2	US president-elect, Donald Trump, vows that "there will be ALL HELL TO PAY" if Hamas does not release its hostages before his inauguration day, January 20, 2025. Meanwhile, Israel fortifies military bases and destroys Palestinian buildings in central Gaza, a step suggesting long-term Israeli control of the area.
December 5	Amnesty International publishes *'You Feel Like You Are Subhuman': Israel's Genocide Against Palestinians in Gaza*, a report finding that Israel continues to commit genocide against Palestinians in the occupied Gaza Strip.
December 8	Opposition forces oust Syrian dictator Bashar al-Assad, who flees from Damascus to Russia. For the first time since the official end of the Yom Kippur War in 1974, the IDF enters Syria to prevent rebel assaults on Israel.
December 10	Charged with bribery, fraud, and breach of trust in three separate but related cases, Benjamin Netanyahu becomes the first Israeli prime minister to take the stand as the defendant in a criminal trial for corruption. Aiming to create a "sterile defense zone" in southern Syria, the IDF announces that it has launched 350 airstrikes on Syrian territory since December 8.
December 15	After the fall of the Syrian dictator Bashar al-Assad, Israel announces plans to increase its settlements in the occupied Golan Heights.
December 16	The Gaza Health Ministry reports that the death toll in the Gaza Strip has topped 45,000, about 2 percent of the prewar population of 2.3 million.

December 17	Standing atop Mount Hermon in Syrian territory, Benjamin Netanyahu states that the IDF will remain in Syria "until another arrangement is found that ensures Israel's security."
December 19	Human Rights Watch issues *Extermination and Acts of Genocide*, a report finding that Israel has deliberately withheld water from Palestinians in Gaza, subjecting them to genocidal conditions. One critic of the report, Gerald Steinberg, calls it "propaganda in the disguise of research."
December 23	High-resolution satellite images show that Israel is engaging in mass demolitions and construction of military fortifications in former residential areas of northern Gaza.
December 25	Displaced Palestinian Christians celebrate Christmas, which coincides with Hanukkah in 2024, while Hamas and Israel trade blame over their failure to conclude a ceasefire agreement.
December 26	*New York Times* investigations show that the IDF significantly loosened its rules of engagement against Hamas after the 10/7 attack, allowing strikes that increased Palestinian civilian casualties. The IDF confirms the rules change but maintains that its practices remain consistent with international law.
December 28	Claiming that Kamal Adwan Hospital was a "Hamas terrorist stronghold," the IDF shuts down and partially destroys the last major hospital in northern Gaza.
December 31	As 2024 ends, no ceasefire halts the Israel-Hamas war, which has damaged but not eliminated Hamas, killed more than 45,000 Palestinians and 1,700 Israelis, and displaced 1.9 million Palestinians and 100,000 Israelis.

Part One
Frank Dialogue

On August 16, 2024, the American president Joe Biden voiced optimism when he said, "We are closer than we have ever been."[1] He referred to prospects for a ceasefire, if not an end, to the Israel-Hamas war, ten months old at the time. As *Stress Test*'s timeline documents, hopes of that kind about the Israeli-Palestinian conflict have a long and mostly futile history, dating back at least to the founding of the State of Israel in 1948.

How will the latest negotiations play out? That question is inseparable from two other August moments in 2024. First, the August 26 cover of *Time* magazine featured the gray-toned gaze of Benjamin Netanyahu, the embattled, 74-year-old Israeli prime minister. "Bibi at War," *Time*'s cover story, quoted Netanyahu's long-standing position: "Our objective is to completely destroy Hamas's military and governing capabilities."[2]

The second August moment, a well-researched Bloomberg report, included the following paragraph, which shows what Netanyahu's policy has entailed in Gaza.

> So far, Israeli air strikes have left **more than 42 million tonnes of debris** across the Strip, according to the UN. That's enough rubble to fill a line of dump trucks stretching from New York to Singapore. Removing it all may take years and cost as much as $700 million. The task will be complicated by unexploded bombs, dangerous contaminants and human remains under the rubble.[3]

Five months earlier, on March 13, 2024, the Council of Centers on Jewish-Christian Relations (CCJR) convened a Zoom meeting. Most of *Stress Test*'s contributors are affiliated with CCJR, which is "committed to interreligious dialogue, the purpose of which is neither to undermine nor to change the religious identity of the other, but rather seeks to be enriched by each other's religious lives and traditions."[4] Prompted by the Israel-Hamas war, the CCJR conversation was called "Sharing Concerns about the Jewish-Christian Dialogue and Relationship in the United States."

Adam Gregerman, professor of Jewish studies at Saint Joseph's University (Philadelphia, Pennsylvania) and chair of the CCJR, began the meeting by acknowledging that the Israel-Hamas war has seriously strained relationships among people committed to improving Christian-Jewish relations. "There have been disappointments, wounded feelings, unmet expectations, and major misunderstandings," Gregerman aptly said, adding that "an appropriate response to these developments is a frank dialogue in which friends and colleagues have a chance to reflect on their current concerns."[5]

What does 'frank dialogue' mean in the context of the Israel-Hamas war and its aftermath, especially in Christian-Jewish relations? The term *frank* connotes honesty, candor, rejection of evasiveness, and refusal to indulge overly polite diplomacy. At its best, frank dialogue cuts to the chase, focuses on what is most vital and important. It encourages clarity, weighs evidence, and pursues truth. Such dialogue is also respectful; it emphasizes careful listening. Done well, frank dialogue also speaks up and speaks out; it seeks truth, defends justice, and minces no words.

Where Christian-Jewish relations are concerned, the Israel-Hamas war creates stress tests because frank dialogue about that war—its causes and casualties, its repairs and reparations—is challenging and difficult. The four chapters that follow acknowledge that fact, build upon it constructively, and model what frank dialogue requires. Like all of *Stress Test*'s chapters, these four intend to provoke no-nonsense discussion, to get people thinking and talking to each other about what concerns them most in the post-10/7 interfaith dialogue between Christians and Jews. That work requires Christians to address challenging issues to clarify what they need to explore with Jewish partners and with Muslim colleagues as well.

Holocaust scholar Carol Rittner's concerns about the Israel-Hamas war include questions about war crimes and crimes against humanity. Specifically, she questions whether the Israel Defense Forces (IDF) have committed gender-based sexual violence against Palestinians in Gaza during the war with Hamas. She also raises concerns about whether the Israel prison service has committed such gender-based crimes against imprisoned or interrogated Palestinians. If dialogue is to be real, she argues, "we Christians and Jews should put all questions related to the Israel-Hamas war 'on the table' for discussion, just as we do when discussing difficult and sensitive questions related to the Holocaust."

The ethicist John T. Pawlikowski examines the impact of the Israel-Hamas war on Christian-Jewish relations by assessing the historical and moral context of the long-standing Israeli-Palestinian conflict. He points out that Jews and Christians often start their analyses of the current war in different places. For Jews, survival of the State of Israel likely comes first; for Christians, just war theory may have priority. Pawlikowski says that frank dialogue about these differences is essential for Christian-Jewish relations to be at their best.

Part One

The Catholic biblical theologian Philip A. Cunningham modestly describes himself as lacking "expertise in tactics, politics, or international law." He declines to "assess the volleying charges and countercharges or propose strategic or legal solutions to the current intolerable situation" of the Israel-Hamas war. But his keen reflections focus on an issue as politically contentious as it is religiously vexing: How should biblical land promises—scriptural warrants suggesting that the land of Israel is divinely promised to the Jewish people—be interpreted during the Israeli-Palestinian conflict?

A longtime Protestant leader in Christian-Jewish relations, Christopher M. Leighton, also wonders about biblical land promises. He analyzes dreams—Jewish, Christian, and Muslim—about a Holy Land that "roughly corresponds, in contemporary geography, to the modern states of Israel and Palestine." Unfortunately, as the Israel-Hamas war painfully shows, dreams about the Holy Land have provoked conflict and drenched the land in bloodshed. The current war makes him question whether the Israeli-Palestinian conflict will ever have a successful resolution.

As the chapters in Part One illustrate, the contributors to *Stress Test* hold diverse views and do not always agree about the impact of the Israel-Hamas war on Christian-Jewish relations. But they all agree that the war must end, the rubble in Gaza must be cleared, homes rebuilt, and lives healed—Israeli and Palestinian alike. These concerns must be at the heart of war-torn Christian-Jewish relations.

To keep sharing those concerns, to give them the priority they deserve, these writers not only insist on frankly presenting what they think but also encourage readers to be frank in assessing these chapters. What do you—the reader—think about what these chapters say? You can advance the dialogue by engaging with its challenges. Done well, such work might help to bring us—Christians and Jews, Israelis and Palestinians—closer than we have ever been.

Notes

1. See Ronen Bergman et al., "Gaza Cease-Fire Talks to Resume in Cairo, as Mediators Race to Head Off Wider War," *New York Times*, August 16, 2024, https://bit.ly/4jrfWIt.

2. Eric Cortellessa, "Bibi at War," *Time*, August 26, 2024, 26.

3. See Fadwa Hodali et al., "Gaza Reduced to 42 Million Tonnes of Rubble. What Will It Take to Rebuild," Bloomberg, August 15, 2024, https://bit.ly/3CcXToR. The report adds that "the majority of the debris is destroyed housing." Boldfacing in original.

4. For further information about CCJR, see its website, https://ccjr.us/.

5. Gregerman's comments are quoted from Carol Rittner's copy of the unofficial transcript of the March 13, 2024, Zoom conversation.

1
Conflicted, Not Confused

Carol Rittner

I am a woman, an American, a Roman Catholic Christian. I am not a Middle East expert, nor am I a theologian or a historian. I am an educator, a scholar who has studied, written, and taught about the Holocaust for more than four decades. Over the years, I have been involved in dialogue with Jewish friends and colleagues about questions and issues affecting both our religious traditions. I have visited Israel more than thirty times, often bringing groups of American Christians—Protestants as well as Catholics—to Israel to meet Jews and Palestinians to try to help them get beyond the headlines they read and hear in the media about the Israeli-Palestinian conflict.

As long as I can remember, I have supported the State of Israel and its right to exist within safe and secure borders. Likewise, for as long as I can remember, I have supported the two-state solution, the right of Palestinians to have their own state within safe and secure borders. I try to follow the ongoing conflict between Israelis and Palestinians in Israel and Palestine, both of whom lay claim to the same patch of land stretching from the Jordan River in the east to the Mediterranean Sea in the west, from Israel's border with Lebanon in the north to Israel's border with Egypt in the south. Christians call this land holy; Israelis and Palestinians each call it theirs; and geopolitical experts call it disputed. The situation is complicated for sure.

I condemn Hamas and its October 7, 2023, massacre of Jews and foreign workers in kibbutzim, villages, homes, and other institutions in Israel bordering Gaza. I support the State of Israel's right to protect and defend its citizens and the foreign workers laboring in Israel, but I am troubled by the extent of the human and physical destruction in Gaza resulting from the IDF's (Israel Defense Forces) massive land, sea, and air bombardment of Gaza in retaliation for the 10/7 Hamas massacre. I am troubled by the IDF's slowdown in allowing the United Nations and other humanitarian organizations to deliver and distribute food, water, medicine, and other life-giving essentials to defenseless Palestinians in Gaza. I am troubled because while all wars are brutal, the current Israel-Hamas war seems more vicious and more brutal than previous wars Israel has fought to defend itself against invasions by Arab nations or attacks by terrorists. I condemn Hamas's repeated drone and missile attacks on Israel since October 7. Likewise, I condemn the April 13, 2024, drone and missile attack Iran launched against Israel.

I believe that Palestinians have a right to defend themselves from unjust attack or incursion into territory internationally recognized by the United Nations as legitimately belonging to Palestinians and Palestine.[1] I am not sure who has the responsibility under international law to defend Palestinians and Palestine—the Palestinian National Authority (PNA), headed by Mahmoud Abbas, president of the State of Palestine, one of the leaders of Hamas in Gaza, or someone else—but a two-state solution could help to settle that question.

Rarely have I tried to wade into debate about the Israeli-Palestinian conflict, but the current Israel-Hamas war in Gaza forces me to confront my long-standing hesitancy to speak about the conflict between Israelis and Palestinians. It forces me to reconsider my hesitancy to speak, forces me to try to say something about the war in Gaza and its implications for Christian-Jewish relations. It also forces me to try to say something about how the war affects me as a woman, as an American, and as a Roman Catholic Christian who is committed to Christian-Jewish relations, supports Israel and the Jewish people, and who also supports the Palestinian people and a two-state solution.

As a Woman

Before October 7, 2023, I did not give much thought to how the Israeli-Palestinian conflict was affecting women and girls, either in Israel or Gaza. I had not given much thought to the issue of gender-based crimes against women and girls during any of the wars and conflicts there. To be honest, before the war in the former Yugoslavia in the early 1990s, I really had not paid much attention to sexual violence during war or even during the Holocaust. I only started to pay attention to gender-based crimes, to sexual violence, to rape as a weapon of war, when I began reading Roy Gutman's Pulitzer Prize–winning news reports coming out of the conflict in Yugoslavia. At the time, he was writing about the atrocities Bosnian Serbs were committing against Muslim and Croat civilians in that country as it was falling apart after the death of strongman Josip Broz Tito (1892–1980).[2]

News reports coming out of Israel after Hamas's brutal attack on 10/7 described the carnage inflicted by Hamas terrorists during their rampage in southern Israel. Stories from Israel revealed that terrorists raped women and girls and committed other forms of sexual and gender-based violence during their invasion and destruction of kibbutzim, towns, and the Nova music festival. I started to pay attention to reports of sexual violence, the desecration of bodies, the mutilation of female and male genitals, and reports about women and girls being raped before they were murdered. Were these accounts true? Or was it fake news, propaganda ginned up by the government of Israel and the IDF to support their decision to massively invade Gaza in retaliation for the horrors inflicted on people in southern Israel on October 7, 2023?

Reports from Israel's Civil Commission of October 7 Crimes by Hamas Against Women and Children and another from the UN Secretary-General's Special Representative on Sexual Violence in Conflict presented evidence confirming that Hamas terrorists had committed sexual violence crimes against women and girls during the October 7 terror attacks. The UN report also said there is "clear and convincing evidence that Israeli hostages being held in Gaza have been subjected to sexual violence, including rape. . .[and] that sexual violence against hostages may be ongoing."[3] I paid attention. Peter Maass is right: "Atrocities tend to rhyme."[4]

Anne Llewellyn Barstow called rape "war's dirty secret."[5] Why? Because it is difficult for victims of sexual violence during war to discuss their experience. This is especially true when it comes to rape.

> Addressing sexual and gender-based violence during war inherently involves a tension between society and the individual. For society, there is a historical, national, and international significance in acknowledging the atrocities that occurred. . . . Survivors should not be demanded to speak out in order to serve people's interest to know. The choice of whether to speak, what to disclose, when, and how should be theirs, and theirs only. . . . The difficulty of disclosing sexual assaults is a well-known and recognized characteristic of the phenomenon even in times of peace. When the assault occurs in the context of war, it seems that additional dimensions of difficulty inhibit disclosure. This aspect is well-known in the research literature on sexual violence during wartime. . . and it is also significantly evident in the current context [the events of October 7, 2023, and after].[6]

UN experts also reported that there were "'credible allegations' that Palestinian women and girls have been subjected to sexual assaults, including rape, while in Israeli detention, and [they] are calling for a full investigation." The UN investigators have "condemned 'unacceptable' violence by the Israeli military against women and children during the ongoing war in Gaza, particularly sexual violence and enforced disappearances."[7] Again I asked myself, was it true? Have members of the IDF and the Israeli prison service engaged in sexual violence crimes against Palestinian women, and children? Or were such reports an example of anti-Zionist propaganda designed to discredit Israel?

I admit that over the years I have tended to discount accusations that members of the IDF or the Israeli prison service sexually abuse Palestinian men, women, and children under their control. Hamas terrorists might do so, members of the military in other countries might do so, but not the IDF or Israeli prison personnel. At least, that is what I thought. What was behind my thinking? What would cause me to think that Israeli men would not engage in such brutish behavior? Rightly or wrongly, but surely uncritically, I assumed the IDF was a well-disciplined army, fighting its wars according to so-called international laws of war, such as the Geneva Conventions, not to mention behaving according to the highest Jewish ethical standards. IDF generals and others may officially order and encourage their troops and personnel to obey the laws of war, order and encourage their soldiers to behave according to the highest Jewish ethical standards and ideals, but members of the IDF and the Israeli prison service are as flawed as are the rest of us human beings. Evidence suggests that they are as capable of committing war crimes and crimes against humanity, including gender-based crimes, as are the rest of us.

Human beings are created in the image and likeness of God (Genesis 1:26–27). This is a foundational belief in Judaism. Rape and other forms of sexual violence violate the most personal, intimate, and vulnerable parts of our embodied lives and spirits. It is as wrong for members of the IDF and the Israel prison service to rape or sexually abuse Palestinian women and girls, men and boys under their control as it is for Hamas terrorists to rape and sexually abuse Jewish women and girls, men and boys under theirs. As a woman, as a human being, I want to believe—I *need to believe*—that perpetrators of gender-based crimes, whether Israeli or Palestinian, Jewish, Christian, or Muslim, will be held accountable and punished by the appropriate military or civilian authorities for committing such crimes at any time and in any place, on a battlefield or in a prison. Otherwise, what hope is there for preventing such crimes from being committed in the future by anyone anywhere?

We Christians and Jews must not shy away from discussing with each other credible allegations of gender-based crimes that may have been committed by Hamas terrorists, members of the IDF, and the Israeli prison service during the Israel-Hamas war. This should be part of our dialogue, not a "dirty secret." We also need to support and encourage governmental and non-governmental organizations such as the UN, Human Rights Watch, and Amnesty International to investigate credible allegations of rape and other forms of sexual violence committed by Hamas, the IDF, and the Israeli prison service in Gaza and in Israel, by anyone anywhere there is war and conflict in the world.

As an American

When Hamas took control of Gaza in 2007, they constructed an underground network of tunnels snaking beneath houses, hospitals, schools, mosques, markets, and other civilian infrastructure. Senior Israeli defense officials estimate the tunnel network in Gaza is between 350 and 450 miles long, with some 5,700 separate shafts exiting near or into Israel.[8] The IDF is determined to destroy this vast tunnel system by bombing and blasting to smithereens wide swaths of territory in Gaza. Photos of Gaza today look eerily like Berlin in May 1945. Rubble is everywhere. Despair is everywhere. Defenseless Palestinians—men, women, and children, the elderly, infirm, and injured—are displaced and on the move everywhere.

In the early summer of 2024, the Gaza Health Ministry, controlled by Hamas, estimated the death toll in Gaza at nearly 37,700 people, including more than 14,000 children (statistics change daily). The numbers of dead are probably higher than currently estimated because there are bodies buried beneath the rubble.[9] More than 77,400 people in Gaza have been wounded since the start of the current war. Food, water, medicine, gas, and electricity are practically nonexistent. More than 85 percent of the Palestinian population in Gaza have fled their homes. Health and hospital services are barely functioning. Those that are functioning report shortages of even the most basic medical supplies. Operating theaters are wrecked; beds for the injured and dying are scarce. The current war in Gaza is the deadliest of the four wars that have been fought between Israel and Hamas. More than 300 humanitarian aid workers have been killed. Many humanitarian organizations have left Gaza because it is too dangerous to work there. The entire population is facing famine.[10]

Eleven days after Hamas's brazen 10/7 attack on Israel, President Joe Biden flew to Tel Aviv. On the Ben Gurion Airport tarmac, he is pictured embracing Israeli President Isaac Herzog and Prime Minister Benjamin Netanyahu. Biden made clear to them, to Hamas, to the world that "Israel is not alone—and with US support it will remain a safe, security [sic], Jewish, and democratic state today, tomorrow, and forever."[11] In the weeks and months following his visit, Biden reiterated his support and that of the American government for Israel. His words have been backed up by providing money, arms, and supplies to Israel. As the journalists Jonathan Masters and Will Merrow report:

> Israel has been using American-made weapons against its foes, including Hamas, Hezbollah, and Iran for decades. Since October 7, the Biden administration has made more than one hundred military aid transfers to Israel, although only two—totaling about $250 million—have met the . . . congressional review threshold and been made public. The Israeli military has reportedly received expedited deliveries of weapons from a strategic stockpile that the United States has maintained in Israel since the 1980s. . . . The extraordinary flow of aid has included tank and artillery ammunition, bombs, rockets, and small arms. In April 2024, news reports said that the Biden administration was considering new military sales to Israel that are valued at more than $18 billion and would include F-15 fighter aircraft.[12]

Christians like me often have engaged colleagues, Jewish and Christian, in discussions, even difficult and delicate ones, about the Holocaust. No topic is "off the table": the role of the Catholic Church during the Holocaust; the puzzling silence of Pope Pius XII; theological supersessionism and anti-Judaism in Christian theology; the Auschwitz convent controversy; and Pope Benedict XVI's lifting of the excommunication of four traditionalist Catholic bishops, including the Holocaust-denying bishop Richard Williamson. We Christian and Jewish Holocaust scholars have debated and argued, agreed and disagreed about the historical impact of Christianity and the Christian churches on the Jewish people and on the Holocaust, but we seem reluctant to discuss with the same vigor the impact of the current Israel-Hamas war on Christian-Jewish relations.

Why do we seem so reluctant to engage each other about the war in Gaza and the American government's support of it, especially President Biden's support? Why are we hesitant to address difficult, even controversial questions regarding the extent of American taxpayer money going into Israel's military coffers to buy weapons the IDF is using to hunt down and destroy Hamas in Gaza? Do we Christians fear losing support from Jewish donors for some of our research projects? Is it because we fear we might be called anti-Israel, anti-Jewish, antisemitic? Responses to these questions are debatable, but if our dialogue is to be real, we Christians and Jews should put all questions related to the Israel-Hamas war "on the table" for discussion, just as we do when discussing difficult and sensitive questions related to the Holocaust. Raising such questions, wanting to discuss such questions does not mean a Christian questioner is anti-Jewish or anti-Israel, a supporter of Hamas, Hezbollah, or Iran. It means she/he wants to engage in dialogue that is more than "diplomatic speak" about real questions and issues.

Then there is the issue of genocide. On December 29, 2023, South Africa submitted a case against Israel to the International Court of Justice (ICJ) in The Hague, Netherlands. South Africa alleged that in direct violation of the 1948 United Nations Convention on the Prevention and Punishment of the Crime of Genocide, Israel was committing genocide in Gaza against the Palestinian people.[13] According to the UN Genocide Convention,

> [G]enocide means any of the following acts committed with intent to destroy, in whole or in part, a national, ethnical, racial or religious group, as such:
>
> (a) Killing members of the group;
>
> (b) Causing serious bodily or mental harm to members of the group;
>
> (c) Deliberately inflicting on the group conditions of life calculated to bring about its physical destruction in whole or in part;
>
> (d) Imposing measures intended to prevent births within the group;
>
> (e) Forcibly transferring children of the group to another group.[14]

The 1998 Rome Statute of the International Criminal Court identifies crimes against humanity as "acts ... committed as part of widespread or systematic attack directed against any civilian population." Such "inhumane acts" include "intentionally causing great suffering, or serious injury to body or to mental or physical health." The Rome Statute also says that war crimes, "committed as part of a plan or policy or as part of a large-scale commission of such crimes" include, among other acts, "Willful killing ... Willfully causing great suffering, or serious injury to body or health ... Extensive destruction ... of property, not justified by military necessity and carried out unlawfully and wantonly ... Intentionally directing attacks against the civilian population as such or against individual civilians not taking part in hostilities."[15]

If it is not genocide that Israel—the IDF—has committed in the Israel-Hamas war, what about war crimes or crimes against humanity? Has the IDF committed those? The current war in Gaza makes people like me ask such questions, if not openly, then in my personal inquiry about Israel and how the IDF is prosecuting its war against Hamas. The International Court of Justice and/or the International Criminal Court in The Hague will issue judgments as to whether or not Israel has committed genocide, crimes against humanity, or war crimes during the Israel-Hamas war. Raising questions about the charges brought against Israel, the deliberations of the international tribunals, and the judgments that eventually are handed down need to be part of Christian-Jewish dialogue about the Israel-Hamas war. Such inquiry should not be frowned upon, dismissed outright, or labeled anti-Zionist, antisemitic, or pro-Hamas.

As a Roman Catholic Christian

I am a Roman Catholic Christian, a member of the Religious Sisters of Mercy. I entered the convent in September 1962, literally on the cusp of Vatican II, an event that revolutionized the Roman Catholic Church. Vatican II transformed the Catholic Church from an inward-looking institution to an outward-looking institution embracing and responding to "the joys and the hopes, the griefs and the anxieties of the people of this age, especially those who are poor or in any way afflicted."[16] Vatican II moved the Catholic Church from a position of isolation in the world to engagement with the world. And one of the ways that engagement took place was through dialogue, that is, through an exchange of ideas and opinions between and among people(s).

Dialogue involves respectful curiosity, asking, and listening. Dialogue demands openness and welcome. Dialogue requires each party to explain its thoughts but also requires each party to listen to the explanation of the situation such as the other party describes it, sincerely feels it, with the real problems that are proper to the party, its rights, the injustices of which it is aware, the reasonable solutions which it suggests.[17] Dialogue is not easy, however. As Patrick Morrow writes:

> [Dialogue] may sound soft, but history suggests it is hard. It takes its toll. It may be pleasant at the beginning (the "bagels and samosas" phase), when parties are delicately getting to know each other. (This is not to dismiss this stage; it is typically necessary.) But the substance of dialogue is serious engagement with difference. It is not impossible that dialogue can lead to

agreement; it is more likely to mean a better quality of disagreement. There is nothing defeatist in this.[18]

In the years since the end of Vatican II (1965), there has been more thinking and development within the Catholic Church about dialogue with others than in previous centuries, resulting in a greater openness on the part of the Catholic Church to others, to their opinions and views, to their lived reality. For years, the Holy See—the Roman Catholic Church—refused to officially recognize the State of Israel, but then in June 1985, the Pontifical Commission for Religious Relations with Jews and Judaism issued "Notes on the Correct Way to Present the Jews and Judaism in Preaching and Catechesis in the Roman Catholic Church."[19] It was the first post-Vatican II text to fully engage the existence of the modern State of Israel. In December 1993, the Holy See and the State of Israel signed a diplomatic treaty, exchanging ambassadors a few months later. (There also was interaction between the Holy See, Palestinians, and the emerging State of Palestine.) None of these developments would have happened without the sustained and difficult work of dialogue between and among Catholics (Christians), Jews, and Palestinians, both religiously and politically. Consider, for example, the discussions that were taking place between Israelis and Palestinians at Camp David in the 1970s, and the discussions taking place between Israelis and Palestinians in Oslo in the 1990s.

Relations between the Holy See and Israel have not always produced a smooth journey. It took the sustained energy and intellectual heft of people like the late Polish Cardinal, Karol Wojtyła, the man who became Pope John Paul II in 1978, to keep the Roman Catholic Church on course. Pope John Paul II not only encouraged dialogue and cooperation between two great religious communities—Christians and Jews—he revolutionized them, doing more to promote Catholic-Jewish dialogue and cooperation than any pope in history. But interreligious dialogue is not just for popes or heads of major Jewish religious organizations. As the 1991 Vatican document, "Dialogue and Proclamation" (n.42) emphasizes, interreligious dialogue also is the preserve of the ordinary believer.[20]

The Impact of the Israel-Hamas War

Christian-Jewish dialogue has two interconnected purposes: to overcome ignorance and prejudice, thus fostering mutual understanding, and to discover the values held in common by these religions, making possible cooperation in support of the common good. Human suffering from disease, poverty, and war does not respect religious divides. People of all religious traditions are affected by plagues, scourges, and wars. Christian-Jewish dialogue cannot do everything. It should not, for example, be expected to bring an immediate solution to a conflict situation. Christian-Jewish dialogue is not a fire brigade that can be called upon to put out a conflagration, like a war, but Christian-Jewish dialogue, indeed, Christian-Jewish-Islamic dialogue, can help to build the trust that is required for joint action to relieve suffering. Such joint action means acting on behalf of peace for all people, not just those of one's own religion. We need to talk to each other across religious boundaries, because if we do not, how shall we deal with the challenges we face in trying to solve wars and conflicts, situations we all contend with irrespective of our religious affiliation? How shall we work on behalf of the common good?[21]

The work of Christian-Jewish dialogue is never-ending and usually difficult. I do not know how to get everyone to embrace a culture of respect for persons who are not of one's own religion. But I am encouraged by the fact that many Christians and Jews of goodwill remain committed to engaging in honest dialogue about even the most difficult issues and questions, including those related to the Israel-Hamas war.

Thinking about the impact of the Israel-Hamas war on Christian-Jewish relations reminds me of two people, Michael Melchior and Hans Küng. Michael Melchior is a rabbi, a man I have known for forty years. He lives in Jerusalem. For many years, he has engaged in dialogue with Palestinians who are fiercely committed to the establishment of a Palestinian state. His Palestinian counterparts do not always advocate peaceful means to achieve their goals. Nevertheless, Rabbi Melchior reaches out to his Palestinian counterparts, even under the most difficult circumstances. He never gives up. He never stops trying to find a way forward toward the common good, toward peace for everyone, Palestinian and Israeli, even when dialogue seems impossible.[22]

Hans Küng (1928–2021), a Swiss Roman Catholic priest, theologian, and scholar taught for many years at the University of Tübingen in Germany. He also was president of the Global Ethic Foundation. Küng was a great proponent of interreligious dialogue. He often said, "No world peace without peace between religions. No peace between religions without dialogue between the religions."[23]

Honestly, I do not know what the impact of the Israel-Hamas war will be on Christian-Jewish relations in the days, weeks, months, even years ahead, but I believe we Christians and Jews must keep talking to each other, keep raising difficult questions and issues with each other, keep listening to each other, even when it seems nearly impossible to do so. I also think we should try to keep in mind a slight paraphrase of Hans Küng's insight about world peace: "No peace in Israel-Gaza without dialogue between Israelis and Palestinians. No peace between Palestinians and Israelis without dialogue between and among Jews, Christians, *and* Muslims."

Questions for Dialogue

1. What questions do you have about the current Israel-Hamas war in Gaza? How do your questions impact Christian-Jewish relations today?

2. Some people think there are two stories, two narratives, two versions of events when it comes to the Israeli-Palestinian conflict. Do you agree, or disagree? If you agree, explain why you agree. If you disagree, explain why you disagree.

3. What role, if any, do you think Christian churches—Catholic, Protestant, Orthodox Christian—should have when it comes to the Israeli-Palestinian conflict in Israel and Palestine?

4. Does South Africa's charge accusing Israel of genocide in Gaza have any merit? Or is the charge a "moral obscenity," as some people have argued? What about charges that Israel has committed war crimes and/or crimes against humanity in Gaza? Do those charges have any merit? Explain.

5. What kind of organization is Hamas? Is Hamas a *genocidal* organization, or, based on the 2017 revision of its 1988 Covenant, has Hamas evolved into a more *traditional* political organization, intent on providing services for its constituents and living in peace with its neighbors? (For the text of the 2017 revised Covenant, see https://bit.ly/40D2kBn). Explain your position.

Further Resources

Ben Johanan, Karma. "There Is a Right Way and a Wrong Way for Catholics to Criticize Israel." *America*, January 18, 2024. https://bit.ly/42tIgnD.

Neuhaus, David. "Anti-semitism and Palestine." *Vatican News*, May 8, 2024. https://bit.ly/3Cx1uhB.

Novick, Tzvi. "The Catholic Church, the Jewish People, and the Current Gaza War." *Church Life Journal*, November 28, 2023. https://bit.ly/3PVRu4E.

O'Connell, Gerard. "An Israeli Jesuit Priest on the War in Gaza, Jewish-Catholic Relations and the Future of the Two-state Solution." *America*, January 5, 2024. https://bit.ly/4gpnPvk.

Notes

1. See further, Lauren Tierney, Laris Karklis, and Daniel Wolfe, "Six Maps Explain the Boundaries of Israel and Palestinian Territories," *Washington Post*, November 17, 2023, https://bit.ly/40rBH2l.

2. Roy Gutman's book, *Witness to Genocide* (New York: Macmillan, 1993) had a great influence on me. Not only did I start to pay attention to Gutman's reports about widespread sexual violence during the conflict in former Yugoslavia, but when genocide erupted in Rwanda in April 1994, I paid attention to reports of massive sexual violence there too. My teaching, writing, and scholarship, since the early 1990s, have been transformed in ways that emphasize sexual violence in war and genocide. See, for example, *Are Women Human? Violence Against Women* (New York: Mercy Global Concern, 2011); *Rape as a Weapon of War* (St. Paul, MN: Paragon House, 2012); *Teaching About Rape in War and Genocide* (New York: Palgrave Macmillan, 2015); *Women, the Holocaust and Genocide* (Greensburg, PA: Seton Hill University Press, 2020).

3. See further, DVORA: Institute for Gender and Sustainability Studies for the CC07 (The Civil Commission on October 7th Crimes by Hamas Against Women and Children) Report and various presentations by Dr. Cochav Elkayam Levy, https://bit.ly/4ghPEpu; and United Nations, *Mission Report, Official Visit of the Office of the SRSG-SVC to Israel and the Occupied West Bank, 29 January–14 February 2024*, http://bit.ly/3WtXeWL.

4. Peter Maass, "I'm Jewish, and I've Covered Wars. I Know War Crimes When I See Them," *Washington Post*, April 9, 2024, https://bit.ly/3EdaA3k.

5. Anne Llewellyn Barstow, ed., *War's Dirty Secret: Rape, Prostitution, and Other Crimes Against Women* (Cleveland: Pilgrim Press, 2000), 3.

6. Carmit Klar-Chalamish and Noga Berger, *Sexual Violence Crimes on October 7* (Tel Aviv-Yaffo, Israel: The Association of Rape Crisis Centers in Israel, 2024), 6, 7, 13.

7. Jianna Cousin and Leah Sarnoff, "UN Report Finds 'Clear' Evidence Israeli Hostages Experienced Sexual Violence in Gaza," ABC News, March 4, 2024, https://bit.ly/3CtBiEm; See also Agence France Presse, "UN Experts Condemn Israel's 'Sexual Assault and Violence' in Gaza," *Barron's*, May 6, 2024, https://bit.ly/3EeVZV5.

8. "Gaza Tunnels Stretch at Least 350 Miles, Far Longer Than Past Estimate—Report," *Times of Israel*, January 16, 2024, https://bit.ly/42q1n1N.

9. Center for Preventive Action, "Israeli-Palestinian Conflict," Council on Foreign Relations, accessed April 24, 2024, https://bit.ly/4jrIcLk.

10. "Duration of Israeli Military Actions in Gaza Strip from 2008 to February 26, 2024," Statista, November 2024, https://bit.ly/42o1ScU.

11. "What They Are Saying: President Biden Visits Israel Following Hamas Terrorist Attacks," The White House, October 18, 2023, "FULL REMARKS: President Biden Visits Israel Amid Israel-Hamas Conflict," posted October 18, 2023, ABC News, YouTube, https://bit.ly/42uNqjh..

12. "Jonathan Masters and Will Merrow, "U.S. Aid to Israel in Four Charts," Council on Foreign Relations, accessed April 11, 2024, https://bit.ly/3WAFdGy.

13. Bill Burke-White, "Explaining the International Court of Justice's Ruling on Israel and Gaza," interview by Perry World House, *Perry World House*, University of Pennsylvania, February 8, 2024, https://bit.ly/3PNQWgT.

14. United Nations Convention on the Prevention and Punishment of the Crime of Genocide, 1948, https://bit.ly/3PKGlTW.

15. Rome Statute of the International Criminal Court July 17, 1998, Article 7.1 and 7.1.k, https://bit.ly/3PMhPC9.

16. See Paul VI, "*Gaudium et spes*, Pastoral Constitution on the Church in the the Modern World," December 7, 1965, #1, https://bit.ly/42ktrne.

17. On these points, see Gregory Baum, *Amazing Church: A Catholic Theologian Remembers a Half-Century of Change* (Maryknoll, NY: Orbis, 2005), 88.

18. Patrick Morrow, "An Anglican-Christian Reflection: Towards a Theology of Dialogue When Dialogue Breaks Down," in *Theological Reflections on the Events That Have Unfolded in Israel and Gaza*, ed. Michael Trainor (International Conference of Christians and Jews (ICCJ), March 12, 2024), https://bit.ly/3WvcQJF.

19. The text of "Notes" is accessible at https://bit.ly/4gelrHC.

20. The text of "Dialogue and Proclamation" is accessible at https://bit.ly/4hiYJ22.

21. For more on these points, see Michael Fitzgerald, "The Promise of Interreligious Dialogue for a World in Conflict," *Studies in Christian-Jewish Relations* 1 (2011), https://doi.org/10.6017/scjr.v1i1.1376.

22. For more information about Rabbi Michael Melchior and his work, see Ron Kronish, *Profiles in Peace: Voices of Peacebuilders in the Midst of the Israeli-Palestinian Conflict* (L.E.A.R.H.N. Peacemaking Publications, 2022).

23. Hans Kung, *Global Responsibility: In Search of a New World Ethic* (New York: Crossroad, 1991), xv.

2
The Impact of the Israel-Hamas War on Christian-Jewish Relations: The Historical and Ethical Context

John T. Pawlikowski

I have sometimes heard Christian scholars criticize Jews for bringing the issue of Israel into the Christian-Jewish dialogue. They argue that such inclusion "politicizes" the theological dialogue. What these scholars fail to recall is that in effect Christian scholars, especially the patristic writers, were in fact the first voices arguing, out of theological considerations, against any notion of a Jewish homeland.

That issue is one of several contextual situations that require understanding if we are to comprehend the current discussion about the impact of the Israel-Hamas war on Christian-Jewish relations. Others that need to be brought into play are the continuing impact of the Holocaust on Jewish self-perceptions, the ethical implications of the Holocaust, the emergence of the just war theory in Christianity, the growing influence of pacifism within Christian churches, and the recent affirmation of human rights as a central component of Christian identity in our day.

In this chapter, I will focus on these contextual issues in my overall analysis of the impact of the war on the unprecedented development of a new, positive connection between the Christian churches and the Jewish people. Will the effects of the war undercut the special bond that has been increasingly recognized between the two religious communities, a bond that Pope John Paul II regarded as unique within the field of interreligious relations?

The Historical Background

My discussion begins with the first centuries of the Common Era. Some of the early church fathers questioned the theological legitimacy of any notion of Jewish territorial sovereignty. The central core of Christianity's theological rejection of Jewish territorial sovereignty was introduced by St. Augustine. Neither Augustine nor the other patristic writers who addressed this question called for genocide against the Jews. Rather, Jews were viewed as an accursed people whose refusal to accept Jesus as their authentic Messiah consigned them to misery and marginalization wherever they might reside in human society. This understanding became so implanted in Western culture that the "wandering Jew" description became commonplace.

While Augustine may be regarded as the father of the "wandering Jew" depiction, he based his view on the teachings of his predecessors. The roots of the perpetual Jewish "wandering" theory can be traced back to the writings of Justin Martyr in the second century, especially in *Dialogue with Trypho,* the first substantive book reflecting on the status of the Jews after the Christ Event.[1]

In his *Dialogue with Trypho*, Justin Martyr raised the issue of the rebuilding of the destroyed city of Jerusalem after the two destructive wars between the Jews and the Roman Empire. Justin's primary focus was on the meaning of Jerusalem's rejuvenation, which he believed would occur for the Christian community. Justin envisioned a thousand-year process of rejuvenation for Jerusalem, integrated with the resurrection of the dead as promised by the prophets Ezekiel and Isaiah. Justin clearly articulated an eschatological vision for Jerusalem.

Importantly, Justin was also responsible for the introduction of the term *Holy Land* for the Jerusalem region. As he saw the situation, Jewish possession of the land under Joshua and his successors was temporary. But the eschatological Jerusalem rooted in the return of Jesus Christ was permanent. Though Christians might not actually possess control over Jerusalem in the short term, the formal title transfer from the temporary one held by the Jews to the eternal one in the hands of Christians had taken place. Sovereignty over the Holy Land had become a central mark of Christianity even if the actual transfer of power was delayed.

The term *Holy Land* reflected the firm conviction that the Christian church had gained the keys to Jerusalem as the result of the failure of the Jews to acknowledge Jesus as the expected Messiah. Jewish dispossession from the land resulted in what Augustine affirmed as the permanent status of the Jews as a perpetually wandering people never again to enjoy national sovereignty. Jewish longings for Zion now became an empty hope for Jews.

It is important to recognize, however, that despite the eschatological orientation of Justin and other patristic writers regarding the Holy Land, Robert Wilken has stressed that this vision also had an actual restorative dimension in human history.[2] For, as Irenaeus insisted, the newly restored Jerusalem would be located "under heaven." This theological vision about the land would eventually serve as the motivation for the medieval crusaders' drive to restore Jerusalem and its surroundings to Christian control.

Other patristic writers, however, especially Origen and Eusebius, did not attribute concrete historical dimensions to the Holy Land concept. For Origen, the biblical land promises were to be regarded as entirely heavenly and spiritual. He criticized those in the Christian community who saw them as having earthly significance upon Christ's return. Such Christians were in fact falling into the flawed understanding held by Jews who mistakenly read these promises as earthly. For Origen, there was no permanency to Jewish hegemony over Jerusalem. The genuine Jerusalem was exclusively a heavenly reality. Origen and Eusebius can be said to have "denationalized" the Jewish community. According to their outlook, no biblical basis existed for the Jewish claims to Jerusalem. The Holy Land was a theological vision that could only be proclaimed within the context of Christianity.

Origen's perspective became critically important to the traditional Christian outlook on the land in light of biblical prophecies. His views found their way into the church's liturgical and prayer life for centuries. They also undercut any appreciation of a continuing earthly interpretation of biblical land texts within contemporary Judaism. I recall a conference in Istanbul, sponsored by the World Council of Churches (WCC), where several Christian biblical scholars strongly argued against any connection between biblical land claims and the State of Israel. In many ways, this Christian understanding of the status of biblical land claims has parallels with the Hamas effort to wipe the State of Israel from the contemporary map even if the religious argument is different from the one advanced by Christianity.

Revised Catholic Views About the Holy Land

The perspectives argued by the church fathers relative to the biblical land promises continued to influence Christian thinking well into the twentieth century. Remnants of that thinking continue in certain circles even today as the comments, mentioned above, by some scholars at the WCC conference in Istanbul demonstrate. Well before that, this classical Christian interpretation was evident in 1904 when Theodor Herzl, a key founder of modern Zionism, made a visit to the Vatican to meet with Pope Pius X in the hope of gaining papal support for a Jewish state in the Holy Land. The papal response to his appeal was negative. The Holy See could not approve of renewed territorial sovereignty for the Jewish people because of their reluctance to accept Jesus as their promised Messiah. This mindset was still evident when Pope Paul VI went to the Holy Land in 1964, after the second session of Vatican II (1962–65). During his stay in the region, the State of Israel was not allowed to welcome him on an official visit even when he briefly entered the Israeli state.

Despite the continued persistence of the Augustinian paradigm on Jews and the land in some quarters of global Christianity, we have seen the emergence of a new positive perspective on Jews and the biblical land tradition both informally and formally. Changes in attitude began to be observed in the Catholic Church's dealing with the State of Israel on a political level. As a form of *de jure* recognition of the State of Israel appeared in Vatican dealings with Israel, two documents furthered the movement toward formal recognition.

First, on Good Friday, April 20, 1984, Pope John Paul II, who wrote more in a positive vein about the Christian-Jewish relationship than any prior pope, issued the apostolic letter *Redemptionis Anno*. It began to jettison the classical Christian outlook on Jews and the land. John Paul II said: "For the Jewish People who live in the State of Israel and who preserve in that land such precious testimonies of their history and their faith, we must ask for the desired security and the due tranquility that is the prerogative of every nation and condition of life and of progress of every society."[3] This statement clearly exhibits a sense of the deep intertwining of faith and land within the Jewish tradition.

Second, "Notes on the Correct Way to Present Jews and Judaism in Preaching and Catechesis in the Roman Catholic Church" was issued on June 24, 1985, by the Holy See's Commission for Religious Relations with the Jews to commemorate the twentieth anniversary of Vatican II's *Nostra Aetate*.[4] Two of its statements are especially relevant for the discussion of the Jewish land tradition and Judaism. The first clearly rejects any notion that the history of Israel came to an abrupt halt in 70 CE when Roman forces destroyed Jerusalem and its temple. Rather, the document affirms that the history of Israel remained alive in various diaspora Jewish communities "which allowed Israel to carry to the whole world a witness—often heroic—of its fidelity to the one God . . . while preserving the memory of the land of their forefathers at the heart of their hope."

The second statement in the 1985 "Notes" affirms that "the permanence of Israel (while so many ancient peoples have disappeared without a trace) is a historical fact and a sign to be interpreted within God's design." These assertions repudiate classical displacement theology. They constitute a growing affirmation of the continuing deep-seated links between the Jewish people and the land of Israel.

The climax of this fundamental Catholic rethinking of contemporary Jewish land claims came to the fore on December 30, 1993, in the "Fundamental Agreement between the Holy See and the State of Israel."[5]

While primarily focused on political arrangements in the Israeli state with regard to the Catholic Church, the "Fundamental Agreement" has been interpreted by leading Catholic and Jewish figures, such as Cardinal John O'Connor and Rabbi David Rosen, as ending the difficult history of Catholic-Jewish relations with regard to Jewish territorial aspirations.

Not all Christian communities operate in the same political context as Catholicism in terms of Judaism and biblical land rights, but in many ways the "Fundamental Agreement" drove the final and permanent nail into the coffin of "perpetual Jewish wandering" theology. While the perspectival change need not eliminate political critique of Israeli governmental policies, it has removed the Catholic Church's theological basis for denying Jews the right to territorial sovereignty. The "Fundamental Agreement" is a vital step in removing barriers to reconciliation, mutual understanding, and friendship between Catholic Christians and Jews.

Other Christian voices contributed to the rethinking of the land issue in the churches before and after the "Fundamental Agreement." Karl Rahner, arguably the leading theologian at Vatican II, held that the council had removed all remaining theological obstacles to the notion of Jewish territorial sovereignty. He did so in response to a letter sent to him by Rabbi Eugene Borowitz, a pioneering Jewish participant in the Christian-Jewish dialogue and founding editor of the Jewish journal *Sh'ma*. In his communique to Rahner, Borowitz asked: Did any remnants of the classical teaching on Jewish territorial homelessness coined by St. Augustine remain valid in the conciliar teachings? Rahner emphatically responded that no prohibition now existed from the standpoint of Catholic theology.[6]

Pope Benedict XVI added an important element to the affirmation of Jewish land rights in an address on Mount Nebo—now part of Jordan—during his visit to that area in May 2009.[7] When he spoke of Moses leading his people within sight of the land that would become their home, one can rightly understand that outlook as applying to the present and legitimating Jewish territorial claims.

Cardinal Pierbattista Pizzaballa, the Latin Catholic Patriarch in Jerusalem, has also affirmed Israel's right to national status. While joining with other Christian leaders in criticizing specific policies of the State of Israel's government, he clearly sees Jews, Christians, and Muslims as possessing rootedness in the area known today as Israel/Palestine. How this co-rootedness is to be shaped in terms of future political borders remains to be determined, but the result will likely involve separation, with the presence of separate territorial entities within an overall framework of mutual recognition, harmony, and collaboration. Cardinal Pizzaballa has publicly supported a two-state solution, a position that presumes legitimacy for a Jewish national state.[8]

Theological and Ethical Reflections

Christians have not sufficiently examined the implications of the patristic era's transfer of Jerusalem from an earthly to a heavenly location. That outlook produced a significant gap in Christian-Jewish understanding. Over the centuries, Jews retained a commitment to the land as the focus of divine activity and as the place where the Messiah would take residence. For Christians, on the other hand, the Jews' earthly existence became depicted as an exilic condition. True followers of Jesus Christ, the narrative held, would want no part of that. This outlook was at odds with Judaism's continuing belief in the sacrality of the physical land. The legacy of these differences is a complexity in Christian-Jewish relations that cannot be adequately explained, let alone resolved, in a single essay, but five key concerns loom large.

First, while Jerusalem retained a special religious dimension for Christians, and many of them dreamed of one day "walking in the footsteps of Jesus," this outlook differed significantly from Judaism's vision of Jerusalem as possessing inherent religious importance. As Christianity became theologically globalized, London, Chicago, Buenos Aires, or Rome had the same potential for the divine presence, presently and ultimately, as Jerusalem. Even while Christianity cherished hegemony over Jerusalem, this feeling never approximated the Jewish tie to Jerusalem.

Focused on persons wherever they might live, Christian priorities differed from Jewish convictions because the former were less grounded in and dependent upon specific claims and hopes about the land of Israel. For Christians, the land of Israel was less significant than it was for Jews. For centuries, Catholicism often limited its concern to formal members of the Catholic Church. I remember a headline in an issue of a weekly Catholic newsletter that was distributed in our primary school classroom: "Tornadoes devastate Mississippi; no Catholics die." This concern took on a revised focus in recent decades with a stress on the basic dignity of all people, whatever their ethnicity, race, sexual orientation, or religious beliefs.

A focus on the centrality of the human person in the encyclicals of recent popes, beginning with John XXIII, is clear. Even a relatively traditional pope such as John Paul II stressed in his first papal encyclical that authentic belief in Christ demanded wholehearted service to one's neighbor. Pope Francis has followed up on this theme, adding deep concern for the well-being of planet earth. While he has also continued the

Catholic Church's move away from transferring Jerusalem to a heavenly status, Pope Francis's concern remains global, with no special theological concern for the earthly Jerusalem. Perspectival disagreement about Jerusalem and the land of Israel may remain as a major difference between Judaism and Christianity. The current Israel-Hamas war is likely to aggravate that difference, and the challenge is to find paths forward that are productive rather than destructive and that enrich both communities' understanding of the sacred.

Hence, a second key issue, an important one in moral theology, requires careful attention. Numerous public statements and published essays about the Israel-Hamas war reveal that Jews and Christians, Catholics in particular, start their analyses in different places. For Jews, there is a solemn responsibility for physical survival and for many—if not most—survival of the State of Israel as a locale of God's redemptive action. For many Christians, *just war theory* serves as a governing paradigm. Historically, theologians have spoken of (1) the right to war and (2) limitations on action during war (*jus ad bellum* and *jus in bello*).[9] Lately, some theologians have begun to add a third dimension, *jus post bellum*, namely, how to respond morally to postwar conditions, including ecological damage as well as destruction of homes and infrastructure.

The just war perspective includes at least eight criteria. For a war to be just, it must be (1) waged for a just cause; (2) declared by a competent authority; (3) carried out in compliance with moral limitations on the war's conduct; (4) fought not simply to retaliate but with the intention to pursue peace; (5) used as the last resort after nonviolent efforts have failed; (6) conducted with a responsible possibility of success; (7) pursued so that good results outweigh the bad; and (8) enacted so that the use and result of violence are not more harmful than the unjust threats that warrant armed resistance against them.

Generally speaking, Jews have not relied upon just war theory, in large part because, until recently, they lacked the political power to wage war. A few Jewish scholars, such as Michael Walzer, have tried to apply just war theory, but most Jewish scholars look to Torah teaching for their guidance.[10] Some Christians, including popes, have moved away from just war theory toward an anti-war, pro-peace perspective. On the papal level, this move became evident in the papacy of John Paul II as he spoke about the Gulf War during the 1990s. During the tenure of Pope Francis, this emphasis on peace has grown even stronger. These differences are rooted, at least implicitly, in Christianity's transfer from the earthly Jerusalem to the heavenly Jerusalem, which resulted in a greater emphasis on protecting the well-being of the individual person rather than securing the sustainability of the state.

Much writing on the Israel-Hamas war reflects the different starting points that Jews and Christians use for their respective analyses. In particular, Christian application of just war theory to the Israel-Hamas war often finds Israeli military strategies wanting. It remains to be seen how intractable the debates and outcomes will be, but controversy keeps swirling around the question: Is Israel's war against Hamas a just war? In late June 2024, for example, the Justice and Peace Commission of the Holy Land issued "Just War?" The document states: "As Catholics in the Holy Land, who share Pope Francis's vision for a peaceful world, we are outraged that political actors in Israel and abroad are mobilizing the theory of 'just war' in order to perpetuate and legitimate the ongoing war in Gaza."[11]

A third element that has brought about differences in Christian and Jewish approaches to the Israel-Hamas war is rooted in the Jewish experience of the Holocaust, either directly or through family memory. There is no question that world Jewry experienced the Hamas attack on October 7, 2023, as akin to the Shoah. Just as the Nazis wanted to make the world free of Jews and their alleged corrupting influences, Hamas's goal, in one way or another, has been to destroy the State of Israel.

If Christians fail to grasp the Holocaust's ongoing traumatic impact on Jews, Christians cannot understand Jewish attitudes about the Israel-Hamas war. Christians need to deepen their awareness of the Holocaust's impact. Only then can they reach out effectively to Jews who are still coping with the traumatic experience of the Holocaust. Done rightly, with sensitivity and in friendship, that reaching out may help Jews to free themselves from overreliance on the Holocaust in evaluating the conduct of the Israel Defense Forces (IDF) during the Israel-Hamas war. Christians can and should encourage movement in that direction, which can be seen in the work of groups such as Rabbis for Human Rights, both in Israel itself and within the Jewish diaspora.

Fourth, details about the State of Israel's population are important. In 2024, about 9.3 million persons lived in Israel. More than 20 percent of that population consists of Arabs, nearly all of them Palestinians from Sunni Muslim or Christian communities. The Israel-Hamas war has been traumatic for them as well as for Israeli Jews. Considerable progress was being made in several sectors of Israeli society toward the integration of Jews and Arabs. This integration was taking place in universities as well as in the housing and employment sectors. The war has intensified fears among the non-Jewish minority that this promising development will collapse. That outcome would be disastrous, because Israeli Jews cannot live in peace without continuing improvement in the positive integration of its minorities into the nation-state.

Fifth, discussion about the Israel-Hamas war also needs to recognize the necessary reorientation of the Christian churches to a far more global context than was the case for centuries when the European/North American setting dominated theological and moral reflection.[12] This reorientation means that in addressing issues such as the Israel-Hamas war, churches will view the situation through a different lens than previously. The effort to decolonize countries in Africa, Asia, the Middle East, and Latin America, plus the rising influence of Indigenous peoples in North America, has altered the issues that dominate theological and ethical assessment. Issues about Palestinian rights as well as Israel's self-defense prerogatives are at play in these developments.

One personal example of such a change in contextualization occurred in 2010. Prior to the annual conference of the International Council of Christians and Jews in Istanbul, Turkey, the World Council of Churches staged a review conference on Christian-Jewish relations as part of its reassessment of its guidelines on interreligious relations. Significant voices from the Global South and the headquarters of the World Council of Churches argued that Christian-Jewish relations were primarily a "North Atlantic" concern (Australia and New Zealand included) with minor relevance at best for the rest of the Christian world. The dialogue with Asian religions was deemed more relevant for many contemporary Christian communities. The argument was also made that there is absolutely no connection between the modern State of Israel and what the Bible has to say about Jewish land promises.

As a participant in that conference, I took strong exception to these two claims, as did several of my Christian colleagues. We did not prevail, although the final statement on these issues was inconclusive. It became clear, however, that Christian scholars like me, who support the globalization of the churches and their missions, will have to find ways of demonstrating the continuing significance of the Christian-Jewish encounter in all parts of the world.

Can Constructive Christian-Jewish Dialogue Survive the Israel-Hamas War?

The answer to the question about the continued possibility of positive encounters between Christians and Jews in the *postbellum* era is complex. Not only do the political and humanitarian circumstances of that time remain undetermined, but also in both communities there will be individuals and organizations who feel that decades of Christian-Jewish discussion about the Israeli-Palestinian conflict have resulted in no permanent constructive change despite statements and policies initiated by prominent leaders. Something of this mindset began to appear in both religious communities prior to the Israel-Hamas war. During and after the war, it is likely that some will walk away from Christian-Jewish dialogue, in part because there is also an overall decline in religious belonging in our present society. Others may feel that Christians failed their Jewish brothers and sisters at the most critical moment for world Jewry since the Shoah or because they saw Jewish leaders calling for unconditional support of Israel's military response to the brutal Hamas attack on October 7, 2023. It is uncertain whether a pro- or anti-dialogue position, or something in between, will gain ascendancy.

For those like me, who firmly believe that the war makes encounters between Christians and Jews even more important and that both communities need the dialogue, we face the challenge as to whether Christian-Jewish relations have thus far produced the depth of understanding that honesty and authenticity require. Among other things, Christians still need to recognize that, despite some important studies and pronouncements, the core of the Christian understanding of Jews and Judaism remains negatively unaltered, especially in worship texts of the various churches.[13]

On the Jewish side, there will need to be greater analysis of the impact of Jewish power and sovereignty on minorities in Israeli society. The Israeli population as well as Jews in the diaspora can defend Israel as a Jewish state. But good integration of the Arab minority can strengthen Israeli society, and, in addition, it can model Jewish-Arab reconciliation in a future two-state relationship—Israeli and Palestinian—and within the greater Middle East as well. American Jewish organizations that have done a commendable job in promoting constructive diversity in North America and elsewhere must do more to promote it in Israel too. If Israel is central to Jewish identity today, as even many secular Jews affirm, then that claim must be clarified and reassessed as part of authentic Christian-Jewish dialogue after the Israel-Hamas war ends. And that discussion must be sociopolitical as well as biblical-theological.

The discussions emerging from the Israel-Hamas war show that numerous issues require further analysis in and through the dialogue, if, in fact, Christian-Jewish dialogue is to be sustained. One of the most important involves military action. As noted above, the Christian tradition has tended to focus on the just war model. While that model has been losing support in recent decades, even among recent popes, it still remains an important framework for evaluating the morality of going to war and its conduct after the initial decision. While Jewish scholars past and present have discussed moral issues in warfare, overall that discussion has not had a parallel to the Christian just war theory.

A hopeful sign is found in the Society of Jewish Ethics, which meets yearly together with the Society of Christian Ethics and its Muslim counterpart. This convergence has encouraged some Jewish scholars who work more along the lines of the Christian framework in the manner of Michael Walzer. This development holds promise for new in-depth conversation between Christian ethicists and these emerging scholars. Among the issues that need attention is the feeling on the side of Christian ethicists that in certain public statements, such as the one sent to Pope Francis by more than 400 Jewish scholars and rabbis, Christians were seemingly asked for a *carte blanche* endorsement of the military response by the Israeli Defense Forces in response to the Hamas attack.[14] Few, if any, Christian scholars reflecting on the morality of war would agree to such a request. I, for one, clearly would not in the case of any warfare situation. And in the Israeli-Hamas war, both sides have clearly violated internationally agreed-upon rules of warfare. Without question, both sides have violated the proportionality principle in just war theory. Christian-Jewish relations cannot be honest if they fail to confront those facts.

Another issue involves examining anew how *land* (including territorial sovereignty) can be interpreted. Land can acquire a sacral dimension as has been the case in a significant part of the Jewish tradition. But there always must be caution about such a designation and whether it might obscure other values inherent to the tradition. Speaking from the perspective of a progressive form of Orthodox Judaism, Yehezkel Landau has argued that while the biblical writers may have defined the parameters of the land identified as sacred, those parameters may need adjustment in light of the sacred value of justice. Moral claims stemming from the Torah's emphasis on justice must be integrated with claims involving the sacredness of land. I fully concur with Landau that if tensions develop between these two values, justice must have priority. Otherwise, a sacred land tradition can devolve into unjust religious nationalism.

A dialogue about the land tradition can benefit each of the two religious communities in different ways. Christians may help Jews navigate the use of political sovereignty in a concrete state framework. Historically speaking, Jews have come rather late to this challenge. For centuries, Jews had to struggle with finding survival in political frameworks dominated by Christians and Muslims. Now they are called to create a political framework that honors the sacrality of the land within the principles of democratic tradition in a territory where the Jewish majority must share space and power with a large non-Jewish minority. As a nation-state, how is Israel to be best defined as a Jewish state? That question remains to be adequately addressed.

From the dialogue on the sacredness of land, Christians can gain an appreciation that their religious community is rooted in our earthly planet even though they may globalize that sacredness in contrast to Judaism's emphasis on a specific space in the Middle East. Pope Francis has stressed the requirement of a "landed theology" in his encyclical *Laudato Si'* and its related document *Laudate Deum*.[15] Christians must also seriously consider the argument that if God's ancient covenant with the Jewish people is irrevocable, even after the Christ Event, then the Jewish tradition's sacral land claims remain integral to that covenant.[16] In the context of the Israel-Hamas war, such an understanding entails an unqualified rejection of Hamas's goal of removing, one way or another, the State of Israel and proclaiming a Palestinian state "from the river to the sea."

Christian-Jewish dialogue must also discuss the creation of a Palestinian state. Christian leaders, including Pope Francis and the Latin Patriarch of Jerusalem, have insisted that there must be active movement on this issue after the war. Work in that direction certainly has and will create tension with many in Israel and in the Jewish diaspora, because Israel's wartime government and many Israeli citizens, even those who have been critical of the governmental leadership during the actual conflict, have strongly resisted the idea of a separate Palestinian state. Such tension, however, should not paralyze efforts to secure a successful two-state solution for the Israeli-Palestinian conflict.

During the Israel-Hamas war, Pope Francis wrote a letter to Israeli Jews offering them his personal support.[17] The letter was a papal response to the "Open Letter to His Holiness, Pope Francis, and to the Faithful of the Catholic Church" signed by more than 400 Jewish academics and rabbis. Pope Francis's letter was well received.[18] The pope's letter, however, focused more on the worldwide growth of antisemitism than on the Israel-Hamas war. In terms of dialogue, the letter was important but inadequate. The issues of a ceasefire and the creation of a Palestinian state were very much on the agenda and should have been referenced, at least, in the papal letter. At the time of the letter's appearance, moreover, the Israeli Foreign Ministry was trashing the Vatican for the critical remarks made by the Vatican secretary of state regarding Israeli military actions in Gaza.[19] Authentic dialogue must deal with the actual realities that are on the table. It requires total candor.

As Christians speak of conditions in Israel/Gaza, they must also challenge the activities and language used by the pro-Palestinian communities. Both Israel and Hamas have engaged in war crimes. If Christians critique Israel for such actions, they must also critique Hamas. In addition, Christians must recognize that Hamas does not represent the totality of the Palestinian people. Israeli military actions and behind-the-scenes support of Hamas by the Israeli government against the Palestine Liberation Organization have been part of an effort to prevent a formal Palestinian state, pushing an increasing number of Palestinians toward Hamas. But I have heard genuine Palestinian activists, such as Jamal Khader, one of the authors of the *Kairos Palestine Document*, eviscerate Hamas for destroying the Palestinian independence movement.[20] Christians must also refrain from heavy reliance on the "settler colonialism" model in their analysis of the Israel-Hamas war. This model does have some value. There were some in the early days of the Zionist movement who envisioned a new Israeli state with Tel Aviv as "Vienna on the Mediterranean."[21] The establishment of the State of Israel, with some 600,000 of its original inhabitants coming from Arab countries and also including a sizable Indigenous Jewish population, is too complicated to be reduced to a "settler colonialism" analysis.

I close with two final and important points. First, whatever critiques Christians may offer regarding Israeli military action in Gaza and the West Bank, Christians are obliged to keep combating antisemitism. Second, Christians and Jews need to continue striving for authentic dialogue, marked by human trust and dignity, that creates space for critical and constructive exchanges about historical and contemporary issues. If the storm is weathered, Christian-Jewish relations can advance in needed ways despite the heavy costs of the Israel-Hamas war.

Questions for Dialogue

1. The patristic writers Justin Martyr and Eusebius moved Jerusalem from a historical realm to a heavenly realm. Does this move affect how Christians and Jews view war and peace issues today?

2. What role, if any, should the State of Israel play in the postwar governance of Gaza?

3. Do you feel that Pope Pius X was mistaken when he rejected Theodor Herzl's request for papal support of the Zionist movement?

4. Are echoes of St. Augustine's notion that Jews should not have territorial sovereignty still heard today?

5. How have Pope Francis's twin roles as both a ministerial prophet and the head of a political state impacted his approach to war/peace issues?

Further Resources

Burrell, David B., and Yehezkel Landau, eds. *Voices from Jerusalem Jews and Christians Reflect on the Holy Land.* New York: Paulist, 1992.

Cunningham, Philip A., Ruth Langer, and Jesper Svartvik, eds. *Enabling Dialogue about the Land.* New York: Paulist, 2000.

Kenny, Anthony. *Catholics, Jews, and the State of Israel.* New York: Paulist, 1993.

Pawlikowski, John T., and Donald Senior, eds. *Biblical and Theological Reflections on the Challenge of Peace.* Wilmington, DE: Michael Glazier, 1984.

Troen, S. Ilan. *Israel/Palestine in World Religions: Whose Promised Land?* New York: Palgrave Macmillan, 2024.

Walzer, Michael. "Israel's Pager Bombs Have No Place in a Just War." *New York Times*, September 21, 2024. https://bit.ly/4aHH4yX.

Wilken, Robert. *The Land Called Holy: Palestine in Christian History and Thought.* New Haven, CT: Yale University Press, 1992.

Notes

1. See Justin Martyr, *Dialogue with Trypho*, ed. Michael Slusser (Washington, DC: Catholic University of America, 1953).
2. Robert Wilken, *The Land Called Holy: Palestine in Christian History and Thought* (New Haven, CT: Yale University Press, 1992), 58–59.
3. John Paul II, "Apostolic Letter *Redemptionis Anno*," April 20, 1984, https://bit.ly/4jv8pbx.
4. The text for "Notes" is accessible at https://bit.ly/3WyGptW.
5. For the full text of the "Fundamental Agreement," see https://bit.ly/4jrBTHt.
6. Borowitz published Rahner's response in *Sh'ma*; See Karl Rahner, "Karl Rahner on Israel," *Sh'ma* 1, no. 16 (1971): 121–22.
7. Pope Benedict XVI, "Holy Land Visit: Arrival in Jordan," *Origins* 39, no. 2 (2009): 17–18.

8. Cardinal Pierbattista Pizzaballa, "May Jerusalem's Peace Be Everyone's," *Vatican Insider* (2016): 2. For additional statements consult the website of the Latin Patriarchate in Jerusalem, https://lpj.org/en.

9. On this topic, see Thomas Narin, "The Peace Pastoral: A Product of the Just War Tradition," in *Biblical and Theological Reflections on the Challenge of Peace,* ed. John T. Pawlikowski and Donald Senior (Wilmington, DE: Michael Glazier, 1984).

10. Michael Walzer, *Just and Unjust Wars* (New York: Basic Books, 2015).

11. See Justice and Peace Commission, "The War in Gaza Is Not a 'Just War,'" https://bit.ly/4haF8l2, the full text of *Just War?* is appended to this article; See also "Israel, Catholic Leaders Clash Over Gaza as a 'Just War,'" *Crux*, July 3, 2024, cruxnow.com; and Jonah McKeown, "Israeli Embassy Criticizes Holy Land Catholic Leaders for Statement on 'Just War,'" *Catholic World Report*, July 3, 2024.

12. Catholic scholar Massimo Faggioli has correctly stressed the importance of this shift; See Massimo Faggioli, "The Effects of the Israel-Hamas War on Jewish-Catholic Relations," *La Croix,* January 11, 2024, https://bit.ly/3Cch0zp.

13. On this topic, see John T. Pawlikowski, "Has Antisemitism Been Uprooted from Christianity? A Catholic Response," *Antisemitism Studies* (2002): 241–59.

14. See Karma Ben Johanan, et al., "An Open Letter to His Holiness, Pope Francis, and to the Faithful of the Catholic Church," Jewish-Christian Relations website, Jewish-Christian Relations, November 12, 2023, https://bit.ly/40wK7Fr.

15. For Francis's *Laudato Si'* (May 24, 2015), see https://bit.ly/40XbURb.

16. A significant statement related to this point appeared on December 10, 2015, when the Pontifical Commission for Religious Relations with the Jews issued "The Gifts and Calling of God Are Irrevocable" (Rom. 11:29): A Reflection on Theological Questions Pertaining to Catholic-Jewish Relations on the Occasion of the 50th Anniversary of *Nostra Aetate* (No. 4)." The text of the document is accessible at https://bit.ly/42nOwgE.

17. See "Full Text: A Letter from Pope Francis to His 'Jewish Brothers and Sisters in Israel,'" *America*, February 3, 2024, https://bit.ly/3WvYYic.

18. See Roberto Cetera, "Rabbis and Scholars Thank Pope for Sowing Friendship Amidst Animosity," *Vatican News*, February 15, 2024, https://bit.ly/40KFIQM.

19. Associated Press, "Israel Complains after Vatican Denounces 'Carnage' and Disproportionate Response in Gaza," February 15, 2024, https://bit.ly/4g8e44t.

20. See Jamal Khader, "Theology of the Land: A Christian Palestinian Perspective," in *Enabling Dialogue About the Land,* ed. Philip A. Cunningham, Ruth Langer, and Jesper Svartvik (New York: Paulist, 2020); For the *Kairos Palestine Document* (December 2009), see https://bit.ly/40AwHs2.

21. See S. Ilan Troen, *Imagining Zion: Dream, Designs, and Realities in a Century of Jewish Settlement* (New Haven, CT: Yale University Press, 2003).

3
Reflections on Catholic-Jewish Relations in Light of the Israel-Hamas War

Philip A. Cunningham

As I write in June 2024, the death toll in the Middle East mounts, and the "fog of war" and disinformation campaigns confound efforts at analysis.[1] Tentative observations are quickly overtaken by unfolding events. Iran's launch of hundreds of drones and missiles toward Israel overnight on April 13–14, 2024, marked an escalation of a covert, decades-long "shadow war" between the two nations.[2] As fears of major military action by Iranian proxy Hezbollah grow, efforts to secure an end to the fighting continue with uncertain chances of success.[3]

These reflections, therefore, are incomplete and provisional. Written by a Catholic biblical theologian without expertise in tactics, politics, or international law, they do not assess the volleying charges and countercharges or propose strategic or legal solutions to the current intolerable situation. Instead, they focus narrowly on what the Israel-Hamas war has brought to light about today's Catholic and Jewish relationship. This might seem the worst time to ponder interreligious dynamics, yet crises can reveal tensions that normally lie beneath the surface.

The Stark Reality of Different Perceptions of History

It has become ever more obvious after decades of dialogue and joint study that Christians and Jews interact with distinct histories, modes of religious thought, and cultures of discourse. These differences unavoidably shape their respective responses to events in the Middle East.

Looming large is the long shadow of the Shoah. The factories of annihilation that slaughtered two-thirds of the European Jewish population in World War II devastated Jews everywhere. In the words of Auschwitz survivor Elie Wiesel, "Not all victims were Jews, but all Jews were victims."[4] After the Hamas assault on October 7, 2023, many remarked that it was the worst slaughter of Jews since the Shoah, whose "horrendous nature ... made the Israeli collective mind inevitably jump back to a past of pogroms and persecutions."[5] Antisemitic rhetoric and physical assaults multiplied against diaspora Jews as the State of Israel retaliated against Hamas.[6] Profound fears intensified among many Jews in Israel and the diaspora.[7] Some also wondered why Israel's immediate counterattack on Hamas received (within a few days of 10/7) massive criticism from so much of the world, when the mass casualties of other conflicts, such as in Syria, Ukraine, Sudan, and Myanmar, did not or do not receive the same public attention.[8]

As for Christians, even if many have heard about the Shoah, most are unfamiliar with the preceding long period of Christianity's "teaching of contempt"[9] for Jews and Judaism. That unfamiliarity may make it difficult for Christians—especially those who are struck by Israel's military might in comparison to stateless Palestinians—to sympathize with Jewish worries about survival.

Christians who are shocked upon learning of their anti-Jewish legacy often painfully ask about "the relation between the Nazi persecution and the attitudes down the centuries of Christians towards Jews."[10] Pope John Paul II did not avoid wrestling with this legacy, saying: "For Christians the heavy burden of guilt for the murder of the Jewish people must be an enduring call to repentance. . . . Guilt should not oppress and lead to self-agonizing thoughts but must always be the point of departure for conversion [away from our anti-Jewish past]."[11] Combined with the notorious complexity of the Israel-Hamas war, American Catholics might tend to avoid speaking about it so as not to take sides or cause pain to their Jewish neighbors.

These factors contributed to the perception among some Jews that Catholic leaders failed to offer sufficient support after 10/7. A November 12 "Open Letter," endorsed by over 400 Jewish academicians and rabbis, expressed "a sense of deep loneliness, and a loss of confidence in the possibility of a life of safety and freedom in the sovereign state of Israel and elsewhere."[12] It asked for the Catholic Church to (1) be "a beacon of moral and conceptual clarity amid an ocean of disinformation, distortion and deceit"; (2) "distinguish between legitimate political criticism on Israel's policy ... and ... hateful negation of Israel and of Jews"; (3) "reaffirm Israel's right to exist"; and (4) condemn and distinguish Hamas's "massacre aimed at killing as many civilians as possible ... from the civilian casualties of Israel's war of self-defense, as tragic and heartbreaking as they are."[13]

Philip A. Cunningham
The Question of "Just War"

Since Pope Francis was the principal addressee of the "Open Letter," his public pronouncements since 10/7 were likely its main, though not only, catalyst.[14] The pontiff regularly states that "war is always a defeat," that women and children are its most tragic victims, that all violence should cease, and that everyone should pray for peace. Less often, but repeatedly, Francis recognizes Israel's right to defend itself, espouses "the two-state solution," voices fears of a wider regional war, and calls for the release of all hostages—without ever naming Hamas. These statements prompted the Chief Rabbi of Rome, Riccardo Di Segni, to ask:

> We all want peace. But ... what kind of peace do you want? A peace in which the workers of evil are not defeated? The workers of evil must be defeated. And we cannot accept the principle that war is a defeat for everyone, because someone has to be defeated, as Nazism was defeated in 1945.... This does not sanction any and all responses, but it must be clear that we must not equate those who are suffering from incredible abuse with those who have committed it.[15]

The rabbi's remarks bear on "just war theory," a set of norms for initiating war and for actions during war. It arose in the Catholic tradition—notably in periods when Christian ecclesiastical and secular rulers had armies at their disposal—but the invention of "modern scientific weapons, especially atomic, biological, or chemical weapons"[16] led to Catholic skepticism about the morality of any war. As articulated by Pope Francis, "it is very difficult nowadays to invoke the rational criteria elaborated in earlier centuries to speak of the possibility of a 'just war.' Never again war!"[17] Catholic leaders concluded that "every act of war directed to the indiscriminate destruction of whole cities or vast areas with their inhabitants is a crime against God and [humanity], which merits firm and unequivocal condemnation."[18] As the Catholic scholar Cathleen Kaveny puts the point: "It may be possible to defend a defensive war—but doing so will require contending honestly with the immense suffering caused by such a war. It is no longer permissible to occlude the suffering by asserting that it is 'proportionate' to the good obtained in accordance with just-war theory."[19] Mary Ellen O'Connell, a Catholic professor of law and international peace studies, observes similarly that although one nation may have the moral and legal right to defend itself, "there's no such thing as a just war ... in certain cases, a state has a just cause to resort to an otherwise immoral action—which is the mass killing of war. You can have a just cause—but war itself is always a moral evil."[20]

Such thinking struck some Jewish observers as otherworldly and impractical, if not suicidal, in real life. To them, the pope's repeated statements were "a rejection of just-war theory and an embrace of primitive pacifism." Citing the principle of proportionality, which "holds that in attacking legitimate military targets—which include military facilities that Hamas has integrated into civilian infrastructure," they counterargued that such attacks "are permitted to cause unavoidable collateral damage to civilians and civilian infrastructure, provided the harm is proportional to the value of the legitimate military objectives being sought."[21]

But how exactly to determine proportionality is unclear. Echoing current Catholic suspicions about just wars, Daniel Reisner, a former Israeli military lawyer, contends that "the rule of proportionality is a very bad rule.... There is no metric that could be the common denominator to calculate military advantage versus civilian harm."[22]

It seems clear that, in general, Jews and Catholics invoke just war ideas in markedly different ways when it comes to the Israel-Hamas war. Catholics, perhaps ashamed of their own violent past, have, unlike Jews, not been viscerally traumatized by the loss of one-third of their entire population during World War II. Moreover, ecclesiastical leaders do not have the duty of a nation-state to provide security for its citizens. Additionally, as John L. Allen Jr. argues, while Pope Francis has long "cultivated close relations with Jews," as the first pontiff from the Global South, he has an "instinctive sympathy for the Palestinian cause."[23]

Thus, it is unsurprising that Catholic and Jewish exchanges since 10/7 are often fraught. For decades, Catholic Church statements have asserted a spiritual relationship, even a brotherhood, with the Jewish people. Yet when it comes to the Israel-Hamas war, the escalating death toll and sympathy for the dire plight of Palestinians (especially the minuscule number of Palestinian Christians) have combined to produce a "jumble of religion and politics" in post-10/7 public Catholic statements.[24]

Catholic Confliction

I suggest that *one* cause of this "jumble" is that a coherent Catholic theology of "the centrality that the land of Israel plays in the historic and contemporary religious life of the Jewish people... appears to be missing."[25] The land and State of Israel are difficult topics for Catholic theology given the perennial Christian assertion that Jews had lost any claim to the land of Israel because of the crucifixion of Jesus. As Pope Pius X is quoted as saying in 1904, "Jerusalem must not get into the hands of the Jews."²⁶ Furthermore, Christians understand themselves as a universalistic community that embraces people from all lands. In contrast, most Jews see themselves "as a [particular] peoplehood that is not solely racial, ethnic or religious, but in a sense a composite of all these.... [and] see this tie to the land as essential to their Jewishness."²⁷ Having no analogous religio-ethnic connection to a particular land as constitutive of their identity, it is hard for Christians to grasp Jews' deep feelings about the land of Israel.

The lengthiest Vatican treatment of the subject is a set of "Notes" issued by the Commission for Religious Relations with the Jews (CRRJ) in 1985. This document invites Christians to understand Jews' biblical and "religious attachment" to "the *land* of their forefathers," without "making their own any *particular religious* interpretation of this relationship." Instead, "the existence of the *State* of Israel and its political options should be envisaged not in a perspective which is in itself religious, but in their reference to the common principles of international law."²⁸ Clearly, the "Notes" wants to distinguish between theology and geopolitics.²⁹

Yet, the "Notes" document goes on to assert *theologically* that the "permanence of [the children of] Israel (while so many ancient peoples have disappeared without trace) is a historic fact and a sign to be interpreted *within God's design*."³⁰ Does this assertion mean that the foundation of the State of Israel in 1948 *could* be seen by Catholics as part of "God's design?" The text is ambiguous.

A pertinent 2018 essay by Emeritus Pope Benedict XVI notes the secular character of the Zionist movement begun by Theodor Herzl and goes on to explain:

> The question of what to make of the Zionist project was also controversial for the Catholic Church. From the beginning, however, the dominant position was that a *theologically understood* acquisition of land (in the sense of a new political *messianism*) was unacceptable. After the establishment of Israel as a country in 1948, a *theological* doctrine emerged that eventually enabled the *political* recognition of the State of Israel by the Vatican. At its core is the conviction that a strictly theologically-understood state—a Jewish faith-state that would view itself as the theological and political fulfillment of [biblical land] promises—*is unthinkable within history* according to Christian faith and contrary to the Christian understanding of the promises. At the same time, however, it was made clear that the Jewish people, like every people, had a natural right [i.e.,

national self-determination] to their own land. . . . In this sense, the Vatican has recognized the State of Israel as a modern constitutional state and sees it as a legitimate home of the Jewish people, the rationale of which cannot be derived directly from Holy Scripture. *Yet, in another sense, it expresses God's faithfulness to the people of Israel.*[31]

Benedict strives to maintain the same distinction between theological and political matters that marked the CRRJ "Notes." So, it is fascinating that he, too, feels compelled to add, almost casually, a tantalizingly ambiguous remark about "God's faithfulness" ("God's design" in the "Notes"). This common impulse points to a premise shared by Benedict and the "Notes" about Jews' covenanting with God.

Catholics, Covenant, and the Biblical Land of Israel

Benedict believes that "the covenant between God and [the children of] Israel is indestructible because of the continuity of God's election [of them]." But viewing the State of Israel as a "new political messianism" is "unacceptable" to him because, from the Christian perspective, Christ has not returned in glory. As Adam Gregerman and I have suggested, "for Benedict, the State of Israel may have *religious* significance as a sign of God's faithfulness to the Jewish people, but not *messianic* significance in our current pre-eschatological history."[32] Yet since Benedict cherishes "God's faithfulness" to covenantal assurances, he does not wish to rule out categorically *any* Christian spiritual meaning of the existence of the Jewish state in pre-messianic times.

The affirmation of the covenantal life between God and Jews is a milestone in post-*Nostra Aetate* Catholic theology, but the Catholic Church has been slow to unpack its implications. Nevertheless, there have been significant developments. In 2002, for instance, Cardinal Walter Kasper viewed "Judaism . . . as a sacrament of every otherness that as such the Church must learn to discern, recognize and celebrate."[33] Pope Francis has also recognized the continuing vitality of Jews' covenanting: "God has never neglected his faithfulness to the covenant with [the children of] Israel . . . through the awful trials of these last centuries, the Jews have preserved their faith in God. And for this, we, the Church and the whole human family, can never be sufficiently grateful to them."[34] He adds that "God continues to work among the people of the Old Covenant and to bring forth treasures of wisdom which flow from their encounter with [God's] word."[35]

Thus, Catholics can be "sacramentally" inspired by Jewish confidence in God's covenantal fidelity—despite "awful trials" past and present—because Catholics themselves, through their own Christ-shaped covenanting with God, trust that, at the End of Days, God will establish the Peaceable Kingdom where the lion lies down with the lamb and warfare ceases. But what does the Catholic affirmation of Jewish covenanting with God mean for a Catholic theology of Jewish attachment to the land that also relates to the State of Israel?[36]

Adam Gregerman's Question

My Jewish colleague Adam Gregerman asks a crucial question: "Is the biblical land promise irrevocable?"[37] It is especially important for Christian-Jewish relations amid the Israel-Hamas war and its aftermath. Catholic theology can consider this question only from within Catholic frames of reference. Today, the Catholic Church teaches that the Bible is "the word of God in human language . . . composed by human authors in all its various parts and in all the sources that lie behind them."[38] Biblical interpretation, therefore, must reckon with the cultural perspectives of these human authors who, although divinely inspired according to Christian faith, were nonetheless conditioned by their specific cultural and linguistic horizons in how they conceptualized and expressed their beliefs. Theologizing biblically, or "actualizing" the meaning of such texts as Genesis 12:7; 13:14–17; 15:18; and 17:8 for the Catholic Church in the twenty-first century requires interacting with the worldviews of writers from more than two millennia ago. "To attempt to bypass [this] when seeking to understand the Bible would be to create an illusion and display lack of respect for the inspired Scripture."[39]

The authors of what Christians traditionally call the "Old Testament" lived over many centuries. In their times, land became even more essential to sustain the larger populations made possible as the Hebrew people transitioned from a primarily herding culture to an agricultural one. The early biblical writers thus conceptualized their covenantal relationship as a nexus between the God of Israel, the tribes of Israel, and the land of Israel. This covenantal interweaving was later intensified by the trauma of the Babylonian exile (586–537 BCE), after which many scriptures achieved their final form. Naturally, in their covenantal "theology," the biblical authors drew upon ancient concepts of divine land grants and the divine selection of kings. Significantly, some scriptures condition Hebrew habitation of the land on the people's proper moral behavior, perhaps most vividly in Leviticus 18:28: "And if you defile the land, it will vomit you out as it vomited out the nations that were before you."

The Pontifical Biblical Commission (PBC) understands that any actualization of the Bible "loses all validity if it is grounded in theoretical principles which are at variance with the fundamental orientations of the biblical text."[40] Therefore, the covenanting between God and the children of Israel, presupposed by all the Hebrew scriptural writers, must be determinative in applying their texts today. Relatedly, the PBC rejects "absolutely" the use of the Bible to justify antisemitism, admonishing all interpreters "to keep unceasingly in mind that, according to the New Testament, the Jews remain 'beloved' of God, 'since the gifts and calling of God are irrevocable'" (Rom. 11:28-29).[41] The last point means that even though the prophetic and other biblical texts severely criticize the behavior of the Israelites, their covenantal life with the ever-faithful God endures because "no human infidelity can nullify" God's promises.[42] The covenant can be violated *but never terminated.*

Therefore, the Catholic answer to Gregerman's question—"Is the biblical land promise irrevocable?"—must be yes. But it does not follow that such a promise can be actualized in 2024 and beyond simply by plopping culturally conditioned ideas about divinely anointed monarchs and land grants on top of the multireligious, multinational, and volatile Middle East or onto the democracy that the State of Israel defines itself to be.

American Catholics and the Israel-Hamas War

This discussion prompts me to underscore Emeritus Pope Benedict's statement that on the basis of national self-determination, "the Vatican has recognized the State of Israel as a modern constitutional state and sees it as a legitimate home of the Jewish people, the rationale of *which cannot be derived directly from Holy Scripture.*"[43] Thus, the irrevocability of the biblical land promises coheres with, *but does not cause,* the Holy See's recognition of the State of Israel.[44] It views the State of Israel as a "legitimate home" of Jews because of the right of self-determination, which accords with the Bible's testimony about the land's being a Jewish homeland for centuries. This biblical witness to Hebrew and Jewish indigeneity, incidentally, mitigates the claim that Jews are foreign colonialist interlopers in the Middle East.[45]

Even though, as Pope Francis insists, "the State of Israel has every right to exist in safety and prosperity," Palestinian Muslims, Christians, and others also have rights on the same land, and, of course, everyone deserves prosperity, security, and respect.[46] For this reason, the Holy See has diplomatically recognized the State of Palestine and has for many years advocated a two-state solution for the Israeli-Palestinian conflict.

I suggested above that the lack of a clear theological position contributed to Catholic uncertainty in the face of the Israel-Hamas war. Although the Catholic Church is torn by its concerns for the many contending peoples in the region, a coherent Catholic position is slowly emerging. However, it is one that necessarily depends on fine distinctions and subtle nuances that cannot be readily communicated in "sound bites" and with which most Catholics, including leaders, are not familiar. Clarity on these matters for the Catholic faithful is urgently needed.

Some years ago, Pope Francis wrote to Christians in the Middle East. His words, I believe, apply also to Catholics in the United States today: "You are called to be artisans of peace, reconciliation and development, to promote dialogue, to build bridges in the spirit of the Beatitudes (cf. Mt. 5:3-12), and to proclaim the Gospel of peace, in a spirit of ready cooperation with all national and international authorities."[47] The relationship between Catholics and Jews "is particular and singular,"[48] but that key understanding does not obscure "the relationship that the Church has with others and the commitment towards them too."[49] With those challenges and commitments in mind, I conclude this chapter with four thoughts about how American Catholics can and should keep faith with our Jewish neighbors and spiritual kindred at a time when our relationship is being "stress tested" by the mass casualties, protests, rage, and racist epithets and attacks that persist amid the Israel-Hamas war and its aftermath.

First, the Catholic Church strives to respect the human dignity of everyone embroiled in the Middle East conflicts. Therefore, it acknowledges the complexities of the region and its history. These involve not only the internal issues between and among Palestinians and Israelis, but also the influence of Iran and other neighboring Muslim states and world powers, including the United States. There are more than "two sides" involved. Peace is not advanced if the multinational character of the Israel-Hamas war is ignored.

Second, all Americans, including Jews, Muslims, Christians, and other groups, have the right to express support or criticism of the foreign policy of the United States or of the actions of any government, including Israel. However, since 10/7, there have been increasing verbal and physical attacks on American Jews—whether or not they were publicly voicing political opinions—as if they, as Jews, were personally accountable for Israeli policy. Such incidents surely fit any definition of antisemitism.[50] Since the Catholic Church "rejects every form of anti-Judaism and anti-Semitism, unequivocally condemning manifestations of hatred towards Jews and Judaism as a sin against God,"[51] American Catholics must be vigilant against its sometimes-subtle appearances.

Third, in conversations about the Israel-Hamas war, American Catholics should respect everyone's religious sensibilities. Concerning Jews, the Catholic doctrine of ongoing Jewish covenantal life with God, including spiritual ties to their biblical homeland, should never be forgotten, even if it is not easy to grasp it fully. Among other things, this sensitivity helps address contrasting views about "just war," but it does not preclude even severe criticism of Israeli policies.

Finally, the present crises must not be allowed to encumber the goal set nearly sixty years ago by *Nostra Aetate*: Catholics and Jews should seek that "mutual understanding and respect which is the fruit, above all, of biblical and theological studies as well as of fraternal dialogues."[52] We have only just begun to learn from each other.

Questions for Dialogue

1. Why do Christians find it difficult to resonate with Jews' attachment to their biblical homeland? What are effective ways to deal with those difficulties?

2. What factors should be considered in determining whether a particular war is "just"?

3. How should Christians interpret biblical "land texts," such as Genesis 12:7; 13:14–17; 15:18; and 17:8 or Deuteronomy 11:13–17; 28:63–65; Leviticus 19:28 or Jeremiah 24 and Hosea 11 with regard to modern events in the Holy Land, including the Israel-Hamas war?

Further Resources

Anderson, Gary A. "How to Think about Zionism. *First Things*, April 2005.

Cunningham, Philip A., ed. *Israel-Hamas War: Selected Texts*, October 2023–Present. https://bit.ly/3PP6OzR.

Cunningham, Philip A., Ruth Langer, and Jesper Svartvik, eds. *Enabling Dialogue about the Land: A Resource Book for Jews and Christians*. New York: Paulist, 2020.

Pontifical Biblical Commission. "The Interpretation of the Bible in the Church." April 23, 1993. https://bit.ly/4hrCK9g.

Notes

1. See Robert M. Dover, "Gaza Is Now the Frontline of a Global Information War," *Conversation*, February 7, 2024, https://bit.ly/40ylRmi.

2. Gerard O'Connell, "After Iran's Attack on Israel, Pope Francis Warns Against 'a Much Bigger War,'" *America*, April 14, 2024, https://bit.ly/4hvkITG.

3. David Brennan, "Israel-Hezbollah War a 'Matter of Time': Ex-official," *Newsweek*, June 6, 2024, https://bit.ly/4hePvEr.

4. See Wiesel's remarks on receiving the Congressional Gold Medal, April 19, 1985, https://bit.ly/42n3Ytr.

5. The quotation is from Raphael Schutz, the Israeli ambassador to the Holy See. See Cindy Wooden, "Amid Prayers for Peace, Vatican-Israeli Tensions Were on Display," *National Catholic Reporter*, June 7, 2024, https://bit.ly/3PPdU7C.

6. See, for example, "U.S. Antisemitic Incidents Skyrocketed 360% in Aftermath of Attack in Israel, According to Latest ADL Data," Anti-Defamation League, January 17, 2024, https://bit.ly/40CfGxY. For links between antisemitism in the United States and the white supremacy movement even before October 7th, see Alon Milwicki, "'Never Again': On Holocaust Remembrance Day, Extremists Are Still Using Nazi Rhetoric and Tactics," Southern Poverty Law Center, April 17, 2023, https://bit.ly/3WzjIWm.

7. See David Meyer, "A Rabbi's Call for Pope Francis and Catholics to Respond to 'Existential Threat' Facing Jewish People," *America*, November 28, 2023, https://bit.ly/4gfqYhk. See also Eugene Korn, "An Immediate Cease-fire in Gaza Will Not Bring Peace to the Holy Land," *America*, May 1, 2024, https://bit.ly/3E6BcDo.

8. For more on issues about reports concerning the Israel-Hamas war, see Nan Levinson, "The Problem With the US Media's Coverage of Gaza," *Nation*, December 20, 2023, https://bit.ly/3WzkhiW.

9. The phrase was coined by the French Jewish historian Jules Isaac. See his *The Teaching of Contempt: Christian Roots of Anti-Semitism* (New York: Holt, Rinehart & Winston, 1964).

10. Commission of the Holy See for Religious Relations with the Jews (CRRJ), "We Remember: A Reflection on the Shoah," §II, https://bit.ly/40IuSdX.

11. "Address to the New Ambassador of the Federal Republic of Germany to the Holy See," (November 8, 1990), quoted in The Saint for Shalom: How Pope John Paul II Transformed Catholic-Jewish Relations: His Complete Texts on Jews, Judaism and the State of Israel, 1979-2006, ed. Eugene J. Fisher and Leon Klenicki (New York: Crossroad, 2011), 200.

12. Karma Ben Johanan, Malka Zeiger Simkovich, Jehoshua Ahrens, Irving Greenberg, and David Meyer, "An Open Letter to His Holiness, Pope Francis, and to the Faithful of the Catholic Church," November 12, 2023, https://bit.ly/3WzkuTg.

13. Johanan, et al, "An Open Letter to His Holiness, Pope Francis."

14. See Pope Francis's comments in "Public Remarks on Israel-Hamas War: October 2023-Present," https://bit.ly/4h8Z5sz.

15. "Address by Rabbi Riccardo Shmuel Di Segni on the 35th Day of Dialogue between Catholics and Jews," Pontifical Gregorian University, Rome, January 17,

2024, https://bit.ly/40Cgyme. Di Segni also criticized a "retrograde theology" that he perceives as reemerging among some Catholics, including bishops.

16. *Catechism of the Catholic Church*, (Washington, D.C.: United States Catholic Conference, 1994), §2314.

17. See the encyclical *Fratelli Tutti* (On fraternity and social friendship) October 3, 2020, §258, https://bit.ly/4huYBwx.

18. Catechism of the Catholic Church, §2314.

19. Cathleen Kaveny, "Can We All Agree to Dignity? Understanding the Audience of 'Dignitas Infinita,'" *Commonweal*, June 7, https://bit.ly/3CnO0Ve.

20. Quoted in Kimberly Heatherington, "Israel's War on Hamas Raises Significant Moral Concerns as Gaza Death Toll Soars," *Catholic Review*, January 4, 2024, https://bit.ly/4juZoiQ. O'Connell's perspective is reflected in Pope Francis's frequent mention of the conflicts in Ukraine, Sudan, Myanmar, along with Israel and Palestine, when he proclaims, "War is always a defeat!"

21. David B. Rivkin and Peter Berkowitz, "The Primitive Pacifism of Pope Francis' Lecture to Israel," *Wall Street Journal*, December 13, 2023, https://bit.ly/3WxF06U. See also Peter Oppenheimer, "A Jewish Perspective on the Catholic Church's Response to the Gaza Conflict," *Catholic Herald*, February 19, 2024, https://bit.ly/42sSiFr.

22. Steven Erlanger, "Under Rules of War, 'Proportionality' in Gaza Is Not About Evening the Score," *New York Times*, December 13, 2023, https://bit.ly/40OLZLn.

23. John L. Allen Jr., "It's Impossible to Ignore Francis's Growing Jewish Problem," *Crux*, November 26, 2023, https://bit.ly/4h7YE1C.

24. Di Segni, "Address on the 35th Day of Dialogue."

25. The quoted statement is from Rabbi David Rosen, noted in David Neuhaus, "Jewish-Catholic Dialogue in the Shadow of the War in Gaza," *La Civilta Cattolicà*, May 27, 2024, https://bit.ly/4jol0xr.

26. See Raphael Patai, *The Complete Diaries of Theodor Herzl*, trans. Harry Zohn (New York/London: Herzl Press, Thomas Yoseloff, 1960), 1602.

27. National Conference of Catholic Bishops, "Statement on Catholic-Jewish Relations," November 20, 1975, https://bit.ly/4hwFy4P.

28. All quotes—the italics are added—to this point in this paragraph are from: CCRJ, "Notes on the Correct Way to Present Jews and Judaism in Preaching and Catechesis in the Roman Catholic Church," §VI, 1, https://bit.ly/4jrjt9H.

29. The text was composed by a commission for *religious* relations with Jews, not the Secretariat of State of the Holy See, which is responsible for *diplomatic* relations with the State of Israel. This distinction reflects a unique feature of the Catholic Church: the Holy See is internationally recognized as a "state" with an ambassadorial corps. This status affects texts issued by any Vatican dicastery because, as Cindy Wooden observes, "in conflicts, the Holy See must adhere to the principle of neutrality, which does not mean being morally indifferent" (Wooden, "Amid Prayers for Peace").

30. CRRJ, "Notes," §VI, 1. Italics added.

31. Benedict XVI, "Grace and Vocation without Remorse: Comments on the Treatise '*De Iudaeis*,'" *Communio* 45 (Spring 2018): 178–79, italics added, https://bit.ly/40yWRLQ.

32. Philip A. Cunningham and Adam Gregerman, "'Genuine Brotherhood' without Remorse: A Commentary on Joseph Ratzinger's 'Comments on *De Iudaeis*,'" *Studies in Christian-Jewish Relations* 14 no. 1 (2019): 19, italics in the original, https://bit.ly/3CzAy0x.

33. "Address on the 37th Anniversary of *Nostra Aetate*" (October 28, 2002), https://bit.ly/3WAy34T.

34. Francis, "Letter to a Non-Believer," September 4, 2013, https://bit.ly/3PRj9Um.

35. See Pope Francis's Apostolic Exhortation *Evangelii Gaudium*, January 24, 2024, § 249, https://bit.ly/4h5z6lJ.

36. See my "Toward a Catholic Theology of the Centrality of the Land of Israel for Jewish Covenantal Life," in *Enabling Dialogue about the Land: A Resource Book for Jews and Christians*, ed. Philip A. Cunningham, Ruth Langer, and Jesper Svartvik (Mahwah, NJ: Paulist, 2020), 303–34. Note that because Jews are a peoplehood and not simply a certain religious community, secularists or even atheists can *as Jews* feel deep personal attachment to Israel, although they would not conceive of their connection in religious terms.

37. Adam Gregerman, "Is the Biblical Land Promise Irrevocable? Post-*Nostra Aetate* Catholic Theologies of the Jewish Covenant and the Land of Israel," *Modern Theology* 34, no. 2 (April 2018): 137–58.

38. Pontifical Biblical Commission (PBC), "The Interpretation of the Bible in the Church," April 23, 1993, §I, A, https://bit.ly/4hrCK9g.

39. PBC, "Interpretation," Conclusion.

40. PBC, "Interpretation," §IV, A, 3.

41. PBC, "Interpretation," §IV, A, 3.

42. CRRJ, "Gifts and Calling," §22.

43. Benedict XVI, "Grace and Vocation," 178–79. Italics added.

44. This perspective distinguishes Catholic approaches from Christians who read the Bible uncritically. See, for example, Charley S. Levine, "Interview: John Hagee," *Hadassah*, October 12, 2007, https://bit.ly/3PPsko4.

45. On this point, see Roger Cohen, "Who's a 'Colonizer'? How an Old Word Became a New Weapon," *New York Times*, December 10, 2023, https://bit.ly/4hvO3NC.

46. See "'Attacks on Jews Are Antisemitism, as Are Attacks on Israel,' Pope Francis Tells Jewish Leader," World Jewish Congress, October 28, 2015, https://bit.ly/3WwZiNZ.

47. "Letter to the Christians in the Middle East," December 14, 2014, https://bit.ly/4js3BUz.

48. Francis, "To My Jewish Brothers and Sisters in Israel," February 2, 2024, a letter in reply to the November 12, 2023, Jewish "Open Letter," cited above, https://bit.ly/42n6v6V.

49. Francis, "To My Jewish Brothers and Sisters in Israel."

50. See "Definitions of Antisemitism" at https://bit.ly/40LmcU5.

51. Francis, "To My Jewish Brothers and Sisters." Such condemnations of antisemitism by Catholic leaders have been reiterated for many decades.

52. Second Vatican Council, *Nostra Aetate*, Declaration on the Relation of the Church to Non-Christian Religions, October 28, 1965, §4. https://bit.ly/4h7wbJ3. See also CRRJ, "Notes," Conclusion: "Mutual knowledge must be encouraged at every level."

4
A Dream Betrayed

Christopher M. Leighton

For thirty-three years, I facilitated deep spiritual conversations between Christian, Jewish, and Muslim leaders as the founding director at the Institute for Islamic, Christian, and Jewish Studies in Baltimore, Maryland. Frequently, I dealt with sharp disagreements.[1] No inquiry, however, generated greater turbulence than exploration about the status and meaning of the Holy Land, a place where the Abrahamic religious traditions hold that ancient, founding events took place. For Jews and Christians, the Holy Land roughly corresponds, in contemporary geography, to the modern states of Israel and Palestine. Muslims orient toward Mecca, in present-day Saudi Arabia, but they too lay claim to land encompassed in Jewish and Christian mapping of the Middle East.

Holy Land: Orientation and Disorientation

The dream of a Holy Land has stirred the human imagination for millennia and given shape to the hope of a home where God and humanity dwell together—secure and sanctified in an economy of mutual blessing. Jews, Christians, and Muslims have distinct visions of a future when peace and justice will come to fruition in such a sacred space. These visions have similarities but also major differences. Each claims that the achievement of its vision will realize God's desire for the human family.

A shadow falls between reality and these dreams. Jewish, Christian, and Muslim claims on the same Holy Land are bitterly contested, and the land itself is defiled by bloodshed. The atrocities unleashed by Hamas against Israel on October 7, 2023, and the ensuing retaliation by the Israeli government and its military have radically altered the political, religious, and cultural landscape—within and beyond the lands cherished as holy. That earth is scorched, and the world confronts a point of no return. However constant the strife between Palestinians and Israelis has been, this moment feels different. Its horizons are more menacing than before.

Current tribulations and prospects are undeniably bound to a long history defined by embittered rivals. The discord not only pits different religious and ethnic communities against one another but also generates deep tensions within each group. Survivors on all sides are captive to traumas, and they see themselves as victims. In addition, the injured are usually certain that they can identify their abusers, at least in terms of their ethnic, religious, or group identities. They know whom to blame and why their own viability seems to depend upon the elimination of their assailants. Any ambiguity is regarded as an enemy of clarity and a distraction from the pursuit of justice.

The dreams that once animated each community converged in the hope for a durable and expansive peace—just over the horizon of here and now. That promise has been betrayed, and so the inescapable question arises: Can a forlorn dream be restored and made more expansive in a land now ruined and rife with lost opportunities? Each religious community is torn by internal divisions and external threats, and the challenge is to find resources within our respective traditions that can revive trust, healing, and hope—or failing that, keep inveterate rivals at a safe distance.

The imperative to resist despair and to rebuild a land of promise falls first and foremost on those who occupy this contested territory, but the struggle is also reconfiguring relationships in North America. Critical work must be undertaken if fragile interreligious bonds are going to endure. At no point in recent history has the turbulence of Israel and Palestine had a more divisive impact among Jews, Christians, Muslims, and other concerned parties. Absent a soul-searching reckoning, no exit from the impasse will be found.

Israel: First Encounters

My wife Betsy and I made our first journey to Israel in the summer of 1982, not long after Ariel Sharon, the Israeli defense minister, had launched a three-pronged invasion of southern Lebanon. The offensive was euphemistically packaged Operation Peace for Galilee, and we were informed that the incursion was purely defensive—a necessary surgical intervention designed to neutralize the Palestine Liberation Organization (PLO). A surfeit of rhetoric about the malicious intentions of Israel's neighbors justified the fear and normalized the military incursion.

I had come to Israel to participate in an intensive summer seminar at Yad Vashem, the World Holocaust Remembrance Center, in Jerusalem. My immersion into the dark night of a nation's soul served both to reveal and to conceal the complexity of the Israeli-Palestinian morass. When the State of Israel was still in its infancy, many Israelis considered the Holocaust a source of embarrassment. The judgment that many Jews went to their death like sheep to the slaughter required reappraisal if not repudiation. The iconic picture of a terrified child with hands aimed at the sky under the brutal gaze of a Nazi warrior could not stand alone. Instead, the story of heroic resistance demanded prominence, and tales of armed and cultural rebellion provided a more promising model for post-Holocaust Israeli Jews. Yad Vashem underwent several overhauls to reconfigure the underlying message.

To give substance to the adage "Never Again," Israeli Jews were determined to shape their own destiny, and they were prepared for the unremitting battle to survive in a world notorious for its indifference and empty gestures of support. The legacy of the Shoah, an often-preferred term to name Nazi Germany's genocide against the European Jews, had enshrined a deep sense of distrust and reinforced the suspicion that alliances are paper-thin and all too often written in invisible ink. Israel must be prepared to stand on its own in a fight to secure its borders.

The Shoah casts a shadow that Jews in Israel and around the world cannot escape. The magnitude of the destruction remains unfathomable, and Yad Vashem became a sacred shrine where grief and mourning are validated and where the steely resolve to defend the nation is fortified. To reinforce this self-understanding, it is almost impossible for visiting dignitaries to avoid a procession to this national monument.

A sizable number of my rabbinic colleagues acknowledge that the Shoah must remain a chapter in world history demanding rigorous scrutiny, and yet they have also expressed concern that concentration on this epoch-making event threatens to eclipse a more comprehensive appreciation of Jewish culture. As Michael Goldberg notes in his book *Why Should Jews Survive?*, the Holocaust narrative all too often shrouds the biblical Exodus story and overshadows the values and practices that bind the Jewish community together. And to the dismay of my rabbi friends, the worst legacy of the Shoah unfolds when the Jewish people forfeit their own sense of agency and assume a forever-victim identity.

During our two-month 1982 sojourn in Israel, we were swept into the whirlwind of Israeli life. We met so many remarkable individuals with astonishing sagas of anguish and triumph, broken dreams and courageous recoveries. I returned home with the conviction that Israel has something of infinite value to teach, something that could not be shared in any other place on earth. In Israel, visitors can learn what it means to be guests housed within a Jewish nation. In so many countries, the majority population is Christian or Muslim. With more than seven million Jews, Israel is the only majority-Jewish country in the world. That fact requires Christians and Muslims living in Israel to discover a different way of being, an unfamiliar range of sensibilities, and an ethos that does not mirror one's core assumptions and cultural dispositions. And one of the most fundamental of these attitudes revolves around the exercise of power and control. In Israel, Christians and Muslims are invited or forced to play by a different set of rules and to live in accord with unfamiliar customs. The experience knocks off balance those who are accustomed to defining the ethos and enforcing the norms of their homelands. Bishop Krister Stendahl once remarked that in God's eyes we are all minorities. Israel affords Christians and Muslims the opportunity to make that disruptive and yet liberating discovery.

And yet, then and now, a question remains: What if the Jewish nation is inhospitable? Or more pointedly stated, how does the State of Israel acknowledge and honor the fact that Jews are not the only people who have long-standing historical and legal claims to the Holy Land? Jews are not the only ones entitled to ownership, and a Palestinian populace is also deeply rooted in the land as its longtime inhabitants and caretakers. It is therefore a massive violation to keep them powerlessly dependent on the majority's beneficence.

This critical dimension of reality was in large measure concealed by my concentration on the legacy of the Shoah. Even after coursework in the history of the region and extended readings about the complex rivalries that continued to inflame tensions from World War II through Israel's declaration of independence and statehood in 1948, I had confidence in the founding Israeli vision of a democracy that affirmed the values of pluralism. The new State of Israel would become a homeland where Jews were assured of refuge and citizenship, but also a country where shared aspirations would eventually animate diverse religious and ethnic communities—inspiring them to build an economic and social order together that protected the rights and dignity of all the inhabitants.

In the wake of Jewish history anguished by the Holocaust, the international dictates of justice, I believed, required this nation to have a Jewish majority. The Jewish attachment to the Holy Land has roots stretching far back into biblical times, and the dreams of a homeland for the Jewish people have been celebrated in ritual and prayer over millennia, reaffirming this intimate and unbreakable connection.

I was also reminded that Israel had absorbed millions of Jews who had fled inhospitable Arab lands as well as those who had escaped the tyranny of the former Soviet Union. While Jewish friends admitted dreadful casualties of war and the catastrophic expulsion of Palestinians, I was told repeatedly this misfortune was not the first massive displacement of an Indigenous people—and lamentably it would not be the last. Why could not the neighboring countries of Egypt, Jordan, Syria, and Lebanon welcome and assimilate Palestinian refugees? Were these Palestinian exiles being used as political pawns to undermine the legitimacy of a predominantly Jewish state? The intractable opposition to a Jewish nation was revealed in numerous terrorist attacks and wars that seemed to demonstrate that a significant segment of the Arab world and Palestinians in particular were making coexistence impossible and equal rights implausible.

These observations coalesced into a narrative that in large measure erased Palestinian claims and framed them as "a problem." The rise of Islamic extremism embedded in the ideologies of Hezbollah and Hamas was increasingly portrayed as normative and representative of a Muslim Palestinian majority. The Christian Palestinian community found itself caught in a crossfire, and many of its outspoken advocates adopted a liberationist position that undermined the legitimacy of the Israeli government and was better aligned with their Muslim neighbors.

The Bible: A Two-Edged Sword

Biblical scholars have identified and explored a deep and enduring tension within Hebrew scripture concerning the land. One narrative strand proclaims the land of Israel to be a divine gift that is unconditional and perpetual. Israel's identity as God's chosen people is tied to this territory, and the bequest cannot be annulled because God remains ever faithful to God's promises. This affirmation, first expressed in Genesis 12:4ff., is later coupled in the book of Joshua with both the expulsion and annihilation of other inhabitants. The exclusivity of this land possession and the quest to avoid defilement are recapitulated in later biblical writings such as Ezra and Nehemiah. Outsiders who espouse idolatrous practices are said to desecrate the land. There are noxious convictions running through numerous biblical texts that denounce neighboring religious communities as sources of contamination and thereby provide a warrant for displacement and dispossession, violence, and even annihilation.

Alongside this exclusionary and unconditional mandate runs a competing stream of thought. According to texts in Deuteronomy, for example, Israel's right to the land depends upon fidelity to the people's covenantal obligations. "Justice, and only justice you shall pursue, so that you may live and occupy the land the Lord your God is giving you" (Deut. 16:20). This obligation to treat the poor and the needy with justice, including "the alien," is grounded in memories of Egyptian enslavement, which define the formative Jewish observance of Passover. Consequently, there is a moral obligation "not to withhold the wages of poor and needy laborers, whether other Israelites or aliens who reside in your land" (Deut. 24:14–15).

Should Israel lapse into immorality and commit sins such as murder, adultery, theft, blasphemy, and bearing false witness, the inhabitants can expect divine judgment, including retribution and even expulsion. The land cannot bear such crimes and will vomit them out (Lev. 18:28; Lev. 20:22).

These two incongruous strands are frequently deployed to serve incompatible ideological agendas. Zealous Jewish Israelis and Christian Zionists alike are apt to invoke texts that establish the ownership of the land as a sacred and inviolate birthright. Christian Palestinians and their supporters cite the subversion of justice and violation of fundamental human rights to disqualify Israel's claims to the land.

As with so many contentious debates, the Bible is enlisted to validate those on both sides of the battlefield. Seeing themselves, and they alone, authorized by God, opponents are locked into uncompromising positions. What strikes some as a political clash over the possession of land and water becomes in the hands of others a sacred duel in which the forces of good are pitted against the denizens of evil. When political struggles are cast in theological categories, and the framework gives apocalyptic import to the struggle, the plunge into total war usually follows—and the distinction between combatants and civilians is erased.

This judgment leads me to resist Christian overtures to impute special theological significance to the land of Israel—most conspicuously advanced by evangelical Christian Zionists. From my Christian vantage point, the entire creation is God's gift, and the obligation to protect and care for the earth has no boundaries. When nations lay claim to an exceptional status and envision themselves vested with a divine mandate, the stage is set for a dangerous militancy. That said, I am acutely aware that for many Jews the land of Israel is holy (and for a significant segment of the Jewish population that includes "Judea and Samaria," an area encompassing the entire West Bank). Classical rabbinic texts highlight the sanctity of this territory by noting that the covenantal life can only be most fully realized within this particular homeland.

Between Christians and Jews, this evaluation constitutes an irreconcilable difference, but one from which both communities have something vital to learn. Jews remind Christians of the importance of landedness and make it unmistakably clear that exile and homelessness are conditions that diminish our humanity. Christians call into question an attachment to land that can slide into idolatry by attributing a sacred significance, which belongs to God alone, to a finite and bounded territory.

Christopher M. Leighton

Coming to Israel's Defense

Over the years, I have spoken and written in defense of Israel as a legitimate nation that deserves worldwide recognition. Efforts to dismantle the United Nations mandate, which underwrote the establishment of the State of Israel, serve as a basis for ongoing grievances and warfare. Arguments that vilify Israel as an imperial and colonial project foisted on inhabitants who had little or no say in its formation are simplistic and moot.[2] These assertions are circulated with polemical intent, and they are laden with lethal aspirations to undo history and disassemble a nation. They stoke the fires of an unending and deadly rivalry.

Christian detractors of Israel have a right and an obligation to advocate for justice on behalf of the Palestinian population, although it is lamentable that criticism is not more evenly distributed to include other abusive countries around the world, including my own. There is no question in my mind that the government of Israel has trampled on the civil rights of Palestinians and created a civil order that renders them second-class citizens at best. The ongoing occupation of the West Bank, the dispossession of the Palestinians' lands with explicit or tacit Israeli governmental approval, and the proliferation of extralegal Jewish settlements are serious violations of international law and a betrayal of ethical norms which my rabbinic colleagues have so often championed as central to the Jewish tradition. More egregiously, the prosecution of the Gaza war now entails violations rightly classified as "war crimes."

Many Palestinian Christian leaders have applauded the censuring of Israel and encouraged American Christians to intensify and broaden their criticism of Israeli policies. Over the course of many years, rhetorical assaults ramped up and branded Israel an apartheid state complicit in ethnic cleansing. Calls for boycotts, divestment, and sanctions (BDS) gained a prominent place on the dockets of mainline Protestant denominations, and strident denunciations of Israel became routine. Calls to roll back and cut financial aid to Israel, most especially military assistance, gave teeth to the demand to "end the occupation." Aside from the self-righteous effrontery built into many of these condemnations, I was convinced that tactics intended to isolate and humble Israel were counterproductive. These strategies stirred up poisonous associations with Nazi policies, amplified fears that Jews could not trust anyone, and generated a defensive backlash that only deepened political and religious divides in North America as well as in the Middle East.

Criticism of the Israeli government all too often repurposes toxic tropes that had a long and ignoble pedigree in the Christian tradition. An image of Israelis was peddled that cast Jews as a vengeful people extracting a pound of flesh from their enemies, and as an ethnocentric tribe consumed by an obsession with power and global control. More notably, Israelis were portrayed as murderous oppressors. Jewish Israelis were once again embalmed in a noxious portrait and charged with the crime of genocide, a charge implicitly, if not explicitly, linked to the accusation of attempted deicide.[3] To dodge the accusation of propagating antisemitism, the critics have transmuted the villains into Judaism's evil twin and identified them as Zionists.

This polemical stratagem serves as the cornerstone of the Israel/Palestine Mission Network (IPMN) and is immoderately displayed in a congregational study guide entitled *Zionism Unsettled*.[4] The demonization of Zionism is given greater traction by more respectable commentators such as the widely revered biblical scholar, Walter Brueggemann.[5] Instead of a nuanced historical account that reveals the complexities and divisions within the movement known as Zionism, a declamatory stereotype is disseminated that features a gang of outlaws as representative of Jews who stand with and support the renegade nation of Israel. They are lumped into a mass and presented as sponsors of a fratricidal campaign. This sweeping account is given currency by suggesting that a straight line can be traced from the early settlers to the extremists now confiscating Palestinian lands, terrorizing the inhabitants, and demolishing their homes. I will return to the catastrophic impact of messianic Jewish supremacists whose religious ideology is shattering the prospect of peaceful coexistence, but for now, let this suffice: the conflation of extremism with Zionism uses an incendiary generalization to slander the larger Jewish community.

Why? Because most Jews in Israel and around the world stand in solidarity with Israel, and the vast majority—whether secular or religious—identify with the hopes and dreams that animate one version or another of Zionism. Knowingly or not, attacks on Zionism lack nuance and register as attacks on the Jewish people. The evidence for this noxious caricature is substantiated with the dramatic rise in antisemitic outbursts, including the intimidation of Jewish students on many college campuses.

An Interreligious Coalition?

The alarming persistence of anti-Judaism has in recent years gained greater scholarly attention, and this pathology has received penetrating scrutiny from academics such as David Nirenberg. In his encyclopedic survey, he demonstrates that "anti-Judaism should not be understood as some archaic or irrational closet in the vast edifices of Western thought. It is rather one of the basic tools with which that edifice was constructed."[6] Walter Russell Mead has enlarged the scope of this analysis and revealed the ubiquity of this fantasy among American critics of Israel. By tracking the long history of Zionist ideas among America's Protestant leaders and by dismantling the argument that Jews are pulling the strings of the American government, he dethrones the prevailing conspiracies of an all-controlling Jewish cabal. Indeed, most of the American Jewish population is opposed to the policies that resulted in the move of the American embassy from Tel Aviv to Jerusalem. They disapprove of the annexation of the Golan Heights, and they have often rejected Israeli justifications for increased settlements in the West Bank.[7]

Furthermore, there has been a growing recognition that militant white Christian nationalism undergirds antisemitism and often goes hand in hand with Islamophobia and racism. This awareness called forth a broader coalition of allies and reinforced the importance of a Christian-Jewish-Muslim dialogue that cuts across ethnic divides. This sense of an interwoven destiny has garnered support against the divisive rhetorical attacks of Donald Trump and his Republican enablers.

The hopeful picture, however, is complicated by significant countervailing tendencies. Prominent advocates within diversity, equity, and inclusion (DEI) coalitions classify Jews as "white," and they regurgitate conspiratorial diatribes about the Jewish quest for domination. The tensions seem to arise from dueling "victimologies," the frantic scramble to elevate one group's suffering by dismissing or minimizing the historical pains of the other.

Despite the shifting currents and undercurrents of interreligious and interracial cooperation, there were until recently strong indications that a constructive dialogue was possible and desirable. A camaraderie born of confrontation linked disparate groups together as they struggled to break the grip of a history that all too often pitted them against one another. Especially in the United States, the conviction that our destiny as Americans is interwoven was reinforced with the growing rate of interfaith and interracial marriages and validated at colleges and universities with the proliferation of interdisciplinary and ethnic studies—all signaling more opportunities of seeing the world through the eyes of others.

Rupture: October 7 and the Bloody Aftermath

Lamentably, ennobling aspirations, including those shared by a broad swath of Americans, were sundered on 10/7 by the atrocities of Hamas and the subsequent Israeli invasion of Gaza. The horrors have left both Israelis and Palestinians traumatized, and the reverberations are shaking the foundations of trust and hope in communities around the world, not least in the United States. The seismic eruption of violence constitutes a watershed event, and the bloody disarray has led almost everyone to conclude that their dreams for the Holy Land have been betrayed.

I need not rehearse the abominations unleashed by Hamas. They demonstrate a commitment to eradicate the Jews from the land of Israel—a cause for which the leaders of Hamas are willing to sacrifice thousands of Palestinian lives. Hamas is executing the intentions etched into its original charter, even though the extremism of Hamas does not reflect the views and conduct of the majority of Palestinians. That fact makes it difficult to comprehend why so many Palestinian supporters in distant lands took to the streets to proclaim that the murderous rampage on 10/7 was justified. It is one thing to hold oppressors liable for their unjust occupation while striving to establish a safe and secure home of their own. But it is another thing to celebrate the rape of Jewish women, the torture of Jewish children, and the brutal roundup of Jewish hostages. For Jews around the world, the Hamas massacre and its laudatory cheerleaders combined to dredge up unbearable memories of vulnerability and devastation, thereby fueling the overpowering sense of the Shoah's proximity. The walls Israel constructed failed to make the nation impregnable, and the promise of a protected haven collapsed.

A harsh and vindictive reaction was predictable within Israel, and the ensuing military incursion has produced Palestinian suffering beyond all imagining. The cycle of violence has spun out of control, and the world has witnessed the consequences: an unconscionable humanitarian crisis for Palestinians in Gaza. Immediately following the horrors of Hamas, the support for Israel coming from the West was substantial, if not unanimous. The magnitude of Israel's military campaign and the scale of the destruction have now substantially reversed public opinion around the world and even in the pro-Israel United States. The polarization has been reflected in the uproar that shook American college and university campuses in 2024 and may continue to do so. And all the while, the grip of messianic zealots within Israel and the occupied territories continues to grow. The voices of the fanatical have become acceptable. For a sizable number of Israeli Jews, the normalization of religious extremism has resulted in the sanctification of conquest and the expulsion of Palestinians as a holy objective.

At the time of this writing in the early summer of 2024, 85 percent of Gaza's two million people have been displaced, and upward of 35,000 of its inhabitants have been killed, including a staggering number of women and children. The enormity of the carnage in Gaza combined with the resurgence of territorial seizures and the rampages of messianic settlers in the West Bank have revealed the underbelly of Israel's exceptionalism.

The claims to democratic and moral preeminence among Middle Eastern nations have imploded under the leadership of Benjamin Netanyahu and his supporters. The blame does not rest on the failures of Netanyahu's administration alone. A troubling right-wing drift infects the larger population of Israeli Jews. According to a January 2024 poll, 94 percent of Jewish Israelis declared that the force deployed against the inhabitants of Gaza was appropriate or even insufficient.[8] The ongoing invasion has turned Israel into a pariah. Hamas has decisively won the propaganda war. Opposition to a two-state solution underwrites a tragic alignment. Hamas and the Netanyahu government share an objective that keeps the two-state vision of coexistence on little more than life support.

Ample evidence exists to demonstrate that military campaigns cannot defeat ideological extremism. A new generation of zealots—on both the Palestinian and Israeli sides—will likely emerge from the ruins. Closer to my American home, what we know is that the divides between Jews and their religious neighbors have deepened, and the relationships between Blacks and Jewish Americans are seriously ruptured.

In conversations with several progressive rabbis, I asked why they have posted "We Stand with Israel" signs on the front lawns of their synagogues. I asked them which Israel they were supporting—the Israel led by Netanyahu and far-right politicians such as Itamar Ben-Gvir and Bezalel Smotrich, who have advocated the resettlement of Palestinians outside Gaza? Or the Israel where hundreds of thousands of other Israelis joined in protest to uphold judicial independence? Israel, the xenophobic state for Jews only? Or a democratic Israel that aspires to defend its minority populations and promote pluralistic values?

I wanted to know how pernicious practices that American Jews would vigorously protest in this country could be ignored or even defended when it came to Israel. How was I to understand the shameful acquiescence to discriminatory policies of Israeli governments going back to the 1973 Yom Kippur War and the ongoing indifference of so many to Palestinian suffering? Did not this passivity leave a disturbing stain on a community that often stood at the vanguard of civic virtue?

My rabbi friends groaned in disappointment and noted that I would never really grasp the vulnerability of the Jewish people or comprehend the imperative to defend a country believed to be on the edge of extinction. In the wake of rising antisemitism that has left Jews isolated and vilified, Israelis and their supporters, it seemed, were forced to embrace the zero-sum logic of war. "I have set before you life and death, blessings and curse. Choose life so that you and your descendants may live" (Deut. 30:19). Were we to take down the signs, the rabbis indicated, we would justifiably be fired for the failure to affirm the indivisible unity and survival of a beleaguered people.

It would nevertheless be a serious mistake to imagine an American Jewish community that marches in lockstep with the Netanyahu government. The stinging March 2024 rebuke of Netanyahu by US Senate majority leader Chuck Schumer, a staunch Jewish supporter of Israel, reflects weighty concerns shared by a great many.[9] The Jewish organization called J Street provides evidence of that, advocating for the establishment of a demilitarized Palestinian state, a massive push for humanitarian relief in Gaza, and a negotiated end to the fighting.[10] For a growing segment of Jews who are routinely reminded that they live in the diaspora, an increased estrangement and disillusionment are the predictable consequence of the Israel-Hamas war. Particularly among the younger generation, Israel decreasingly occupies a prominent role in the formation of Jewish identity.

In the United States, and in other countries as well, conflicting reactions and interpretations among and within religious and ethnic communities have widened a chasm that separates Jews from their neighbors. The grievous events are also splintering significant segments of the Christian community and spilling into the public at large. The frictions, for instance, have exposed and alienated American Muslims. The rise of Islamophobia and antisemitism goes hand in hand. Despite a shared vulnerability, the polarized and embittered factions have congealed and lost a sense of common ground. A Holy Land made unholy by bloodshed is the legacy of the current Israel-Hamas war. Everyone's dreams are being betrayed. Or worse, have the dreams rested on specious fantasies now exposed—as critics have long maintained?[11]

Whichever narrative of right and wrong wins popular assent, the restoration of trust will require unprecedented labor. New levels of cooperative engagement, coordinated resolve, and concerted action to rebuild among the wreckage will require more than noble intentions, no matter what the outcome of Israel's campaign to destroy Hamas turns out to be.

A Midrash on the Question of Separation

I find myself thinking a great deal about the biblical story of Jacob and Esau, most especially their saga of betrayal. Jacob—renamed Israel after contending with a mysterious stranger at the River Jabbok—is returning to his homeland after cheating his brother Esau out of his birthright. Esau greets his brother with an army of four hundred warriors, and Jacob has good reason to anticipate a bloody confrontation. But the story takes a surprising turn. The estranged brothers embrace; reconciliation seems near. A happy ending to a sordid family saga, it would appear. But Jacob instructs his brother Esau to head home without him lest he slow his brother down. Jacob says he will follow but moves elsewhere instead, to a place at some distance from Esau and the brothers' parents.

Why, I often wonder, did Jacob refuse to return and reside with his larger family? Was Jacob once again dissembling? Was the rapprochement nothing more than a useful fiction? Or did Jacob have an intuition that truces are fragile and sibling rivalries remain risky? Did Jacob suspect that he and Esau might reenact the murderous story of Cain and Abel? Was keeping a safe distance the most viable option? Did the best path forward require separation?

Amid the Israel-Hamas war and its aftermath, cooperating Jewish, Christian, and Muslim religious communities may need to make a counterintuitive choice and affirm the distances that separate one from the other. In the story of Jacob and Esau, the two were disconnected until the day they came together to bury their father. Perhaps we Christians, Jews, and Muslims must remain at a distance until the day arrives when we too are called upon to bury the dead. Whatever else we come to share, we start with grief. And perhaps, in these tumultuous circumstances, when religion authorizes indiscriminate killing, the One we will discover we buried is none other than Our Father.

Questions for Dialogue

1. What, if anything, makes a land holy, and how is this attribution understood by Jews and Christians? In what ways do Jews, Christians, and Muslims have different stakes in the Holy Land? To what extent do our religious traditions aggravate disagreements and conflicts? If passions are inflamed by religious attachments, how might the sacred be reimagined to moderate the combustible rivalries?

2. What fears, resentments, and memories most painfully affect Jewish Israelis and Palestinians in Israel, the West Bank and Gaza? What role might Christians and Jews in the United States play to rebuild trust and interreligious cooperation—at home and abroad?

3. How do you and your community overcome the binary thinking that animates zero-sum logic? How might we break the grip of dividing the world into two warring categories: winners and losers, oppressors and victims, colonizer and colonized, innocent and guilty?

4. Is the separation of embattled Palestinians and Jewish Israelis possible or desirable? How can a division be established that does not result in

the segregation, ghettoization, and oppressive marginalization that we associate with an apartheid state?

Further Resources

Ezra Klein Show. "The Sermons I Needed to Hear Right Now." Interview with Rabbi Sharon Brous. *New York Times*, November 17, 2023. https://bit.ly/3CwKIz8.

Manekin, Mikhael. *End of Days: Ethics, Tradition, and Power in Israel*. Brookline: Academic Studies, 2023.

McCann, Colum. *Apeirogon*. New York: Random, 2021.

Mead, Walter Russell. *The Arc of a Covenant: The United States, Israel, and the Fate of the Jewish People*. New York: Knopf, 2022.

Notes

1. For more on this point, see Christopher M. Leighton, *A Sacred Argument: Dispatches from the Christian, Jewish, and Muslim Encounter* (Eugene, OR: Wipf and Stock, 2024).

2. The massive influx of Jews fleeing Arab lands and the former Soviet Union in addition to those who escaped the Nazi genocide does not amount to a cohesive plot line that can be characterized as a colonial project driven by the greedy ambitions of imperial powers. If Israel is branded and condemned as a heinous example of "settler colonialism," then the overwhelming majority of North Americans are also living in illegitimate states and, accordingly, are worthy of denunciation.

3. On the latter point, see, for example, Saleh Vallander, "The Crucifixion of Palestine," *We Exist*, December 3, 2023, https://bit.ly/3WyH4vp.

4. Walter T. Davis, ed. *Zionism Unsettled: A Congregational Study Guide* (New York: Curtis Brown, 2016). See also Donald E. Wagner and Walter T. Davis, eds., *Zionism and the Quest for Justice in the Holy Land* (Eugene, OR: Wipf and Stock, 2014. The IPMN website for *Zionism Unsettled* is accessible at https://bit.ly/3PRmJxu.

5. See, for example, Walter Brueggemann, *Chosen? Reading the Bible Amid the Israeli-Palestinian Conflict* (Louisville, KY: Westminster John Knox, 2015).

6. David Nirenberg, *Anti-Judaism: The Western Tradition* (New York: Norton, 2013), 6.

7. Walter Mead, *Arc of a Covenant: The United States, Israel, and the Fate of the Jewish People* (New York: Knopf, 2022), 6.

8. See Megan K. Stack, "The View Within Israel Turns Bleak," *New York Times*, May 16, 2024, https://bit.ly/4gbGkmW.

9. Schumer said that Netanyahu had "lost his way" and was an obstacle to peace. See Aamer Madhani, "Schumer's Rebuke of Netanyahu Shows the Long, Fragile Line the US and Allies Walk on Interference," Associated Press, March 16, 2024, https://bit.ly/42sjnbJ.

10. See "J Street's Ongoing Response to the Israel-Hamas War and Israeli-Palestinian Crisis," https://bit.ly/3E80O2N.

11. An extensive *New York Times* investigative report highlights the dangerous drift into religious extremism that has been gaining momentum since the 1995 assassination of Yitzhak Rabin. If not checked, this extremism will inflame violence for generations to come. See Ronen Bergman and Mark Mazzetti, "The Unpunished: How Extremists Took Over Israel," May 16, 2024, https://bit.ly/4jvgNb1 .

Part Two
What We Owe Each Other

As the Israel-Hamas war escalated in the spring of 2024, protest and disruption, antisemitism and anti-Palestinianism, encampments and arrests engulfed American colleges and universities from coast to coast. On more than 100 campuses, demonstrators demanded an end to Israel's war in Gaza, insisted that their colleges and universities scrap financial ties with Israel, and upset commencement ceremonies. Jewish students and faculty members felt besieged as antisemitism skyrocketed. Palestinian protesters and their allies complained that administration reactions, including interventions by police, were heavy-handed and in violation of free-speech rights.

Summer arrived, but its calm did not last. On August 14, 2024, days before the fall semester began, Minouche Shafik abruptly resigned as president of Columbia University, a position she had held for little more than a year. Shafik joined Claudine Gay of Harvard University and Liz Magill of the University of Pennsylvania as academic leaders who could not survive the firestorm of dissent and disorder that swept through their elite institutions during the Israel-Hamas war.

Columbia University was scarcely alone, but its New York City location put the students' pro-Palestinian and anti-Israeli demonstrations in media prime time, especially on April 30, 2024, when New York police in riot gear entered the campus to remove protesters barricaded inside a university building. A week later, Columbia canceled its main commencement ceremony. Three months later, Shafik was gone.

On August 13, 2024, the day before Columbia's president announced her resignation, a Palestinian father, Mohamed Abuel-Qomasan, went to a government office to register the birth of his newborn twins, a girl named Ayssel and a boy named Asser. That journey's joy tragically turned to grief when he learned that an Israeli air strike had killed them and Joumana Arafa, their mother.[1]

Early on, Abuel-Qomasan and his wife had followed Israeli warnings to evacuate Gaza City. They took refuge near the city of Deir al-Balah only to have disaster strike. The bereaved Palestinian father has birth certificates but not his children or his wife.

The Israel Defense Forces insist that they work diligently to prevent civilian casualties, contending that Hamas bears responsibility for them because it uses human shields. That narrative elides the deaths of Ayssel and Asser.

The Israel-Hamas war stress tests Christian-Jewish relations in diverse places. College and university campuses are among them. That is true because many of the leaders in Christian-Jewish dialogue are teachers and scholars who work in academe. So, as Ayssel and Asser are remembered, it is also important to note what Minouche Shafik said when she resigned. Emphasizing the toll that war-related unrest had taken on the Columbia community, Shafik nevertheless stressed optimism that "differences can be overcome through the honest exchange of views, truly listening, and—always—by treating each other with dignity and respect. That," she concluded, "is what we owe each other."[2]

Shafik's assertion is an imperative, but did she speak frankly enough? If Israelis, Palestinians, Americans, and others treated each other with dignity and respect, listening truly and exchanging views honestly, would the Israel-Hamas war end? Will Gaza be rebuilt? Will two states emerge, safe and sound, one for Israelis, one for Palestinians? Or is it naïve, academic wishcasting, a fool's errand to think and hope for any of that?

What do we owe each other? Before our heads nod too easily in agreement with Shafik, her assertion/imperative raises that key question for Christian-Jewish relations and for human relations of every kind. Versions of this question govern the four chapters that follow.

Widely recognized for her contributions to Christian-Jewish relations, Mary C. Boys is a professor of practical theology at Union Theological Seminary, which is only blocks away from Columbia University. "It's not the protests *as such* that elicit my personal disequilibrium," she writes, "but rather the unmitigated denunciation of Israel and concomitant absolution of Hamas. Among the dominant voices, it is assumed that Israel is 'genocidal,' and Zionists are 'settler colonialists.' Hamas, in contrast, is seen as a liberating force. I have discerned little, if any, empathy for Israel's moral quandary: exercising its right to self-defense against a well-funded terrorist organization operating out of an elaborate tunnel system."

According to historian and theologian Massimo Faggioli, what we owe each other includes advancing frank Christian-Jewish dialogue by exploring and criticizing how the Holocaust, Nazi Germany's genocidal destruction of the European Jews, is used and abused to legitimate the

State of Israel and its defense. He argues that the future of Christian-Jewish relations—especially the Catholic aspects of those relations—"depends significantly on the Catholic Church's ability to find the best ways through political and theological minefields. The minefields include . . . a postcolonial shift that erodes conviction that the Holocaust justifies the State of Israel's policies regarding Palestinians and the current Israel-Hamas war."

Drawing on her Iona University experience in teaching about Christian-Jewish relations, Elena Procario-Foley indicates that we owe each other a reliable assessment of what sound education can and cannot do in response to the Israel-Hamas war. She emphasizes that "brutal terror attacks, such as Hamas's attack on Israel, deny that those attacked are worthy of life. The attackers do not recognize that those attacked share a common humanity with them. In the fog of war, however, it is also difficult to recognize the attackers' humanity." As Procario-Foley's chapter shows, interreligious dialogue at Iona University could not stop atrocities or create a ceasefire in the Israel-Hamas war, but it can support such efforts by encouraging people to keep standing in solidarity with one another.

Underscoring that the suffering and grief unleashed by the Israel-Hamas war have reverberated far and wide, the sociologist James G. Paharik echoes Procario-Foley. "The work of interreligious dialogue," he argues, has "never been more challenging." But that fact is what makes such dialogue timely and necessary. He ends on a much-needed hopeful note, one that we owe each other: interreligious dialogue may never be more rewarding than in these troubled and troubling times of ours.

Have these four authors written frankly, insightfully, helpfully? Have they made good cases for what we owe each other? They hope that their readers will engage those questions in dialogue that honors Ayssel, Asser, and all the defenseless children—Jewish as well as Palestinian—who are threatened and lost in crushing circumstances because of human failure to respond well to the decisive question: What do we owe each other?

Notes

1. Chantelle Lee, "Newborn Twins Killed in Israeli Airstrike in Gaza, *Time*, August 14, 2024, https://bit.ly/4h73ufn. See also Camilla Alcini and Diaa Ostaz, "As a Father Was Registering His Twins' Birth in Gaza, an Airstrike Killed the 3-day-olds and Their Mother at Home," ABC News, August 15, 2024, https://bit.ly/40K72P8.

2. For the full text, see "Announcement from President Minouche Shafik," Office of the President, Columbia University, August 14, 2024, https://bit.ly/4axGAvi.

5
Protesting the Israel-Hamas War: Implications for Relations Between Christians and Jews

Mary C. Boys

The Israel-Hamas war suddenly unleashed a massive outpouring of support for Palestinians and a torrent of harsh criticism of Israel, galvanizing multitudes into the streets in protest. The sheer number and intensity of pro-Palestinian demonstrators catapulted this conflict to the worldwide stage for months.

I find this confounding: How did this terrible, tragic conflict so swiftly ignite the passions of large numbers of people who know little of Middle East history, geography, and politics beyond headlines? Why this degree of vehemence, particularly in the midst of all the other vile and violent conflicts in our world meriting protest? How did the Palestinian cause become the overriding issue of justice in which Israel has been cast as its implacable, diabolical enemy?

Because I believe the impassioned protests against "genocidal Israel" hold important implications for relations between Christians and Jews, they serve as a focal point for my reflections. My analysis is intertwined with thorny questions and layered with years of involvement, scholarship, institutional commitments, and deep friendships. I can think of no single topic on which I have written in recent years that touches upon such onerous issues that seem impossibly professional and personal, pressing yet premature. At best, mine is a vision dimly perceived in the mirror of the present (see 1 Cor. 13:12) as filtered through the specifics of my own situation.

Every war is unspeakably tragic, yet each is distinct in its catastrophic consequences. In the Israel-Hamas war, ordinary people are its principal victims. Initially, they were Israelis on the border with Gaza who were brutally attacked on October 7, 2023—raped, murdered, and taken hostage. Then the Israeli counterassault against Hamas also killed vast numbers of defenseless Palestinians in Gaza. Palestinian homes were reduced to rubble. Disease and famine consumed much of Gaza's civilian population. There is an apocryphal saying: "The first casualty when war comes is truth." Yes, but are not children war's greatest casualty?

What to Say in the Face of Tragedy?

Months after that fateful 10/7 attack, it is necessary to ponder what the Israel-Hamas war portends for another relationship that is deeply scarred by the wounds of history: the "tormented" history between Christians and Jews.[1] This relation requires grappling with multifaceted issues about Jewish identity and Israel, a topic I have long wrestled with, particularly since living for six months in Israel in the mid-1980s and witnessing some of the complexities regarding Palestinians.[2] I consider myself a friend to Israel—and, as with my other friends, I have high expectations while acknowledging we all fall short.

Being a friend to Israel proves to be difficult during the times of the Israel-Hamas war. At the time of this writing in July 2024, the war's outcome is far from certain, and thus its ramifications are unclear as well. Will a ceasefire, still in negotiation, take hold and become the hiatus opening to some sort of peaceful resolution? Or will this war develop on another front, such as an intensification of the tensions on the Lebanon-Israel border with Iranian-backed Hezbollah, inciting an all-out war in the Middle East with dire global implications? What will become of postwar Gaza and its Palestinian residents after such unspeakable death and destruction? What further effects will the war have—on West Bank Palestinians and their years-long conflicts with Israeli settlers? On Israel itself, roiled by internal conflicts over the governing policies of Prime Minister Benjamin Netanyahu and his cabinet, yet resolute in its hope to "be a free nation in our land / the Land of Zion and Jerusalem"?[3] On the hostages as yet unreleased? On the kibbutzniks and other Israelis who had to flee to northern areas for their safety after the atrocities of 10/7 and who remain unable to return to their homes?

The current state of the conflict in Gaza weighs heavily on me. I fear for the future of the State of Israel *and* for that of the Palestinian people in Gaza and the West Bank. There seems to be a dearth of leadership, as recent articles attest. An astringent *New York Times* analysis by Thomas Friedman, for example, insists that US leaders should stop "debasing" themselves in their diplomatic outreach to Netanyahu, whom Friedman accuses of having sold his soul in order to form a government with far-right Jewish extremists eager to control all the territory between the Mediterranean Sea and the Jordan River, including Gaza.[4] A *Washington Post* article cites a spokesman for the Israeli Defense Forces, Rear Admiral Daniel Hagari, criticizing the Israeli government's failure to articulate a political strategy for postwar Gaza.[5]

In the Israeli newspaper *Haaretz*, the former prime minister Ehud Barak, also Israel's former chief of staff of the army, accused the current government of "risking a multi-front war that would include Iran and its proxies. All this is happening," he continued, "while in the background the judicial coup continues, with its goal of establishing a racist, ultranationalist, messianic and benighted religious dictatorship." Barak maintains that the vow to win an "absolute victory" over Hamas is merely an "empty slogan" in view of the "most serious and dangerous crisis" in Israel's history led by a government and prime minister that are "patently unfit for their offices."[6] When the battle-weary Israeli military urged a ceasefire, Netanyahu rebuked it as defeatist.[7] Meanwhile, Bezalal Smotrich, Israel's finance minister, proposed construction of some 6,000 new housing units in West Bank settlements to further forestall a Palestinian state.[8]

As for Hamas, success in damaging Israel's reputation makes questionable whether it will negotiate an end to the fighting. In addition, the Israel-Hamas war has stalled, if not stopped, reconciliation work between Israelis and Palestinians, which advanced in promising ways over the last fifty years. Testimony about the setbacks for those with a long commitment to advocacy for peace is poignantly provided in Masha Gessen's *New Yorker* article (June 10, 2024) about the intentional living community of *Wahat al-Salam/Neve Shalom*.[9] Some Palestinians in Gaza have spoken against Hamas for its failure to give any attention to the safety of Gazans while Hamas fighters return to the relative safety of their tunnels, seemingly indifferent to the unspeakable suffering of Palestinians. Protest, however, must be uttered with care, as Hamas brooks no dissent.[10]

It's not only sources like these that contribute to my unease. It's my Israeli friends and Palestinian contacts. It's my deep bonds with beloved Jewish colleagues, companions in the work for ameliorating relations between our two traditions and who themselves love Israel and grieve its flaws.

It's the protesters, however, who sound the notes of greatest dissonance with their ardent advocacy for a Palestine "free from the river to the sea"—protests not simply manifest in ample news coverage but mere blocks away from my home. I work and live in New York City's Upper West Side. I have taught for more than thirty years at Union Theological Seminary, two blocks north of Columbia University's main gate on Broadway and a block south of the Jewish Theological Seminary of America (JTS). The Columbia campus has been the site of vociferous protests. Many Union students have participated alongside academic neighbors who chant, "From the river to the sea, Palestine shall be free!"

Unsurprisingly, the JTS campus has been quieter, as its students, nearly all with family and friends in Israel, negotiate the tensions within Jewish life regarding the Israel-Hamas war while also confronting virulent antisemitism, which has, in many cases, accompanied the pro-Palestinian protests. Particularly for JTS students enrolled in joint programs at Columbia, the past academic year—and perhaps the 2024–25 year as well—has included experiencing overt antisemitism unleashed by the war, antisemitism expressed not only by student protesters but also by some faculty members.

It's not the protests *as such* that elicit my personal disequilibrium, but rather the unmitigated denunciation of Israel and concomitant absolution of Hamas. Among the dominant voices, it is assumed that Israel is "genocidal" and Zionists are "settler colonialists." Hamas, in contrast, is seen as a liberating force. I have discerned little, if any, empathy for Israel's moral quandary: exercising its right to self-defense against a well-funded terrorist organization operating out of an elaborate tunnel system. Nor do I sense concern that Hamas has emerged from its underground reserve primarily to attack Israelis rather than to defend Gazans, thus leaving the Palestinians vulnerable to Israeli assaults by ground and air. What provisions has Hamas made for protecting Palestinians in Gaza?

A Case in Point

My unease intensified at a regular meeting of Union's faculty on March 27, 2024. Representatives of the Student Senate reported on the adoption of the following resolution:

RESOLVED

As students of Union Theological Seminary, we call on the Union Theological Seminary administration to immediately divest and cut off all economic and academic stakes in Israeli settler-colonialism. Our demands are as follows:

1. In line with the historical continuum of divesting, i.e., Fossil Fuels and South African Apartheid, the Union Theological Seminary divest from their current investments in all entities that profit from Israeli settler-colonialism, which currently include but are not limited to [there follows the names of various banks and capital groups].

2. End all promotion of Israeli settler-colonialism via academic ties, including but not limited to Fulbright Israel, as well as hosting any Zionist speakers amplifying settler-colonialist propaganda.

3. Recommit to vigorously protecting and upholding the academic freedom and right to political speech of students, staff, and faculty as they face McCarthyite smear campaigns. Accordingly, the seminary must maintain and create further policies so that students are able to organize gatherings and events on campus under urgent circumstances, such as in response to the genocide in Palestine.

I was stunned. Acknowledging my own grave reservations about the effects of Israel's continued bombardment of Gaza, I questioned the assumption that Israel was genocidal while Hamas remained innocent, despite its statements about destroying the State of Israel.[11] I learned that my criticism was unwelcome—one of the various ironies of the third element of the resolution.

Regarding divestment, the faculty was informed at the April 2024 faculty meeting that discussion about divestment had been underway among the Board of Trustees since November 2023. On May 9, 2024, the board passed a resolution to divest.[12] While I personally disagree with that decision and know I am not alone in that viewpoint, it is the right of the board to take action in this regard. The final paragraph of the board's statement reads as follows:

> To be clear, as we [Union's Board of Trustees] take these actions, we remain unequivocal in our denouncement of the horrific killing by Hamas of Israeli citizens on October 7, 2023, and call for the immediate release of all hostages. With respect to both Palestine and Israel, we affirm their right to secure existence and self-determination. We also remain committed in all we do to stand against all forms of hatred, including antisemitism and Islamophobia. Our investment policies will continue to adapt, guided by our values, to strengthen the resolve that undergirds our decision today. We do not take this step lightly, and we do so with all humility, recognizing that our work on the global stage is far from finished. Although our investments in the war in Palestine are small because our previous, strong anti-armament screens are robust, we hope that

our action today will bring needed pressure to bear to stop the killing and find a peaceful future for all.

No such qualification was ever apparent from Union's Student Senate. At its final meeting of the academic year, the following resolution was proposed:

RESOLVED:

that the students of Union Theological Seminary condemn the actions by Hamas, and by any individuals or groups affiliated with or acting in support of Hamas, on October 7, 2023.

This resolution *failed*: 1 yes, 30 no.

To say that I found the Student Senate's failure to condemn the actions of Hamas on 10/7 dispiriting is an understatement of considerable proportions. I do not know, however, the context in which the resolution was discussed, nor am I involved in Student Senate discussions—and student groups have a right to their own discussions and judgments. My concern here is what the thinking of a substantial proportion (or so I estimate) of the student body presages for relations between Christians and Jews. I am conscious, as well, of many students less sure of their opinions about the war and consequently reluctant to speak out.

In the wake of these resolutions, as well as in our own continuing concerns, the Union faculty met to have a frank airing of our various perspectives. As might be expected, the sharp differences among us elicited lengthy, lively debate. And yet, the tone was one of respectful listening, recognition of the complexity of issues, and reluctance to present ourselves as speaking as if we were experts. Following this meeting, one person drafted a statement that underwent extensive edits in online exchanges. Because the online editing had been so wide-ranging and challenging to keep up with, we decided to meet in person one more time (with some attending via Zoom). After still more edits, several days later, we voted on a final version of the faculty statement, which passed with twenty-three votes in the affirmative and one in the negative. I think none of us regard the statement as flawless; it was a consensus statement, which meant that those who voted in the affirmative agreed we could live with the statement, imperfect though it might be. The lone dissenter saw the statement as undermining principles of liberation theology but expressed gratitude for the robust discussion we had had. In a book such as this one, which focuses on the Israel-Hamas war and Christian-Jewish relations, this statement of the Union Theological Seminary faculty (April 29, 2024) merits, I believe, quotation in full.

Dear Union Community,

As we approach the end of an academic year, we members of the faculty are struggling, like many of you, to concentrate on our own work amid the heartbreaking devastation that Palestinians in Gaza are suffering every day. We grieve the horror Hamas unleashed on Israel on October 7, 2023. We also grieve the terrible oppression and suffering of Palestinians since 1948, when Israeli militia drove 750,000 Palestinians from their homes, resulting in their ensuing exile. Decades of Israeli government brutality against the Palestinians and the intensifying violence of both sides have led to ever more dire political consequences.

We affirm that two historic peoples with different narratives must share the land of Palestine/Israel and respect each other's right to self-determination, respect, and safety. As a progressive Christian seminary defined by its interreligious commitments and its emphasis on justice, we acknowledge that Christian antisemitism resulted in centuries of contempt for Judaism and Jewish persecution in Europe. The Nazi regime exploited this contempt in its extermination camps and its ruthless "Final Solution," resulting in the death of six million Jews. Many Holocaust survivors were among the founders of the State of Israel. Moreover, Christian antisemitism and Islamophobia have contributed to the abyss of the present in Gaza and the West Bank. Additionally, we acknowledge that institutions in the United States, including in higher education, have participated in the marginalization and targeting of Muslim and Jewish communities in a way that has contributed to the current conflict.

We faculty members do not agree on some crucial aspects of the crisis in Israel/Palestine, including the use of the term "genocide." But we agree that we must stand against the ongoing destruction of Gaza and its people. We commend the moral passion of our students in demanding that U.S. Americans take responsibility for our complicity in the ongoing bombardment and pulverization of Gaza. We are grateful to President Serene Jones for standing up for academic freedom and against the use of any police force on our campus.

Those who seek to silence protest play into the hands of those who attack the teaching of Black history, including Critical Race Theory. Liberal education itself is under attack. The indiscriminate leveling of charges of antisemitism against all who oppose the policies of the current Israeli government should not silence protest, lest it occludes the widespread antisemitism in American public life. We join calls for an immediate and lasting ceasefire, the release of all hostages and political prisoners, and a radical reevaluation of the terms of the U.S. government's military support of the State of Israel.

Implications for Christian-Jewish Relations

Neither my New York City context nor my experience at Union Theological Seminary represents the totality of responses at Union to the Israel-Hamas war or defines the complexity of my own perspectives. Nevertheless, the issues raised by protesters, both explicitly and implicitly, deserve explication insofar as they intensify stress in relations between Christians and Jews, particularly with regard to liberal-leaning Christians. Three of those issues are especially troubling: the mischaracterization of Israel as a singularly unethical, racist, and colonial power; a simplistic, if not distorted, grasp of Zionism and its complicated role in Jewish identity; and inattention to the pernicious, persistent, and protean nature of antisemitism.

Although the United Nations was crucial to the establishment of the State of Israel, it has also played a significant role in problematic depictions of Israel. An egregious example, the 1975 Resolution 3379, equated Zionism with racism. While the UN's General Assembly annulled this resolution in 1991 via Resolution 46/86, the 2001 World Conference against Racism in Durban, South Africa, under the auspices of the United Nations, revived the charge, although it was removed from final documentation. A related conference, however, the NGO [Non-Governmental Organizations] Conference for Human Rights, which met concurrently in Durban with the one on racism, issued a resolution on September 2, 2001, describing Israel as a "racist apartheid state" guilty of "war crimes, acts of genocide and ethnic cleansing."[13]

I contend that apartheid is falsely applied to Israel, which includes a 20 percent Arab population with rights as citizens; this is not to deny the problem with unjust treatment of Palestinians in the West Bank, a problem that the most recent Netanyahu government has exacerbated. To claim Israel is distinctly racist among the nations distorts the reality of its multicultural population and shrouds the pervasiveness of racism in numerous other nations. Nevertheless, it has become commonplace on the left simply to assume a Jewish state is racist, an assumption that abets a slide into the charge of "genocide." Today's protesters, shaped by what British historian Simon Sebag Montefiore terms the "new identity analysis," seem to view history through an understanding of race derived from the context of the United States:

> The argument is that it is almost impossible for the "oppressed" to be themselves racist, just as it is impossible for an "oppressor" to be the subject of racism. Jews therefore cannot suffer racism, because they are regarded as "white" and "privileged"; although they cannot be victims, they can and do exploit other, less privileged people, in the West through the sins of "exploitative capitalism" and in the Middle East through "colonialism."[14]

The assertion that Israel is a colonial power originates from a misleading account of its founding in 1948. Jews, primarily from Europe and including large numbers of Holocaust survivors, returned to their ancestral homeland and fulfilled their centuries-long yearning for Zion, a key part of Jewish prayer and liturgy. The conflict over land occupied by Palestinians for generations and their resulting displacement and expulsion created bitterness for Palestinians, for whom this experience was the Nakba, an ongoing catastrophe. Granted the grave injustices suffered by Palestinians in 1948, depiction of Jews as "colonists" ignores the deep historical connection between Jews and the Land of Israel, overlooks the concomitant expulsion of Jews from Arab lands, and elides the reality that Jews did not come to appropriate the land's resources for another power—that is, to colonize—but rather to recreate what they regarded as an ancestral homeland.

Current protesters frequently use the term *settler colonialists* in their criticism of the State of Israel. That concept may be appropriate in part when applied to Israel's settlements in the West Bank since 1967. Applied to Israel as a whole, however, the term *colonizer* is problematic. As Roger Cohen aptly argues:

> The colonial stereotype is of invading white occupiers, but Israel is, and has long been, a very diverse, multihued society. While the French could withdraw from Algeria to France, there is no such "metropole" for a Jew expelled from Iraq. Indeed, at the core of the Israeli-Palestinian conflict lies the fact that both peoples are historically indigenous and neither has anywhere else to go, even as delusional dreams persist on both sides of the disappearance of the other.[15]

Zionism has similarly become a term of opprobrium that is unmoored from its history in late nineteenth-century Europe, including the Dreyfus Affair in France, the anti-Jewish pogroms in Eastern Europe, and the growing hostility toward Jews in Germany, which led the journalist Wilhelm Marr to coin the term *antisemitism* in the 1870s. European Jews dreamed of coming to Israel not to colonize but to find a land where they could live safely and freely—a dream made all the more vivid and vital after the nightmare of the Shoah. Zionism seems now to be conflated with what Jonathan Karp terms "anti-Israelism": an "irrational feeling of repulsion" against Israelis, a blanket disapproval of all things Israeli, attributing "inherent negative characteristics to an entire national group." Israel, he adds, is "a tiny country whose all-too-real flaws have been blown into cosmic significance in the global imagination. Anti-Israelism, then, is not a mere policy stance with which one might agree or disagree . . . . It is a prejudice, a sweeping judgment of an entire people, country, state, and culture that we would not tolerate if it were directed at anyone else."[16]

Karp distinguishes anti-Israelism from antisemitism. While from my vantage point it does seem that anti-Israelism is the primary driver of hostility in the protests I have observed, antisemitism lurks in overt and subtle ways within them.[17] Accounts abound of Jewish students being taunted and accused of complicity in the alleged genocide of Palestinians. I was struck by "In Our Name: A Letter from Jewish Students at Columbia University." This early May 2024 open letter responded poignantly to what Jewish students experienced on a campus "riddled," as the letter put it, "with hateful rhetoric and simplistic binaries." Deeply feeling that their concerns about antisemitism had been rebuffed and discredited, they wrote:

> The evil irony of today's antisemitism is a twisted reversal of our Holocaust legacy; protesters on campus have dehumanized us, imposing upon us the characterization of the "white colonizer." We have been told that we are "the oppressors of all brown people" and that "the Holocaust wasn't special." Students at Columbia have chanted "we don't want no Zionists here," alongside "death to the Zionist State" and "go back to Poland," where our relatives lie in mass graves.[18]

In early July 2024, Columbia announced the removal of three deans for exchanging texts that manifested well-worn antisemitic tropes.[19]

In general, the perfidious and protean nature of antisemitism is largely unrecognized in American society. While I suspect the majority of protesters neither view nor intend their actions to be antisemitic, history provides a caution. Long ago, when members of the Jewish movement that would eventually emerge as Christianity sought to distinguish themselves from (other) Jews in the second and third centuries, they initially characterized Judaism as superseded by the Christ. By the fourth century, however, the claims about Judaism had become in many cases *antagonism to Jews themselves*—thereby setting in motion the theological antisemitism that has corrupted Christian moral integrity, with disastrous results for Jews.[20] I fear that the condemnation of Israel may mutate into full-blown denunciation of Jews, particularly given the upsurge of antisemitism in the United States and elsewhere that has accompanied the Israel-Hamas war.

As a Christian in the Roman Catholic tradition, I draw the following implications for work in deepening relations between Christians and Jews in stressful times. We Catholics involved in Christian-Jewish relations need to:

- Take seriously the widespread and ardent advocacy for Gaza's Palestinians by so many people, including a broad swath of younger liberal Christians. This awareness requires us to deepen our own grasp of the political, religious, and cultural ramifications of the Israel-Hamas war by becoming more knowledgeable about the history and conditions that ignited it and the steps that must be taken to rebuild and reconcile relationships once it ends.

- Encourage expanding the categories by which the war is discussed and take issue with the limitations of binary formulations such as oppressor/oppressed.

- Inform ourselves about the ethical issues at stake in this war, including exploring ways in which Catholic theologians have moved beyond the category of "just war" theory, as some of my Catholic colleagues do in their essays for this volume.

- Seek to understand the varying ways in which Jews of past and present understand themselves in relationship to Israel.

Since 10/7, I have talked with learned friends of varying perspectives and read numerous commentaries as a way of grappling with my own turmoil about the conduct and consequences of the Israeli-Hamas war and its potential impact on relations between Christians and Jews. I am grateful for all I have learned. Yet clarity, let alone certainty, is elusive. Writing this essay at this juncture of the situation in the Middle East suggests the need for humility about my own limited grasp of the situation and for acknowledgement that whatever conclusions I draw are necessarily tentative and subject to modification as the conflict changes.

Nevertheless, basic core beliefs will not change. I am committed to the flourishing of Israel and the Palestinian people. I believe there are no innocent parties to this conflict and that it is vital for a solution to be found before a wider conflict leads to even further devastation. It seems to me that for many Jews, "longing for Zion" lies deep in their psyche, as is evident in the *Siddur* (Jewish book of prayer). That yearning, however, does not amount to a one-size-fits-all Jewish consensus regarding the State of Israel. Palestinians also yearn to live in peace, safety, and prosperity. Honoring the longing of both peoples calls for wise leaders committed to judicious and empathetic negotiation.

Despair and cynicism are temptations increased by the devastation of the Israel-Hamas war. To resist them, we should recall a vision from the prophet Zechariah, expanding it beyond Jerusalem to Gaza, the Palestinian Authority, and Israel: "Old men and old women shall again sit in the streets of Jerusalem, each with staff in hand because of their great age. And the streets of the city shall be full of boys and girls playing in its streets" (Zech. 8:4–5).

Questions for Dialogue

1. What concerns you the most about the Israel-Hamas war? Why? What resources might best speak to your concerns?

2. On what dimensions of the Israel-Hamas war are you least informed? What resources might prove helpful in increasing your understanding of this war's complexities?

3. In your own situation, what possibilities exist for dialogue, and what might be the most promising way to carry on constructive interactions about the war and its aftermath?

Further Resources

The Atlantic. This monthly publication and daily postings (available with a subscription) offer much stimulus for thought.

Sacks, Rabbi Jonathan. *Not in God's Name: Confronting Religious Violence*. New York: Schocken, 2015.

Teter, Magda. *Christian Supremacy: Reckoning with the Roots of Antisemitism and Racism.* Princeton: Princeton University Press, 2023.

Notes

1. See "We Remember: A Reflection on the Shoah," the 1998 statement by the Vatican's Commission on Religious Relations with the Jews, which underscores that "the history of relations between Jews and Christians is a tormented one." https://bit.ly/40IuSdX.

2. See Mary C. Boys and Sara S. Lee, *Christians and Jews in Dialogue: Learning in the Presence of the Other* (Woodstock, VT: SkyLight Paths, 2006), 151–68.

3. The quoted phrase is from *Hatikvah* (The Hope), Israel's national anthem. See Dalia Marx, "*Tikvatenu*: The Poem that Inspired Israel's National Anthem, *Hatikva*," *The Torah,* https://bit.ly/3WA2450.

4. Thomas L. Friedman, "American Leaders Should Stop Debasing Themselves on Israel," *New York Times,* June 18, 2024, https://bit.ly/3EbSMWs.

5. Adela Suliman, "Rift Grows between Netanyahu and Israeli Military over Hamas Elimination," *Washington Post,* June 20, 2004, https://bit.ly/3EcnoY0.

6. Ehud Barak, "Israel Must Oust Its Failed Government Before It Sinks into the Moral Abyss," *Haaretz,* June 13, 2024, https://bit.ly/4h3Sj7g.

7. Ron Kampeas, "Netanyahu Pushes Back against Reports of Army Pressure to End the War, Accusing Officials of 'Defeatism,'" Jewish Telegraphic Agency, July 2, 2024, https://bit.ly/3PQwz2F.

8. Yael Freidson, "Israel Advances over 6,000 Housing Units in West Bank Settlements," *Haaretz,* July 3, 2024, https://bit.ly/3Cp0pIv.

9. Masha Gessen, "How a Palestinian/Jewish Village in Israel Changed after October 7th," *New Yorker,* June 10, 2024, https://bit.ly/4ht2x0T.

10. See Anas Baba and Daniel Estrin, "In Gaza, Anger Grows, Along with Fury at Israel," NPR, February 8, 2024, https://bit.ly/4hbvI8U.

11. Interpreting the various statements from Hamas is complicated. Its 1988 "Covenant of the Islamic Resistance Movement" says that "Israel will exist and will continue to exist until Islam will obliterate it." Similarly, the charter includes the claim that "the Day of Judgment will not come about until Moslems fight Jews and kill them." In 2017, the Islamic Resistance Movement (Hamas) issued a "Document of General Principles and Policies" that redirects the criticism against Jews to the "Zionist project," which the document describes as a "racist, aggressive, colonial and expansionist project based on seizing the property of others." Not only is the Zionist project "hostile to the Palestinian people" but also the "Israel entity is the plaything of the Zionist project and its base of aggression." For the full wording of both documents, see the website of the Wilson Center, https://bit.ly/3WAlc2U. See also Mohamed Nimer, "Charting the Hamas Charter Changes," *Insight Turkey* 11, no. 4 (2009): 115–30; Issam M. A. Adwan, "Hamas Charter: Changes and Principles," *Politics and Religion Journal* 13, no. 1 (2019):

15–37; and Kali Robinson, "What Is Hamas?" Council on Foreign Relations, October 17, 2024, https://bit.ly/4h6VZoZ.

12. For the board's full resolution, see https://bit.ly/4atTB9b.

13. For these documents see, https://bit.ly/3PQeIJe.

14. Simon Sebag Montefiore, "The De-colonization Narrative is Dangerous and False, *Atlantic*, October 27, 2023, https://bit.ly/4aw58F2.

15. Roger Cohen, "Who Is a Colonizer?" *New York Times*, December 12, 2023, https://bit.ly/3PWG7ZX.

16. Jonathan Karp, "Anti-Israelism," *Jewish Review of Books*, Winter 2024, https://bit.ly/4h81svL. See also Jonathan Karp, "What's Going on with Antisemitism? *Jewish Review of Books*, May 16, 2024, https://bit.ly/42tfvaB.

17. See Mary C. Boys, "Antisemitism and the Contemporary Catholic Tradition in America," *Antisemitism Studies 6*, no. 2 (Fall 2022): 324–41.

18. Four Columbia students co-authored the letter, which was signed by at least 450 students. See,https://bit.ly/40D2DfI.

19. Katherine Rosman, "Columbia Removes Three Deans, Saying Texts Touched on 'Antisemitic Tropes.'" *New York Times*, July 8, 2024, https://bit.ly/40v3Pl8.

20. See Guy G. Stroumsa, "From Anti-Judaism to Antisemitism in Early Christianity?" in *Contra Iudaeos, Ancient and Medieval Polemics between Christians and Jews*, ed. Ora Limor and Guy G.Stroumsa (Tübingen: J.C.B.Mohr, 1996), 1–26.

6
Catholic-Jewish Relations and Their Discontents: The Israel-Hamas War, the Holocaust, and a Globalized World

Massimo Faggioli

The October 7, 2023, Hamas attack against Israel and the military response ordered by the Israeli government against Gaza ruptured the modern history of Christian-Jewish relations. The events unleashed by 10/7 are particularly important in the history of the bilateral and multilateral relations between different political and religious entities, and for each of them within themselves: Judaism, the State of Israel, world Christianity, the Catholic Church, and the Vatican.

For the Catholic Church and the Vatican, these wartime events burden an already fragile state of affairs in their relations with Judaism and the State of Israel. The Israel-Hamas war and its reverberations are blocking and even reversing the positive momentum toward dialogue and understanding initiated by the Second Vatican Council (1962–65) and accelerated by the pontificate of John Paul II (1978–2005). The consequences of 10/7, moreover, are complicated by the fact that they are unfolding amid the uncertainties of a transition to "Global Catholicism," a reality more complex and difficult to govern than the "world Church" that Vatican II imagined.[1]

The Catholic Church, the Holocaust, and the Post-Colonial World

Two public intellectuals in the Anglo-American world have devoted significant attention to Catholicism and Pope Francis—with two completely different interpretations. One is Ross Douthat, a Catholic columnist for the *New York Times*. The other is the Indian writer Pankaj Mishra. After 10/7, they have also offered two completely different interpretations of the situation in Israel and Gaza.[2] Douthat's unapologetically Western view of Israel stands in stark contrast to Mishra's anti-colonial critique of Zionism. Taken together, their conflicting views form a telling sequel to a narrative that the American historian Charles Maier saw at play more than twenty years earlier.[3]

As the twenty-first century began, Maier saw two opposing narratives vying to explain how the twentieth century developed. He called one the "Western narrative." It centered on the Holocaust. The other—Maier called it "postcolonial"—did not. Paradoxically, the Holocaust-centered narrative included the story that the West advances the values of humanism, enlightenment, and progress. In this narrative, the Holocaust is a catastrophic aberration, a fall into barbarism, a danger that would continue to infest Europe if reactionary forces were still allowed to proliferate. This narrative justifies the defense of liberal democratic values. The postcolonial second narrative criticizes the centering of the Holocaust or Stalinism and Communism as pivotal and decisive in the historiographical and civil interpretations of the twentieth century. As Maier contended, such emphases seem "parochial . . . to many observers from outside the Atlantic world . . . . Their moral-atrocity narrative maintains that the domination of the West over the massive societies of what once could be called the Third World established the preeminent historical scaffolding of the century."[4]

Within ecclesial and religious consciousness, especially in Catholicism, the postcolonial second narrative has irrupted during the last quarter of a century. Back in 2000, the postcolonial narrative, in which the Holocaust has no unique and universal value, had not yet *internally* affected the Catholic Church. But now it has, and 10/7 and its aftermath must be confronted to understand what began to be visible in Catholicism with the election of Pope Francis in 2013.[5]

Pope Francis's pontificate embodies and represents the largely unstated difficulties of the Catholic Church to reconcile—not only in its official teaching but also in its theological thinking, and not just among academics but among the faithful—the historical-theological uniqueness of the Holocaust during World War II and the upsurge of post-colonial views of history. Postcolonial historical narratives relativize European history in diverse ways and even jettison the concept of the uniqueness of the Holocaust in the context of other genocidal events in the history of modern empires. There are delicate theological developments connected with and dependent on accepting a certain uniqueness of the Holocaust for the history of Christianity and theology. Among these theological developments are the legacy of the 1965 Vatican II document, *Nostra Aetate*, the Catholic Church's "Declaration on the Relationship of the Church to Non-Christian Religions," and the post-conciliar growth in the understanding of the importance of Catholic-Jewish relations from an intra-ecclesial perspective.[6]

The relationship between the role of the Holocaust in twentieth-century history and the global, post-Western political-theological narratives, with which the Catholic Church must interact, has changed since October 2023 in ways in which they never did before or since Vatican II. When Al Qaeda attacked the United States in September 2001, the reception of the conciliar declaration *Nostra Aetate* was not interrupted—if anything, its importance in connection with other Vatican II documents, especially *Dignitatis Humanae*, Pope Paul VI's "Declaration on Religious Freedom," was reaffirmed.[7] The 9/11 attacks and the US "war on terror" that followed came after the highest phase in the rapprochement between Catholicism, Judaism, and Islam under the incredibly authoritative (on that matter) reign of Pope John Paul II (from his 1980 speech in Mainz to his May 2001 trip to Syria). The Polish pope also took a very clear position against the attempts of some who saw the US-led wars in Iraq I (1991), Afghanistan (2001), and Iraq II (2003) as a crusade or a war of civilizations against the Arab and Muslim world.[8] The Catholic Church's early theological and religious responses to 9/11 engaged in interreligious dialogue and encouraged Catholic-Jewish relations in coping with a new interfaith agenda.

Neither did the Russian invasion of Ukraine in 2022 put Catholic-Jewish relations directly on the table, even though the issue of Europe's divided "political memories" of World War II and the Holocaust had already begun to emerge, and Francis applied the term *genocide* to the Russian war in Ukraine.[9] But 10/7, the Israel-Hamas war, and their reverberations are different. They are producing a theological crisis that puts at risk the Catholic-Jewish accomplishments of Vatican II.

Holy See-Israeli Relations at an All-time Low

The uncertainties and disconnects between the Vatican, papal diplomacy, and the Catholic Church's representatives in Israel have contributed to a deterioration of the relations between the Holy See and the State of Israel. For example, according to a group of Palestinians who met privately with Pope Francis on November 22, 2023, he called Israel's military offensive against Gaza "a genocide." Even though the Vatican issued a denial, the alleged comment plunged relations between the Holy See and Israel to an all-time low.[10] In these tragic circumstances, it is not surprising that no Israeli celebrations commemorated the thirtieth anniversary of the "Fundamental Agreement between the Holy See and the State of Israel" (December 30, 1993), which had officially established diplomatic relations and mutual recognition between the two states.[11]

Since 10/7, the Catholic Church's relations with Judaism and Islam have changed a great deal. Importantly, these changes take place during the pontificate of the first non-European pope in modern times and the first-ever pope from the Global South, one whose relationship with Europe is much more detached compared to that of previous popes. Francis's pontificate is making clear that the Catholic Church is neither a satellite nor a surrogate of the Western world. Part of this shift includes a break with the historical-political narratives that Western Europeans have embraced since 1945, including their emphasis on the Holocaust, and a more general collapse of collectively shared historical narratives in the West. "As the historian Enzo Traverso has argued," the journalist Adam Shatz observes, "a particular version of Holocaust remembrance, centered on Jewish suffering and the 'miraculous' founding of Israel, has been a 'civil religion' in the West since the 1970s. People in the Global South have never been parishioners of this church, not least because it has been linked to a reflexive defense of the State of Israel, described in Germany as a *Staatsräson*."[12]

The weakening role of the Holocaust in master narratives about global history is not only a result of the Catholic Church's de-Europeanization. It also results from abuses of the Holocaust to justify problematic policies of the State of Israel and to equate criticism of Israel with antisemitism. "The memory of the Shoah as 'civil religion,'" Traverso argues, compromises "its pedagogical virtues .... Combatting antisemitism will be more and more difficult after having disfigured and distorted [the Holocaust] so brazenly."[13] Anticipating Traverso, the late Tony Judt argued in 2012 that Israel might "devalue, undermine and ultimately destroy the meaning and serviceability of the Holocaust.... The farther away you get from the shores of the United States," Judt aptly added, "the more Israel's behavior looks like simply political exploitation of a victim narrative. Eventually, of course, you get so far away that you arrive in countries and continents—East Asia, Africa—where the Holocaust itself is an unfamiliar abstraction."[14]

These warnings are important for the Catholic Church, whose relationship with Judaism and the State of Israel has been built, during and after Vatican II, on acknowledgment that Christianity and Catholicism bear responsibility for the anti-Jewish hostility that eventually culminated in the Nazis' racial antisemitism and the Shoah or Holocaust during World War II. In addition, Pope Francis and his aides are dealing with a more militant and violent State of Israel than the one with which Pope John Paul II opened full diplomatic relations in 1993. And democratic backsliding in much of the world does nothing to curb ethno-nationalist narratives that seek domination in Israel and even the United States as well as in Russia, Turkey, and India.

The Catholic Church's most urgent problem concerning its relations with Judaism and Islam is to protect all that has been gained since the Second Vatican Council (1962–65) and its positive legacy. But the Catholic Church, the papacy, and local Catholic churches represent dramatically different levels of authority to address the issue of the relations (religious and political) with Judaism and Israel, Islam and Palestinian statehood. Those Catholic constituencies also have different views about the issues themselves. Consider, for example, how serious the situation has become in terms of the resurgence of antisemitism in often ambiguous relations involving tensions between anti-Zionist views and Christian and Catholic Zionism.

The pope, the Holy See, and the Catholic Church must now walk a precarious line. On one hand, it is essential not to give an inch to the old forms of anti-Jewish and antisemitic sentiments that are resurfacing. There is a difference between anti-Zionism, anti-Judaism, and antisemitism, but their mutual boundaries have shifted. It is imperative to defend the legacy of *Nostra Aetate* and its doctrinal augmentations made possible by all the popes since Vatican II—a major shift in Catholic teaching that was also made possible in the early 1960s when Catholics began reckoning with their responsibility for the Holocaust.[15]

On the other hand, Catholicism must remain alert about the danger of instrumentalizing the Holocaust and devaluing its significance. Political debates in the West are often guilty of both. In addition, the Catholic Church must guard against "strategic philosemitism," as Pankaj Mishra calls it, which is "parasitic on old antisemitic stereotypes."[16] The Catholic tradition can be affected problematically (if it has not been already) by the call that "Never Again Is Now," which politically "memorializes" the Shoah by defending the position that Israel must do whatever it takes to defeat Hamas and its intention to destroy, one way or another, the State of Israel. A misguided philosemitism is a serious risk for the preservation of what the Catholic Church has learned theologically from the Shoah. Unless carefully watched, philosemitism could trap the Catholic Church into favoring, even legitimating, unjust Israeli policies against Palestinians.

"Political Memories" of the Holocaust and a Non-European Pope

With a non-European pope in globalized circumstances, the Catholic Church faces new challenges to keep alive the lessons of the tragedies of anti-Judaism, antisemitism, and the Holocaust. While firmly resisting antisemitism, the Catholic Church cannot indulge uncritical philosemitism or pro-Israeli positions that are likely to inhabit now-decaying "political memories" of the Holocaust as part of the "civil religion" in Europe and the West. This problematic centering of the Holocaust has made the political elites in the West indifferent or callously cynical to the fate of innocent Palestinians. As the journalist Masha Gessen has rightly suggested, the politics of memory of the Holocaust in Europe can obscure what we have seen in Israel and Gaza during and after October 7, 2023.[17] A pope such as Francis, who looks at the West with an evident detachment and leads a Catholic Church that is no longer a satellite of the post-1945 liberal order, is in a unique position to reassess the relationship between political memories of the Holocaust and the ecclesial, theological tradition about the Holocaust. At the same time, the current papacy's important and unique role is also precarious.

Signs of the complexity are evident in Francis's January 2024 address to ambassadors to the Holy See, which took place amid Israel's devastating military offensive in Gaza. The pope's words merit lengthy quotation.

> Here, in your presence, I cannot fail to reiterate my deep concern regarding the events taking place in Palestine and Israel. All of us remain shocked by the October 7 attack on the Israeli people, in which great numbers of innocent persons were horribly wounded, tortured, and murdered, and many taken hostage. I renew my condemnation of this act and of every instance of terrorism and extremism. This is not the way to resolve disputes between peoples; those disputes are only aggravated and cause suffering for everyone. Indeed, the attack provoked a strong Israeli military response in Gaza that has led to the death of tens of thousands of Palestinians, mainly civilians, including many young people and children, and has caused an exceptionally grave humanitarian crisis and inconceivable suffering.
>
> To all the parties involved I renew my appeal for a ceasefire on every front, including Lebanon, and the immediate liberation of all the hostages held in Gaza. I ask that the Palestinian people receive humanitarian aid, and that hospitals, schools and places of worship receive all necessary protection.
>
> It is my hope that the international community will pursue with determination the solution of two states, one Israeli and one Palestinian, as well as an internationally guaranteed special status for the City of Jerusalem, so that Israelis and Palestinians may finally live in peace and security.

The present conflict in Gaza further destabilizes a fragile and tension-filled region. In particular, we cannot forget the Syrian people, living in a situation of economic and political instability aggravated by last February's earthquake. May the international community encourage the parties involved to undertake a constructive and serious dialogue and to seek new solutions, so that the Syrian people need no longer suffer as a result of international sanctions. In addition, I express my profound distress for the millions of Syrian refugees still present in neighboring countries like Jordan and Lebanon.[18]

The January 2024 speech to the diplomatic corps can be seen as a rebalancing of his "Urbi et Orbi" message on Christmas Day 2023, when Francis used the term "little Jesuses" to describe Palestinian children killed in the current war:

In the Scriptures, the Prince of Peace is opposed by the "Prince of this world" (*Jn* 12:31), who, by sowing the seeds of death, plots against the Lord, "the lover of life" (cf. *Wis* 11:26). We see this played out in Bethlehem, where the birth of the Savior is followed by the slaughter of the innocents. How many innocents are being slaughtered in our world! In their mothers' wombs, in odysseys undertaken in desperation and in search of hope, in the lives of all those little ones whose childhood has been devastated by war. They are the little Jesuses of today, these little ones whose childhood has been devastated by war.[19]

Those who are committed to Catholic-Jewish dialogue worry about the possible consequences of the pope's referring to Palestinian children as "little Jesuses." Does this then mean that the Israeli Defense Forces, the State of Israel, and—by extension—the Jewish people, are directly responsible for the death of these "little Jesuses"? That interpretation would harken back to the historical accusations of *deicide*, which *Nostra Aetate* strongly repudiated (albeit without using the word).

Francis cannot credibly be accused of reversing the teaching of this important Vatican II document, the first conciliar text he cited at the start of his pontificate in March 2013.[20] But, in light of what is happening in Gaza, the pope's every word matters, especially given the problematic posture taken toward the Israel-Hamas war by many Western leaders, including Joe Biden, the second-ever Catholic to be president of the United States. At the same time, it is clear that Catholic-Jewish dialogue has suffered from Jewish dissent against Francis because he allegedly seems unfairly pro-Palestinian. Francis has used language typical of Palestinian Christians, intending to support them, which is his responsibility. Catholic-Jewish dialogue, which may unavoidably contain fundamental disagreements, must recognize that the pope's work involves multiple contexts, commitments, and audiences.

One lesson the Holy See learned in the twentieth century is that the papacy and the Catholic Church can never again be silent or complicit in facing murderous ethno-nationalism. In the twenty-first century, successful responses to that challenge must recognize that the fog of war has become the smog of cyber and information warfare—a 24/7 cycle of crowdsourced disinformation and propaganda—that makes it almost impossible to avoid seeing images and videos of conflicts, but even more difficult to know the truth of what is happening.

The Holy See has resources to cut through that smog. The Catholic Church needs to defend the theological gains of the post-World War II period from the denialism and relativization of the Holocaust, and that means defending the State of Israel's right to exist and defend itself. But at the same time, the Catholic Church needs to detach itself from the instrumental use of the memory of the Holocaust, and it must use responsibly the freedom to criticize Israel's policies without fear of allegations that it is antisemitic, bigoted, or indifferent about the Holocaust's Never Again imperative.

Catholic-Jewish Dialogue in the Disruption of Globalization

The social teachings of the Catholic Church have much to say about the conduct of war, efforts to avoid it, a nation's right to self-defense, and the protection of civilians during wartime. How to interpret and apply those teachings with regard to the Israel-Hamas war, however, is complicated because that war is taking place at a time when Catholic progressive and peace movements flow into the wider river of political culture marked by the divisions and changing alignments that characterize globalization and identity politics.

Far from having unified or unifying outlooks, twenty-first-century Catholicism inhabits and contributes to a world that is immensely unsettled and unsettling. It must cope with issues about gender and patriarchy, sexuality and abuse, that are more acute than a few decades ago. It must deal with technology, including artificial intelligence (AI), that increases threats of misinformation and disinformation and the destabilization that accompanies them. The Catholic Church also must be accountable for its colonial history and legacy at a time when post-colonial theology sees Catholicism as having a uniquely toxic tradition to overcome (if it can), one that still affects Catholic-Jewish relations, including how the current Israel-Hamas war should be understood and assessed.

The Israel-Hamas war affects the Catholic Church's relationships not only with Judaism but also with Islam. Hamas, for instance, represents a form of Islam. In one way or another, a militant Islam is the flag-bearer of the Palestinian cause. That fact creates a situation different from the Muslim situation that confronted John Paul II, Benedict XVI, and even Francis at the beginning of his pontificate. The State of Israel keeps changing too—10/7 saw to that. It is more right-wing, more determined than ever to destroy Hamas, less likely to support a two-state solution, and more inclined to support Jewish settlements in the West Bank. The Catholic Church is dealing with a vastly different Israel in 2024 and beyond compared to the Israel of 1965 and the Vatican II Declaration, *Nostra Aetate*, or even to the Israel of 1993 when the "Fundamental Agreement between the Holy See and the State of Israel" was reached. The legacy of post-Vatican II Catholic-Jewish dialogue should never be taken for granted. Its future depends significantly on the Catholic Church's ability to find the best ways through political and theological minefields. The minefields include changes within the Catholic Church itself since 1965 and 1993. The twenty-first century's globalization includes a post-colonial shift that erodes conviction that the Holocaust justifies the State of Israel's policies regarding Palestinians and the current Israel-Hamas war.

Catholic Education Can Help

In 2024, the Israel-Hamas war produced turmoil that engulfed American college and university campuses as protests erupted, antisemitism increased, and marginalization of Palestinian students took place. Relative calm, however, was apparent on Catholic campuses in the United States. Students at those colleges and universities were not indifferent about the Israel-Hamas war, but they were influenced by Catholic traditions that helped them to discern and act upon differences between what *can* be said and done and what *should* be said and done in profoundly difficult and volatile circumstances.

The Catholic Church has vast resources for research and education that can help to address the twenty-first-century upheaval that the Israel-Hamas war has increased and intensified. Catholic educational institutions are skilled at cultivating and encouraging the habits of ethical inquiry, critical thought, and constructive action that engage religion and secularism, culture and politics, even the long-standing Israeli-Palestinian conflict in creative ways that resist the temptation to embrace blindly the polarizing ideologies of the day.

The resources of Catholic education can help especially to find ways forward when the Israel-Hamas war ends and the rebuilding of Gaza begins. The spirit of Catholic education at its best will be important in nurturing the good Christian-Jewish relations that will be much needed in the war's aftermath.

Questions for Dialogue

1. In (Catholic and Jewish) schools and higher education, what is the status of the teaching of the history of the Holocaust and of the (Christian/Catholic) theological responses to it?
2. How would you advise the pope to deal with the Israel-Hamas war and its aftermath?
3. How is globalization affecting responses to the Israel-Hamas war and to Christian-Jewish relations? How can the effects be beneficial instead of harmful?
4. How can misinformation and disinformation about the Israel-Hamas war be detected and combatted?
5. How can Catholic education encourage the Christian-Jewish relations that will be especially needed after the Israel-Hamas war ends?

Further Resources

Faggioli, Massimo. "The Church After Gaza. " *La Croix International*, November 7, 2024. https://bit.ly/3CiKpbf.

Hartog, François. *Chronos: The West Confronts Time*. Translated by Samuel Ross Gilbert. New York: Columbia University Press, 2022.

Judt, Tony, with Timothy Snyder. *Thinking the Twentieth Century*. New York: Penguin, 2012.

Traverso, Enzo. *Singular Pasts: The "I" in Historiography*. Translated by Adam Schoene. New York: Columbia University Press, 2023.

Notes

1. On these points, see Massimo Faggioli and Bryan Froehle, *Global Catholicism: Between Disruption and Encounter* (Leiden: Brill, 2024).

2. See, for example, Ross Douthat, "The Justice of Israel's War in Gaza Will Depend on How It Ends," *New York Times*, March 2, 2024, https://bit.ly/4gfF42c https://bit.ly/4gfF42c https://bit.ly/4gfF42c. See also Pankaj Mishra, "The Shoah After Gaza," *London Review of Books*, March 21, 2024, https://bit.ly/40Y2Zip.

3. See Charles S. Maier, "Consigning the Twentieth Century to History: Alternative Narratives for the Modern Era," *American Historical Review* 105, no. 3, (2000): 807–31.

4. Maier, "Consigning the Twentieth Century to History," 826.

5 See Massimo Faggioli, *The Liminal Papacy of Pope Francis: Moving Toward Global Catholicity* (Maryknoll, NY: Orbis, 2020).

6. For the full text of *Nostra Aetate*: Declaration on the Relationship of the Church to Non-Christian Religions, see https://bit.ly/4jvLKvS.

7. For the full text of *Dignitatis Humanae, Declaration on Religious Freedom*, see https://bit.ly/3Ea4lNX. It is worthwhile to note that the Vatican does not have a monopoly on the translation of conciliar documents. For alternative translations, see Austin Flannery, ed., *Vatican Council II: The Conciliar and Postconciliar Documents* (Collegeville, MN: Liturgical, 2014), and Norman P. Tanner, ed., *Decrees of the Ecumenical Councils: Trent to Vatican II* (Washington, DC: Georgetown University Press, 1990).

8. See Andrea Riccardi, *Giovanni Paolo II: La biografia* (Cinisello B.: San Paolo, 2011).

9. See Francis X. Rocca, "Pope Francis Compares War in Ukraine to the Holocaust," *Wall Street Journal*, December 7, 2022, https://bit.ly/4aEXlET.

10. Elise Ann Allen, "Pope Calls Gaza War 'Terrorism,' but Vatican Denies He Said 'Genocide,'" *Crux*, November 22, 2023, https://bit.ly/4azTnND.

11. The text of the "Fundamental Agreement between the Holy See and the State of Israel" is accessible at https://bit.ly/42vA46e.

12. Adam Shatz, "Israel's Descent," *London Review of Books*, June 20, 2024, https://bit.ly/4gemp6E.

13. Enzo Traverso, *Gaza davanti alla Storia* (Roma-Bari: Laterza, 2024), 53–54 (translation mine).

14. Tony Judt, with Timothy Snyder, *Thinking the Twentieth Century* (New York: Penguin, 2012), 123, 134.

15. On this topic, see John Connelly, *From Enemy to Brother. The Revolution in Catholic Teaching on the Jews, 1933–1965* (Cambridge MA: Harvard University Press, 2012).

16. See Pankaj Mishra, "Memory Failure," *London Review of Books*, January 4, 2024, https://bit.ly/42vi0Jw.

17. See Masha Gessen, "In the Shadow of the Holocaust," *New Yorker*, December 9, 2023, https://bit.ly/4h9GDQi.

18. Pope Francis, "Address to Members of the Diplomatic Corps Accredited to the Holy See," January 8, 2024, https://bit.ly/40NiDNd.

19. Pope Francis, "Urbi et Orbi" message of Christmas 2023, December 25, 2023, https://bit.ly/3WAVTO1.

20. See Pope Francis, "Audience with Representatives of the Churches and Ecclesial Communities and of Different Religions," March 20, 2023, https://bit.ly/4ggi2YO.

7
Learning and Lamenting:
At the Corner of Union and Division

Elena Procario-Foley

The war that erupted on October 7, 2023, when Hamas perpetrated a terrorist attack on Israel, sparked a variety of protests around the world. With their strong traditions of free speech and religious freedom, university campuses in the United States saw protests take many forms. Major research universities were in the media spotlight. There were accusations of antisemitism, Islamophobia, hate speech, violence, and the suppression of free speech. In some cases, classroom instruction was moved to online formats, and in-person commencement ceremonies were suspended. Not all campuses, however, experienced disruption.[1]

I have taught at Iona University for over twenty-five years. We did not experience polarizing demonstrations. I cannot state why our campus remained free from the unrest experienced at other campuses during the 2023–24 academic year, and I cannot predict that the same will hold true in the 2024–25 academic year. We enroll approximately 3,700 students of different races, ethnicities, and religions, the majority of whom are undergraduates. There are many Catholics (nominal and active) because Iona's Catholic heritage is an important part of its identity. But legally, we are a non-sectarian institution that embraces students and staff of all faiths. Demographic statistics about religious identity are not gathered. Based on my classroom experience, I would estimate that we have more Muslim than Jewish students, but both populations on campus are relatively small. This *Stress Test* chapter explores the response of Iona students and staff to the Israel-Hamas war from the perspective of interreligious dialogue informed by Catholic theological anthropology.

A Theologian's Contribution

I am not a political scientist, historian, or expert in abating geopolitical conflicts. I was reluctant, therefore, to accept the invitation to contribute a chapter to *Stress Test*. Unresolved issues about Israeli and Palestinian statehood were complicated before the 10/7 Hamas attack on Israel. They are becoming even more complicated and emotionally fraught as the Israel-Hamas war enters its eleventh month, as of this writing. What could I offer from the perspective of Christian-Jewish relations and the limited view from my campus experience that would be meaningful in the face of this war?

As a Catholic theologian, I concentrate on Catholic-Jewish relations, taking seriously my obligation to repair the harm that anti-Jewish theology has wrought on Jews for millennia.[2] While not ignoring Islamophobia, working for understanding between Christians and Jews is one way I have of trying to alleviate the dizzying dimensions of the catastrophic Israel-Hamas war, a war that has caused people to retreat into ideological camps. While teaching undergraduate students, I direct a program in Jewish-Catholic Studies that highlights an annual series of public education lectures for Iona and its wider civic community. In response to the Israeli-Palestinian conflict, I support a two-state solution. Israelis *and* Palestinians have experienced brutal suffering over their very long histories. Both Palestinians and Israelis need and deserve safe homelands. Specifically, in terms of the Israel-Hamas war, I believe an immediate and durable ceasefire is necessary, and the hostages (both those still living as well as those who are dead) must be released immediately. I believe that my best contribution to achieving these goals is to continue teaching in my small corner of the world, laboring to keep open the doors of dialogue between and among Jews, Christians, and Muslims on my campus and in the communities beyond my campus.

Crossing Borders

I was barely awake on Saturday, October 7, when I picked up my cell phone to check the time. I was jolted by a push notification from the *New York Times*: "We are at war." For a horrified and frenzied second, questions raced through my mind: War? With whom? Why? I quickly realized it was not the United States that was at war. It was Israel. I tried to absorb the news of the horrific Hamas terror attack on Israel. I remember the feeling of fear that washed over me that morning. It reminded me of the fear I felt on 9/11 when al-Qaeda attacked New York and Washington, DC, and I thought that the United States was, or soon would be, at war. Remembering that feeling keeps me aware of the fear Palestinians and Israelis must feel and have lived with every day since 10/7.

A few weeks after 10/7, I was doing errands. Stopping for the traffic light at the corner of Union and Division avenues, I was overwhelmed with the thought that I was exactly where the world is: perched upon the precipice of union *and* division. Within a stone's throw of that intersection are two churches, a hospital, and a train station—all places that can either unite or divide, either bring people together or tear people apart. Union and Division. The traffic reminded me that people can either continue going in the same direction when they are lost, or they can change course and find a new way forward.

Streets and roads go in many directions, including toward and through borders. Borders—physical, metaphorical, legal, intellectual—are human creations. They can be crossed. People who cross them are "border crossers." They carry ideas, traditions, and gifts back and forth from one place to another, for good or for ill. People who cross borders encounter new people and new ideas. Such encounters can change people for good, enriching them, even making them better human beings. When people cross borders violently, however, everyone loses because everyone's humanity is diminished by violence. But if one crosses borders to dialogue with "others," to learn from them, good things can happen. Does dialogical border crossing happen at a university? Can it promote union over division?

Undergraduate students cross many borders when they come to college. Some live on campus, others commute, but they all cross borders. Students travel back and forth across the borders of late adolescence and early adulthood. They cross intellectual borders. They cross from the familiar worlds of their parents and peer groups into new worlds of thought and interpretation as professors and fellow students challenge them to grapple with new ideas and engage with persons from diverse ethnic, economic, racial, religious, and non-religious backgrounds. College students constantly cross, or refuse to cross, many borders—intellectual, spiritual, and personal.

Interreligious dialogue is a key way to encourage students to be good border-crossers. Pope Francis reflects on dialogue as follows:

> An element that I consider essential for facing the present moment is constructive dialogue. Between selfish indifference and violent protest there is always another possible option: that of dialogue . . . . I consider fundamental for this dialogue the contribution made by the great religious traditions . . . . When leaders in various fields ask me for advice, my response is always the same: dialogue, dialogue, dialogue. The only way for individuals, families and societies to grow, the only way for the life of peoples to progress is via the culture of encounter, a culture in which all have something good to give and all can receive something good in return. Others always have something

to give me, if we know how to approach them in a spirit of openness and without prejudice. This open spirit, without prejudice, I would describe as "social humility," which is what favors dialogue. Only in this way can understanding grow between cultures and religions .... Today, either we take the risk of dialogue, we risk the culture of encounter, or we all fail; this is the path that will bear fruit.[3]

During the first week of the fall semester, new and returning college students often encounter each other at club fairs. At these events, returning students recruit their peers to student organizations. I helped some Jewish students at Iona to form a campus club under the auspices of the Jewish-Catholic Studies program I direct. Given the small minority of Jewish students on campus, it was not surprising that when they met for the first time, a few of those Jewish students said, "I thought I was the only Jew here." During Sukkot, the weeklong Jewish holiday that occurs five days after Yom Kippur, a *sukkah*—a foliage-covered booth where Jews eat their meals during the days of this holiday—was built on the lawn of the university's campus ministry house.[4] Everyone—Jewish and non-Jewish—was invited to participate in events celebrating Sukkot. "Come learn about religious diversity on campus" was the invitation's tagline.

The campus events surrounding Sukkot were an opportunity for students to cross religious borders as they learned about different Jewish religious practices and met students from different religions or from none. Non-Jewish students crossed borders as they got to know their Jewish fellow students, faculty, and staff. Jewish students, faculty, and staff crossed religious borders, too, as they got to know people from other traditions. Sukkot ended the evening of Friday, October 6. The next day, Saturday, October 7 (Shabbat for Jews), Hamas attacked Israel. How did the Iona community learn and lament in the aftermath of that horrible event?

Learning and Lamenting

As a first step, the offices of Mission and Ministry and Jewish-Catholic Studies worked together to plan a multireligious prayer service. It was held outdoors in the campus's central quad. Students provided music and offered readings from different religious traditions. A Reform rabbi, an imam, and the university's Catholic chaplain, as well as a Muslim woman who leads interfaith dialogue in the local county, offered reflections. Both the rabbi and the imam—who had not consulted with one another prior to the prayer service—spoke eloquently, emotionally, and in mutually reinforcing ways, emphasizing that the Hamas terror attack was unjustified and condemning its atrocities as perversions of Muslim tradition. They stressed that the death of innocent people must be mourned. They urged all communities to join together in prayer and to work for peace.

The Catholic chaplain, a Franciscan priest, offered reflections on peace from Pope Francis. The Muslim woman, a medical doctor, spoke about the moment she looked into her microscope, saw a single cell, and remembered a Qur'anic teaching: all humans are created equal. Fighting back tears, the Muslim doctor echoed ideas from the other speakers. She grieved the senseless loss of life. Speakers clearly opted for union, not division. They opted for crossing borders to heal and repair rather than retreating into national, ethnic, or religious tribalism to intensify separation and isolation. For those who attended the prayer service—Jews, Christians, and Muslims—the prayers and reflections allowed them to witness the possibility of union, to see that people can engage across religious borders, even when their hearts are breaking. The service was a moment of learning while lamenting.

In the evening, a much smaller and specifically Jewish service was provided for Jewish students, faculty, and staff, although members of other traditions were present as well. It was important for Jewish students on campus, many of whom had only just discovered each other, to gather, to meet supportive Jewish faculty and staff, and to pray with traditional Jewish texts. Some participants shared painful personal details. Amid the laments, non-Jews learned about how the attacks on October 7 affected Iona's Jews and their families. Jews learned that their university cared about them and about what happened in Israel. They said they did not feel so alone.

A specifically Muslim service was not held. That was a loss. Those of us involved in interreligious efforts on campus should have worked harder to find our Muslim students and to respond specifically to them and their pain. Although there is no specific Muslim student club at Iona, a group called SAME (South Asian and Middle Eastern Cultures) includes Muslim students. Given the small Muslim campus population and, in the absence of a specific Muslim student group, the authentic need for a specifically Muslim prayer service was, regrettably, overlooked.

In the weeks that followed the original prayer services, members of the Jewish student group and the Muslim leader of SAME did reach out to each other. They tried to organize a social event so students could get to know each other, have an opportunity to learn about campus ethnic and religious diversity, and cross those borders of diversity. Unfortunately, scheduling conflicts prevented that event from happening, but other student events did take place. In November 2023, for example, SAME held a bake sale to support relief for Palestinian refugees. That event was held in conjunction with the campus United Nations club's information session on the history of the Israel-Hamas war. The UN club's student panelists provided multiple sources for information about the conflict. Students of different religions and nationalities attended and participated in the discussion. Nothing controversial transpired. The UN club sponsored a similar session during the spring semester. Catholic, Jewish, and Muslim students also tried to organize a session called "Talking Better Together" as a way for them to learn about religious diversity. Unfortunately, that event did not happen, again due to scheduling issues, but through the process of working together on the program, students learned about each other. In all these examples, students were able to find ways to cross borders, to encounter each other without prejudice in a spirit of Pope Francis's "social humility."

In late October 2023, some faculty members communicated by email to ask if those of us who had planned the first prayer service were planning anything else. Faculty members wanted to organize an event acknowledging the thousands of Palestinians killed in the wake of Israel's war on Hamas. Unfortunately, organizing by email, rather than in person, quickly became complicated. One faculty member reported that some Muslim students did not approve of a draft flyer that mentioned both Hamas and Israel. Other faculty members recounted that some Palestinians and Muslims would not attend an event that did not focus on the many Palestinian dead. But everyone on the email thread agreed about two commitments: all events must assure the safety of each of our students; each event must stress the importance of all lives. *Every* life lost—Israeli and Palestinian—must be mourned. Everyone also agreed that every event should bear witness for the living and the dead, not be a protest gathering. But significant issues remained.

A faculty-staff Zoom meeting was organized. It was a difficult meeting, but the discussion was respectful as well as emotional. We listened; we learned; we lamented. We acknowledged the desire of some faculty and staff members to speak more directly to the enormous loss of life suffered by Palestinians in Gaza. People shared their stories about how the Israel-Hamas war was affecting them. We learned about the safety concerns gripping Palestinian, Muslim, and Jewish students. We agreed to organize another service for reflection and prayer: "Bearing Witness When Worlds Are Shattered: The Iona Community at Prayer for Our Wounded World."

As before, this service was held outdoors in the main campus quad. A bagpiper began the service with a musical lament. A faculty member gave an opening reflection on bearing witness in a global world riven by violence. Other faculty recited verses from different religious traditions. Mindfulness bells were struck between each reading to encourage silent reflection. The prayer service ended with participants writing their laments, their hopes, their memorials on tree tags, then hanging those tags on a campus tree. The tags served as visual symbols of loss, bearing witness, and hope.

The prayer service did not propose solutions to the Israel-Hamas war. It did, however, respond to a need on campus to address the ongoing tragedy. Was it perfect? Did it address all the issues some wanted to address? No. But in its planning and conduct, the service allowed people to cross borders, to learn together, to grieve together, to recognize each other's different perspectives, and to come together as a campus community trying to make one small statement for peace. This second interreligious service advanced the experience of living at the corner of union and division. We opted for learning while lamenting and for union amid differences.

Sponsored by the Jewish-Catholic Studies program and the campus office of Mission and Ministry, another faculty-led event occurred in the 2024 spring semester: Iona's first-ever interreligious Iftar, the evening meal breaking the fast of Muslims during Ramadan. I invited Muslim faculty and staff to take the lead in developing the program for the evening, an event intended to support our Muslim students and colleagues and to educate non-Muslims about Islam. Enthusiastically, faculty and staff warmly embraced the invitation to plan the Iftar. They created a wonderful evening in a collaborative interreligious effort. Faculty and staff supplemented the university meal with a variety of homemade traditional foods. An imam from the local community was invited to reflect on the meaning of Iftar. Muslim faculty, staff, and students also joined in, offering reflections and prayers. The new student president of SAME, a Palestinian Muslim, spoke about his family's traditions. He said the campus celebration was important to him because "my people are going through something they have never gone through before." Muslim, Jewish, and Christian students sat together at table, fully aware of the war. Yet, by the evening's end, everyone was discussing how to plan for next year.

Yet another faculty-initiated event occurred in April 2024. Some faculty took the lead on organizing and holding a service to continue bearing witness to the overwhelming Palestinian suffering in Gaza and in Israel. They purchased olive-wood hearts made by traditional artisans in Bethlehem. Held again on the campus quad, the event was designed to be a time of silent solidarity as participants held the hearts.[5] Perhaps public acts of silent lament are the most appropriate response when people are overwhelmed by an intractable global conflict and words seem inadequate to express the depth of one's feelings.

The Advice of Robert Masson

In a very different context, that of intense conflict between theologians and the Vatican, the philosophical theologian Robert Masson penned an essay about taking stands. His observations are useful to those who must decide what to do on our particular campuses as the Israel-Hamas war continues to take a devastating toll. Masson observes:

> On the one hand, we know from classroom experience that genuine learning requires taking stands. Nothing undermines the fruitful engagement of students quicker than evasiveness, obscurity, equivocation or sophistry about where things stand—whether on the teacher's part or the student's. On the other hand, nothing shuts down learning in class more surely than stands taken one-dimensionally, one-sidedly, insensitively, polemically, or coercively—even if only by one party.
>
> [Q]uestions about "where we stand" are best answered by asking how we can use our own voice and voices to create a constructive intellectual and social space within our classrooms, colleges and universities, church and civil society where people of conviction can better discern the truth in complicated issues and in the difficult circumstances of a deeply wounded world.[6]

It seems to me that Iona followed Masson's sage advice. Our student groups, faculty, and staff worked together to provide "constructive intellectual and social space." We leaned into complexity and lament. We respected differences. Faculty members advocated for their positions and their students in staking out what was important to them; they asked for clarity and rejected obscurity. They did not take one-dimensional stands. As a community we were able to create public services to mourn the victims of war. We demonstrated an ability to unite in bearing witness when it would have been so easy for us to divide into particular "stands."

Masson's advice is that we should first ask how we can create constructive spaces to explore difficult questions rather than foreground our personal "stands."[7] It is advice well taken when colleges and universities cope with the variety of issues that arise relative to the Israel-Hamas war. Such a method does not hide from difficult conversations but allows them to occur in ways that might yield insight over ire. It allows us to care for our students and colleagues, hear and learn from their different narratives, and stand with them in their pain. At Iona, we keep trying to provide constructive spaces where learning and lamenting can proceed in parallel and intersect productively. We encourage opportunities for people to listen, to engage with new ideas, to respond, and to cross borders of learning. Such efforts can be transformative for everyone involved.

Each college and university has a particular history that shapes responses to cataclysmic events. According to the National Center for Education Statistics, there were 5,916 colleges and universities in the United States in the 2020–21 academic year.[8] "One-size-fits-all" recommendations simply do not exist for designing campus responses to the Hamas-Israel conflict for so many diverse institutions. Perhaps it was dumb luck that Iona escaped conflict; we will never know. But I do not think we were unique in our intentional use of multireligious prayers and interreligious dialogue as a response to 10/7.

Even at schools where conflicts garnered media attention, border crossers who engaged in dialogue made progress toward understanding each other. For example, just prior to 10/7, Elijah Kahlenberg, a Jewish student at the University of Texas at Austin, founded Atidna International. *Atidna* combines Hebrew and Arabic words to form a word meaning "our future."[9] The website states that Atidna is a "dialogue initiative that seeks to solidify Arabs and Jews as cousins, one unified family, and not enemies." After 10/7, some Jews and Palestinians left the organization; but others stayed and organized vigils to mourn all people who died. As the University of Pennsylvania erupted into controversy, some of its Jewish and Arab students sought instead to engage in thoughtful dialogue. They founded a chapter of Atidna. Students Tova Tachau and Faresi Alfaresi organized the first meeting in February 2024. Arab and Jewish students discovered that simply by risking attending the meeting and engaging in dialogue they immediately drew one step closer to understanding each other. Using the Atidna model, students at two major universities created the intellectual and social spaces for border crossing. They listened to people of diverse cultures and religions. They put aside personal "stands" in the pursuit of truth in a dangerously polarized world. They demonstrated that deliberate and respectful dialogue yields transformative possibilities.

Theological Anthropology and Dialogue

For such transformation to happen, however, a shared understanding of what it means to be human is crucial. In his magisterial work *Christ: The Experience of Jesus as Lord*, the late Belgian Catholic theologian Edward Schillebeeckx describes a system of interlocking anthropological coordinates/constants that helpfully analyzes the human condition.[10] His anthropology can guide how we treat each other, encourage interreligious dialogue, and support the transformation that is needed to respond to the Israel-Hamas war.

"Our relationship with nature and our own corporeality come up against *boundaries* which we have to respect if we are to live a truly human life," says Schillebeeckx, stating the first of his constants. "What is technically possible has not by a long way been an ethical possibility."[11] Boundaries are necessary limits to protect humanity. In particular, boundaries (ethical and legal) must constrain the technologies of war so that the human boundaries blinding us to a common humanity can be crossed and open us to the possibility of a unified, not divided, humanity.

A second constant is our relationship to the other. Being human means being "*destined for* others," for treating every person as an end and not as a means. When we recognize this essential element of human existence, we seek "norms without which whole and livable humanity is impossible here and now. This also implies that well-being and wholeness, complete and undamaged humanity, must be universal, must apply to each and every individual, and not only a privileged few."[12]

Brutal terror attacks, such as Hamas's attack on Israel, deny that those attacked are worthy of life. There is no recognition by the attackers that those attacked share a common humanity with them. In the fog of war, however, it is also difficult to recognize the attackers' humanity. After 10/7, Israeli officials vowed to cut off water, electricity, and food to Gaza. Such policies, as well as terror attacks, disrespect the anthropological constants of corporeality and the intrinsic relatedness of all humans. Interreligious dialogue cannot solve the tactical problem of how to create a ceasefire, but interreligious dialogue grounded in an anthropology focused on the other can help to keep communities concerned about Israelis and Palestinians talking to each other. The dialogue can explore how Christian anti-Judaism and Islamophobia have historically caused Christians to deny the full humanity of Jews and Muslims. Christian theologians have a responsibility to teach about repentance for that history and to show how Christian, Jewish, and Muslim traditions can contribute to recognizing and honoring a shared humanity.

Schillebeeckx's first two constants lead to further reflection on the inherently social dimension of human life. Humanly created, social and institutional structures arise to support human existence. They are changeable, not immutable. "This gives rise," Schillebeeckx writes, "to the specific ethical demand to change them where, as a result of changed circumstances, they enslave and debase [persons] rather than liberate them and give them protection."[13] People involved in interreligious dialogue have the possibility of using a rich theological anthropology to help question whether political or military structures are aiding or harming the development of human flourishing. The importance of the interpretative question of what it is to be human is not to be underestimated. The more those of us who are not on the ground in a war zone can use dialogue to engage people in discussions about the meaning of being human in the spirit of Pope Francis's "social humility," the more chance we have of crossing borders and embracing the humanity of the other, especially those with whom we disagree most vehemently. It is at the point of touching the humanity of the other who we see as an enemy that we may best find ways to end conflict, even the Israel-Hamas war.

Schillebeeckx's additional anthropological constants include the inescapability of being conditioned by time (history) and space (geography); the dialectical relationship between theory and practice; and human religious consciousness. Running through these constants is the key insight that being human is an ongoing interpretative process, one that seeks understanding. But our being embedded in time and space means that "adopting a standpoint outside *historical* action and thought is a danger to humanity."[14] Standing within our historical and religious situations, however, we can find sound interpretations that add meaning to our lives. At their best, religious traditions help us in that quest. They affirm that something more than the individual or community helps to move humanity to fulfillment. They encourage faith that provides and grounds hope. As Schillebeeckx affirms, "faith and hope—whatever their content—are part of the health and integrity, the worthwhileness and 'wholeness' of our humanity."[15]

The cacophony in the United States surrounding debates about Hamas, Israel, and Palestine is fueled in part by vastly divergent understandings of the many narratives involved. How people approach a community's interpretation of history and geography, how people think about the best relationships between theory and practice—these considerations affect judgments about what is *justified* and who is *right*. Although the Israel-Hamas war and the hostility between Israelis and Palestinians that stands behind it need to be resolved by appropriate diplomatic and political means, religion in the form of interreligious dialogue can help create the constructive spaces that are necessary for people to move beyond violence and to find healing. Interreligious dialogue based on a theological anthropology that is grounded in the present while looking to the future offers people a chance to consider the position of the other.

Schillebeeckx's theological anthropology emphasizes the need to identify and heed norms of behavior that will enhance our common humanity. He recognizes the pluralism that attends determinations of such norms. "One of the tasks of a livable modern humanity will be that of learning to live with different conceptions of specific norms for a worthwhile human life. . . . The pain of this pluralism is part of our *condition humaine* . . . . We must cope with it and not by means of the dictatorial rejection of other conceptions."[16] Amid the Israel-Hamas war and its aftermath, which will require long and dedicated efforts to rebound and rebuild, coping constructively with the pluralism that Schillebeeckx identifies is important work for Christian-Jewish (and Muslim) relations to do.

Union and Division Revisited

Entire communities have been internally displaced in Israel and Gaza. Conflicts on a variety of borders threaten to erupt into additional wars. Jewish communities around the world feel threatened, alone, and abandoned. Humanitarian aid to Palestinians—especially for women and children, the disabled and the elderly, indeed all the non-combatant civilians in Gaza—has been inconsistent and insufficient. Christians must oppose the alarming increase in antisemitism and Islamophobia and take responsibility for the long arc of Christian triumphalism. Grief and pain abound. Yet, I am not without hope that we may be able to find our way through this crisis. Schillebeeckx's Catholic anthropology offers common ground in a pluralistic world.

My institution does not have any special insight about how to navigate the difficult issues and questions related to the Israel-Hamas war. I do think, however, that our practice of engaging in interreligious dialogue as an educational institution in the Catholic tradition has informed how we tried to meet the challenges following the events of October 7. In a variety of ways, Iona people with many different views—religious, political, cultural—came together during the weeks and months after 10/7. They crossed borders—ideological, religious, emotional. They tried to listen to each other respectfully. Education was able to continue.

Faculty and staff focused on the well-being of all students—Jewish, Christian, and Muslim. We held prayer services and vigils, information sessions instead of protests. We sat down together interreligiously at Iftar and at Shabbat dinner. People learned together while being religious interreligiously.[17] The understanding and respect that were built through such interreligious engagement fostered learning amid lament. It created space for disagreement without the campus falling into disunity and disarray. Some colleagues wanted students to protest. There are many reasons why protests did not happen, but one stands out: people made choices, difficult though they were, to honor each person's humanity. People engaged in dialogue with the social humility urged by Pope Francis. They were helped to do so by Iona's tradition, nurtured by a Catholic anthropology, of multireligious reflection and prayer. Will such practices end the Israel-Hamas war? Will they cause conflict between Israelis and Palestinians to cease? No, but these practices encourage border-crossing for the sake of coexistence. And at Iona, they have enabled us to keep lines of communication open between and among Christians, Jews, and Muslims—at least so far.

Peace is possible—in Gaza, Israel, the Middle East—if people recognize and respect the humanity of "the other." No better image for this hope can be offered than the embrace of Maoz Inon (an Israeli), and Aziz Abu Sarah (a Palestinian) with Pope Francis in Verona, Italy, on May 18, 2024.[18] Peace activists, Maoz and Aziz both lost family members in the Israel-Hamas war, but they did not retreat into ideological camps. They crossed borders for the sake of peace that honors human life, including the loss of their loved ones.

Union or division? The choice is ours. Interreligious dialogue and sound Christian-Jewish (and Muslim) relations can encourage choices that foster peace.

Questions for Dialogue

1. How would you respond to Robert Masson's question, "How can we use our own voice and voices to create a constructive intellectual and social space within our classrooms, colleges and universities, church and civil society where people of conviction can better discern the truth in complicated issues and in the difficult circumstances of a deeply wounded world?"

2. Will creating understanding between Christians, Jews, and Muslims on the local level make a difference to the Israeli-Palestinian conflict and the current Israel-Hamas war?

3. Is mutual understanding about what it means to be human necessary for productive interreligious dialogue?

4. Is there a situation of union and division in your community that would benefit from interreligious dialogue?

Further Resources

For Heaven's Sake. Podcast. https://bit.ly/40S0GwZ.

Fredericks, James L., and Tracy Sayuki Tiemeier, eds. *Interreligious Friendship After "Nostra Aetate."* New York: Palgrave Macmillan, 2015.

Kronish, Ron. *Coexistence and Reconciliation in Israel: Voices for Interreligious Dialogue.* New York: Paulist, 2015.

McCarthy, Eli. *A Just Peace Ethic Primer: Building Sustainable Peace and Breaking Cycles of Violence.* Washington, DC: Georgetown University Press, 2020.

Shreiber, Maeera Y. *Holy Envy: Writing in the Jewish Christian Borderzone.* New York: Fordham University Press, 2022.

Notes

1. For more on these points, see, for example, Colbi Edmonds, Anna Betts, and Anemona Hartocollis, "What to Know About the Campus Protests Over the Israel-Hamas War, *New York Times*, April 28, 2024, https://bit.ly/40z2iKI. See also Robin Hattersley, "Which Colleges and Universities Are Experiencing Pro-Palestine Protests?" *Campus Safety*, May 16, 2024, https://bit.ly/4hm5fFy.

2. On this point, see "A Sacred Obligation: Rethinking Christian Faith in Relation to Jews and Judaism," https://bit.ly/4hm5oc4.

3. Address of Pope Francis, Rio de Janeiro, July 27, 2013, §3, https://bit.ly/40v8L9B.

4. In 2023, the Jewish holiday of Sukkot, a festival of thanksgiving and a commemoration of the forty-year period when the biblical people of Israel wandered in the desert after leaving slavery in Egypt was observed from September 29 to October 6.

5. Because I was included on the email thread inviting faculty to this gathering, I am aware that at least one faculty member screened the following video in class: https://bit.ly/3Wx2ysB. It is a record of a December 28, 2023, ecumenical service in Bethlehem commemorating the Feast of the Holy Innocents. Participants in that ecumenical event held 8,000 olive-wood hearts to mourn and symbolize the children who had been killed in the Israel-Hamas war.

6. Robert Masson, "When Stands Are Taken, Where Do We Stand?," *Horizons: The Journal of the College Theology Society* 32, no. 2 (2005): 204, 209, https://bit.ly/42MFxpF.

7. See further, Masson, "When Stands Are Taken, Where Do We Stand?"

8. See "Fast Facts," Institute of Education Sciences/National Center for Education Statistics, https://bit.ly/3EbARzj.

9. The Atidna International website is located at www.atidnainternational.com. For more on Atidna at the University of Texas, Austin and the University of Pennsylvania, see Erin Gretzinger, "Meaningful Conversations," *Chronicle of Higher Education*, May 22, 2024, https://bit.ly/4hacS1N.

10. See Edward Schillebeeckx, *Christ: The Experience of Jesus as Lord*, trans., John Bowden (New York: Seabury, 1980).

11. Schillebeeckx, *Christ,* 734.

12. Schillebeeckx, *Christ*, 737.

13. Schillebeeckx, *Christ*, 738.

14. On these points, see Schillebeeckx, *Christ*, 739, 740.

15. Schillebeeckx, *Christ*, 741.

16. Schillebeeckx, *Christ*, 743.

17. On this point, see Peter Phan, *Being Religious Interreligiously: Asian Perspectives on Interfaith Dialogue* (Maryknoll, NY: Orbis Books, 2004).

18. For more on this story, see "An Israeli and Palestinian, Both Victims of Gaza War, Embrace Before Pope Francis," PIME Asia News, May 18, 2024, https://bit.ly/4hlXzmy.

8
The Israel-Hamas War: Challenges and Opportunities for Interreligious Dialogue

James G. Paharik

The attack by Hamas on Israel on October 7, 2023, along with the ensuing retaliation by Israeli forces, reverberated far and wide. As graphic details of the Hamas assault became known, and as reports documenting the scale of human suffering in Gaza were disseminated, people around the world became deeply distressed, particularly those with ties to the region. Emotions have run high, and political leaders as well as the citizens of many nations have expressed sharply differing opinions about the causes of the violence and when and how it should end.

Attitudes have hardened into absolutist positions that are sharply either pro-Israeli or pro-Palestinian, with little nuance or shades of gray. Exacerbating tensions further, acts of discrimination and hate directed at Jews, Muslims, and Palestinians have become increasingly common in the United States and abroad.[1] These acts have brought the war to our American and Christian doorsteps, making it more difficult to view events in Israel and Gaza dispassionately.

Confronting Differences

Christian, Jewish, and Muslim organizations in the United States that are committed to interreligious understanding, as we are at the National Catholic Center for Holocaust Education (Seton Hill University), have always had to carefully navigate differences of opinion related to the conflict between Israelis and Palestinians. Often, we Christians have set such issues aside for fear that discussing them would interfere with the important work of furthering interreligious understanding in our own communities, where many of us have made valuable progress over the years. But the events surrounding the Israel-Hamas war have rendered it all but impossible to avoid the topic, which now seems to be the "elephant in the room" that must be confronted.

The need to address the war in interreligious circles—not only Christian-Jewish but also including Muslims—became apparent in the immediate aftermath of the Hamas assault, which left many Jews feeling terrified and alone. Some who had been involved in interreligious dialogue for decades were upset by the lack of empathy expressed by their Muslim dialogue partners, prompting them to wonder "whether years of bridge-building efforts had meant anything at all."[2] Rabbi Ellen Nemhauser, president of Interfaith Atlanta, noted that some Jewish members of her organization were "wounded and confused" when their Muslim colleagues did not reach out to them after the Hamas attack. "Some questioned why," she said, "after devoting their time, energy, and money to various causes, they felt a cold shoulder from people they considered friends or allies, people they thought shared a similar view of the world."[3] A leader of the Pittsburgh branch of the Daughters of Abraham, a women's interfaith book group intended to foster dialogue among Jews, Christians, and Muslims, told me that several Jewish members also left her group for this very reason.[4]

The strong feelings that the war produced made it difficult in the weeks following 10/7 for some organizations to continue their work as planned. For example, a trip to Spain and Morocco that was co-sponsored by the Islamic Society of North America and the National Council of Synagogues was abruptly canceled. The pilgrimage, intended to celebrate the history of tolerance between Jews and Muslims in the region, no longer seemed feasible due to the raw emotions of many participants. Some were personally affected by violence impacting friends or family members in Israel or Gaza. Even more disturbing was the fact that, for some Jewish members, the brutality of the attack surfaced memories of the Holocaust, while for some Muslim participants, the bombing of Gaza was reminiscent of the destruction of Palestinian communities in the 1948 Arab-Israeli war. According to one of the trip's organizers, these powerful emotional responses produced "a cooling" in the willingness to engage with those of other faiths and a desire to retreat into the safety of their cultures of origin.[5]

Trauma and Misinformation

It is not surprising that the Israel-Hamas war has evoked long-held cultural memories of betrayal, loss, and injustice. These memories, however authentic and justified they are, pose an impediment to honest engagement in dialogue and to the expression and sharing of grief for personal losses. In their work on the psychological barriers that impede understanding between those whose sympathies lie primarily with Israelis or Palestinians, Raja Khory and Jeffrey Wilkinson argue that trauma plays a central role. "Trauma," they contend, acts like a force field that repels narratives that appear threatening to our own perspectives. The respective traumas—incurred by Jews through millennia of exile, culminating in the Holocaust, and by Palestinians through mass displacement during the Nakba—have kept us each in our camps, resistant to viewing the other and the other's pain. Trauma is formed not just from the loss and grief of the present but also reflects past grief and fears of future grief. It is a very real obstacle to reaching out beyond our own painful stories and to grasping the depths of the other's pain.[6]

The experience of grief and resentment not only diminishes empathy for others but also encourages adherence to simplistic and extreme views of the conflict. The ideas that all Palestinians are "terrorists" who seek the destruction of Israel, or that Israel is perpetrating a "genocide" of Palestinians, are serious distortions of a reality that is highly complex and requires a sustained effort to properly comprehend. A balanced history of the region and a sensitivity to all the victims of the violence are much needed. The effort to achieve accurate understanding also entails intellectual humility, which is a mindset that recognizes one's intellectual limitations and "encourages us to seek out and evaluate ideas and information in such a way that we are less influenced by our own motives and more oriented toward discovery of the truth."[7] Psychological trauma, however, is not conducive to an attitude of openness or the exploration of diverse points of view.

Unfortunately, the present media environment reinforces the tendency to view issues from a single, often biased perspective rather than encouraging the development of a fact-based, comprehensive understanding of the issues. Those who regularly use social media for news about the war receive a daily dose of information that is, at best, incomplete and, at worst, deliberately false.[8] News reports are typically "decontextualized"—that is, they lack the historical perspective required to illuminate the underlying causes of the violence. Even the choice of language employed in news reports can introduce bias. A study of BBC coverage of the Israeli-Palestinian conflict found that inflammatory terms like "atrocity" and "brutal murder" were often used to characterize violence perpetrated by Palestinian militants but not to describe lethal force inflicted by Israeli forces. According to the same study, the BBC was more likely to describe Israeli victims as having been "killed," while Palestinians who were killed were simply said to be "dead"—a significant difference.[9] When members of interreligious discussion groups adopt such linguistic practices, perhaps unconsciously, barriers to effective communication arise. Often employed carelessly and uncritically in the media, terms such as *Zionism, antisemitism, terrorism,* and *genocide* convey emotional weight likely to make dialogue participants feel accused and defensive.

Despite these challenges, most groups devoted to furthering interreligious understanding appear to be staunchly committed to continuing their work. Many of us—Christians, Jews, and Muslims—are convinced that our efforts are even more essential now, in what has been termed "the worst crisis ever" to face our organizations.[10] The task is to determine how best to overcome these obstacles and to forge deeper bonds among dialogue partners. Such work is essential for good Christian-Jewish relations amid the Israel-Hamas war, and those relations increasingly need to include Muslim partners. To do such work well, I contend, requires us—Christians, Jews, and Muslims—to take the following steps: 1) establish a foundation of personal relationships and trust; 2) listen empathetically to accounts of the suffering of others; 3) draw upon the experiences of peacemakers; and 4) affirm the human rights of all parties to the conflict. These directions confer responsibility on American Christians who are committed to encouraging crucial interreligious relationships. Keeping that fact in mind, I discuss each of the four in turn.

Personal Relationships and Trust

The Sisterhood of Salaam Shalom is one of the largest organizations devoted to Jewish-Muslim dialogue in the United States. Several years ago, group leaders began organizing "Building Bridges" excursions to places where people have endured human rights abuses, including Bosnia and Albania, European nations that were experiencing a refugee crisis, and the United States border with Mexico, where they studied the plight of migrants. In the process, a commitment to shared values emerged, along with the formation of personal bonds within the group. Only then did the organization begin in a systematic way to address the Israeli-Palestinian conflict.[11] The organization's executive director told me that, though conversations about the current Israel-Hamas war have been very difficult, the approach of beginning by establishing personal relationships among participants has been a clear benefit.[12]

In some cities, the strong ties among interfaith leaders that facilitate tackling difficult issues such as the war are the result of tragedies that occurred in the past. In the aftermath of the 1995 bombing of the federal building in Oklahoma City, suspicion was at first directed at the Muslim community, spurring a wave of anti-Muslim violence. One of the alleged suspects was Imad Enchassi, a Palestinian immigrant. When it turned out that he was unjustly accused, the city rallied around him. Enchassi became a highly respected scholar and spiritual leader. He chairs the Islamic studies program at Oklahoma City University and is a leader of the city's interreligious movement. Enchassi stated that, in Oklahoma City, "we have what I call a 'faith NATO': An attack on one faith is an attack on all faiths." Executive director of the Oklahoma Faith network at the time, Reverend Shannon Fleck explained that "a lot of roots sprung out of [the 1995 bombing], and one of them is interfaith conversation and engagement. . . . Oklahoma City's interfaith community is so close and tight knit because we have to be."[13] A similar dynamic has occurred in Pittsburgh, Pennsylvania, where new relationships that were formed—particularly between Muslims and Jews—in response to the 2018 Tree of Life Synagogue murders have aided the community in dealing with a rise of antisemitic and anti-Muslim acts, as well as with contentious campus protests.[14]

Another example of the value of friendship in dialogue is the work of NewGround, which is a Los Angeles-based organization led by Aziza Hasan, a Muslim of Palestinian origin, and by her associate director, Andrea Hodos, who is Jewish and a former resident of Israel. The intimate friendship they have developed guides their approach to cultivating interreligious understanding. In the weeks after the war broke out, they led fruitful discussions, which they are convinced were possible only because of the personal relationships they have nurtured over the years. They have found that "in the absence of that relationship, one person becomes defensive in a discussion, and whoever they are speaking with from the other side entrenches and gets defensive back quickly. When there's a relationship, there are moments of softening . . . and a little more care."[15]

Stories of Suffering

In my experience, a sure way to undermine discussion of the Israeli-Palestinian conflict is to begin with an exchange of political views, complete with preferred policy approaches to address the problems. Before long, disagreements surface among participants, and their selective knowledge and entrenched convictions prevent them from truly listening to one another. To avoid this danger, many groups follow a set of guidelines for dialogue that was developed several decades ago by Leonard Swidler, long-time professor of Catholic thought and interreligious dialogue at Temple University. The foundational principle of his approach is that "the essential purpose of dialogue is to learn, which entails change."[16] And one of the most effective means of learning from others is to listen to their stories. Stories have a unique ability to capture the attention of listeners, and to engage their empathy.[17]

Therefore, once a level of trust has been established in a group, members can begin to give voice to their personal attitudes and feelings toward the Israel-Hamas war. They may wish to describe their emotions when they first heard about the Hamas attack, or when they learned of the international aid workers who were killed in the bombings of Gaza.[18] If they have a personal connection to people affected by the violence, they may be willing to share those stories. A methodology like Narrative 4, which has been used to facilitate dialogue in many types of settings (and is employed by many of us at Seton Hill University) can provide useful guidance in the process of story exchange.[19] And though participants may find it painful, they should also read and listen to the first-hand accounts of those who have been directly impacted by the war. As long as the accounts are accurate and not sensationalized, they can provide observers with an indispensable window into the war's impact on ordinary people.

An appropriate place to begin is with the website that has been created by the USC Shoah Foundation. The website provides testimonies from the survivors of the Hamas attacks. More than 100 videos have been posted, and the archive is growing.[20] By viewing these videos, even a small fraction of them, one can gain valuable insight into the severity of the trauma suffered by a wide range of Israeli citizens. Various media outlets have also recorded survivor stories, like that of a young Israeli woman who, in trying to escape the carnage at the Nova Music Festival, was trapped in a shelter underneath dozens of bodies. She escaped, but nearly all of those huddled in the shelter with her were murdered, including her companion.[21] And though they are agonizing to read, the observations of volunteers who retrieved the bodies of victims offer an important record of the crimes that were perpetrated by Hamas.[22] This is also true of the disturbing eyewitness accounts of gang rapes and the other forms of sexual violence that occurred.[23] Painful as it is to encounter them, these stories must be told, and they must be heard.

Participants can then proceed to listen to the stories of victims of the Israel Defense Forces (IDF) assault on Gaza. They might begin with the reflections of the priest of Holy Family Catholic Church about his two parishioners who were murdered while walking on parish grounds.[24] They should read too about the frustrations of José Andrés, who has tried to get food to starving Gazans, and about the enormous challenges facing parents who are struggling to protect and care for their children amid so much destruction.[25] With these disasters in mind, they may wish to discuss the pointed moral question posed by journalist Nicholas Kristof: "What can we possibly say to the children of Gaza?"[26] In the West Bank as well, a wave of violence has been unleashed against Palestinians.[27] It is imperative to hear the accounts of those victims.[28] Finally, participants can read the heartbreaking story, and view the photo, of the father who cradled his dead son, and refused to let him go.[29]

By engaging with these narratives, participants confront the truth that no one group in this conflict has a monopoly on suffering, and that no one's suffering is more important than the suffering of anyone else. They will understand how inaccurate and unfair it is to make sweeping assertions that place blame exclusively on one side or the other and will not be as ready to advocate solutions that are likely to result in still more violence and destruction. Instead, they can begin to grapple with the terrifying reality of the war, recognize its dreadful human toll, and grieve along with its victims.

Lessons of the Peacemakers

As difficult as it is in the United States to discuss the Israeli-Palestinian conflict in a way that acknowledges the suffering on both sides, for those whose lives have been directly affected by the violence, doing so is far more daunting. And yet, despite the personal traumas they have endured, there are many in the region who have devoted decades to pursuing interreligious dialogue and to making peace. As we, in our organizations, struggle to address the war in a way that deepens our empathy for one another, there is a great deal that we can learn from these peacemakers.

One such person is Yitzhak Frankenthal, whose beloved son, Arik, who was serving in the Israeli Defense Forces, was murdered by Hamas kidnappers in 1994. Since then, Frankenthal has devoted his life to bringing Israelis and Palestinians together in meaningful dialogue. He founded the Parents Circle–Family Forum as a place for bereaved families to grieve, and to heal, together. In an interview, Frankenthal said that his work for peace and reconciliation is guided by his deep faith, and by the conviction that all human life is sacred. He sees no difference in the inherent value of an Israeli and a Palestinian life. He also opposes violence in all forms, particularly the killing of innocent civilians that so often occurs when one side or the other attempts to retaliate for previous acts of violence.[30]

Today, members of Parents Circle–Family Forum focus on fostering dialogue among families who have lost loved ones in the war, and they continue to advocate for peace. They helped to organize a ceremony to remember all of the war's victims, and they spoke about the futility of continuing the cycle of violence and revenge. One participant, Michal Halev, whose son was killed by Hamas militants on October 7, addressed the audience, saying, "There are, and will be, no winners in this war. We have all already lost. . . . May we always choose compassion and love over everything else."[31]

Liat Atzili is an Israeli high school teacher and educator at Yad Vashem, the Holocaust remembrance institution in Jerusalem. On October 7, she was kidnapped and held in Gaza for nearly two months. During that time, she feared what had happened to her family. After her release, she learned that her three children had survived, but her husband had been killed. Her home and her entire community were also destroyed.

Atzili has discussed the concept of *tekumah*, or rebirth, as it relates to her experience. "Tekumah," she explained, "provides us with the vital life lesson of how to move on with dignity and purpose after experiencing a tragedy, and it is perhaps the most important gift that the [Holocaust] survivors gave us." She has argued for the need for *tekumah* today, imparting this remarkable and inspiring message:

> Without tekumah, we will only sink further into the cycle of mutual anger and victimhood that has plagued our relationship with the Palestinians for too long. That is not the approach that the survivor generation chose, and in their spirit, I do not seek revenge for what I have been through. I am humbled by how my fellow Israelis put their lives at risk to fight my kidnappers, but I do not feel any catharsis in seeing the destruction of Gaza. Instead, I want to focus on building a better future for my three children—and for the children of Gaza.[32]

Human Rights

As they conclude their study of the war, dialogue groups can benefit from examining their findings from a human rights perspective. To do so is to realize how thoroughly and callously the human rights of both Israelis and Palestinians have been violated.

At the time of this writing in July 2024, the war continues with no sign of a cessation of hostilities. Hamas is now waging war as a guerilla force in Gaza, with small groups of fighters and, in some cases, lone individuals, launching surprise attacks on Israeli soldiers.[33] Meanwhile, the Israeli military, in its search for Hamas militants, continues to injure and kill non-combatants. After two months, its "limited" siege of Rafah, a refuge for more than a million Palestinians, made the city uninhabitable.[34]

A Palestinian writer from Gaza has poignantly described what it has been like to lose the home where he grew up—with all of its memories.[35] His story could be repeated a thousand times over. Enormous swaths of Gaza have been destroyed, including homes, shops, businesses, and churches. For this reason, some have accused Israel of *domicide*, which is defined as the "massive, arbitrary destruction of civilian housing in a conflict." Even before the current war, the office of the UN High Commissioner for Human Rights argued that domicide should be considered a crime under international law.[36] Whether a formal crime or not, it is surely a tragedy.

As we study the facts of the war carefully, we recognize that both Hamas and Israel have committed crimes against civilians. An investigation by the Holy Land Justice and Peace Commission has concluded that neither Hamas's October 7 assault nor Israel's "indiscriminate" response meet the definition of a "just war." The report explained that a just war must "clearly differentiate between civilians and combatants," which neither party to the conflict has consistently done. The Commission also stated that in a just war, there is a "proportionate" use of force, and argued that this "cannot be said of a war in which the Palestinian death toll is tens of thousands of people higher than that of Israel, and one in which a clear majority of the Palestinian casualties have been women and children."[37]

The excessive violence of this war, and the awful and lasting damage it has done to survivors and their communities, is deeply distressing. It is a great disappointment that despite many calls from the international community and citizens of Israel and Palestine for a ceasefire and a return of hostages, a resolution remains elusive.

Those of us who practice interreligious dialogue must affirm these truths and honestly confront the enormity of the suffering the war has caused. And while we likely will not agree on some specific issues, at least we can find common ground in our belief in the rights and inherent dignity of all those who have been affected by the conflict. We can also express our support for the peacemakers of the region, who are working so bravely for an end to the vicious cycle of violence and revenge.

Perhaps we can also agree with members of the Sisterhood of Salaam Shalom who conducted an extensive discussion of the war. After participating in the process, one of the members concluded, "I believe in my religion, and I believe . . . that any innocent life killed is a crime. . . . Regardless of who does it, we have no right." To this, another participant added, "This intractable problem has been going on for 70 years—we're not going to solve it. But we can maintain our relationships, and not lose sight of each other's humanity."[38]

Finally, we should recommit ourselves to the task of learning about one another's faiths with open hearts and minds, and to deepening our friendships. The work of interreligious dialogue was never more challenging, or necessary and rewarding, than it is right now.

Questions for Dialogue

1. What roles do friendship and trust play in interreligious dialogue? Why are they important to its success? Do Christians have a part to play in encouraging good Jewish-Muslim relationships?

2. Why are narratives and stories effective at creating empathy in various types of groups?

3. What are the dangers and benefits of discussing the Israel-Hamas war in interreligious groups that include Muslims as well as Christians and Jews?

Further Resources

Daniel, Ari. "A Holocaust Survivor Identifies with the Pain of Both Sides in the Israel-Hamas War." NPR, January 30, 2024. https://bit.ly/4ghEh0D.

"Daughters of Abraham." *On the Brink*. Posted April 25, 2024. PBS, YouTube. https://bit.ly/40PWUV0.

Khouri, Raja J., and Jeffrey J. Wilkinson. *The Wall Between: What Jews and Palestinians Don't Want to Know About Each Other*. Northampton, MA: Olive Branch, 2023.

Rehman, Sabeeha, and Walter Ruby. *We Refuse to Be Enemies: How Muslims and Jews Can Make Peace, One Friendship at a Time*. New York: Arcade, 2021.

Swidler, Leonard. "The Dialogue Decalogue: Ground Rules for Inter-Religious, Inter-Ideological Dialogue." *Journal of Ecumenical Studies* 20, no. 1 (Winter, 1983): 1-4.

Notes

1. See Timothy Jones, "Antisemitism Rising Dramatically Across the World—Report," *Deutsche Welle* (*DW*), May 5, 2024, https://bit.ly/4g96c2F; Nadine El-Bawab, "Anti-Muslim Incidents Climbed Sharply Last Year, Civil Rights Group Says," ABC News, April 2, 2024, https://bit.ly/40xDLph.

2. Louis Keene, "War Is Putting Jewish-Muslim Relationships to the Test. Some Religious Leaders Are Determined to Protect Them," *Forward*, October 27, 2023, https://bit.ly/40zSekP.

3. Dave Schechter, "Holding the Monsters at Bay," *Atlanta Jewish Times*, November 5, 2023, https://bit.ly/3CphCBG.

4. Leila Richards, interview with the author, June 3, 2024.

5. Tom Gjelten, "A Cooling: Jewish-Muslim Interfaith Work after October 7 and Gaza," *Moment*, February 23, 2024, https://bit.ly/3WxSOhC.

6. Raja G. Khouri and Jeffrey J. Wilkinson, "Trauma Is Shaping Our Reactions to the Violence in Palestine and Israel," *Walrus*, October 26, 2023, https://bit.ly/40L0HD1.

7. The quotation is from "Intellectual Humility," John Templeton Foundation, https://bit.ly/40FDVeq.

8. Tom Hanson et al., "Teens Struggle to Identify Misinformation about Israel-Hamas Conflict—World's Second 'Social Media War'," CBS News, December 19, 2023, https://bit.ly/4ju0xHw.

9. Yasemin Giritli İnceoğlu, "'Dead' vs. 'Killed': A Closer Look at the Media Bias in Reporting Israel-Palestine Conflict," *Wire*, November 1, 2023, https://bit.ly/40KRNWa.

10. Judy Maltz, "'Worst Crisis Ever': Jewish-Muslim Partnership Groups in U.S. Become Another Victim of Gaza War," *Haaretz*, January 10, 2024, https://bit.ly/3Qbkzt3.

11. Atiya Atfab, "Why and When We Officially Began Israeli-Palestinian Dialogue," Sisterhood of Salaam Shalom, May 21, 2024, https://bit.ly/3WxXDI2.

12. Tahija Vikalo, interview with the author, June 4, 2024.

13. Quoted in Marc Ramirez, "As War in Gaza Tests Interfaith Bonds in the US, Some Find Ways to Mend Relationships," *USA Today*, April 4, 2024, https://bit.ly/3EkGtHg.

14. Erin Yudt and Betul Tuncer, "Amid Antisemitism and Islamophobia, Faith Communities and Students Try to Tamp Down Tension," *PublicSource*, November 28, 2023, https://bit.ly/3CdNBot.

15. Kurt Streeter, "'I Love You. I Am Sorry': One Jew, One Muslim and a Friendship Tested by War," *New York Times*, October 21, 2023, https://bit.ly/4ggCFEv.

16. Leonard Swidler, "Dialogue Principles," https://bit.ly/4js6nch.

17. See Paul J. Zak, "How Stories Change the Brain," *Greater Good*, December 17, 2013, https://bit.ly/4avlVrC.

18. See Ishaan Tharoor, "Israel's 'Unintentional' Strike on Aid Workers Stirs Global Outrage," *Washington Post*, April 3, 2024, https://bit.ly/3CrGvN3.

19. See Larisa Epatko, "The Barrier-Breaking Power of Learning Someone Else's Story," PBS, July 13, 2017, https://bit.ly/3PQiz9a.

20. "Survivors of the October 2023 Hamas Terrorist Attacks," USC Shoah Foundation, https://bit.ly/4gjHhtf.

21. "Nova Survivor Bravely Revisits the Shelter of Horrors Where She Escaped Death on October 7," i24NEWS, May 13, 2024, https://bit.ly/4OomU8k.

22. See Ido Efrati, "Confirming the Worst Hamas Atrocities: Inside Israel's Center for the Identification of the Dead," *Haaretz*, October 15, 2023, https://bit.ly/4gfkqPR.

23. Josh Breiner, "Israeli Police Collect Eyewitness Testimony of Gang Rape During Hamas Attack," *Haaretz*, November 8, 2023, https://bit.ly/40v77F0.

24. Antonella Palmero and Roberto Cetera, "Gaza Catholic Priest: 'I Knew Victims of Attack on Catholic Church,'" *Vatican News*, December 18, 2023, https://bit.ly/4g7PwIY.

25. See José Andrés, "José Andrés: Let People Eat," *New York Times*, April 3, 2024, https://bit.ly/4joGnid. See also Louisa Loveluck and Hajar Harb, "Parenting in Gaza Today is So Much More Than Keeping Your Children Alive," *Washington Post*, April 30, 2024, https://bit.ly/4jtrn2p.

26. Nicholas Kristof, "What Can We Possibly Say to the Children of Gaza?" *New York Times*, February 3, 2024, https://bit.ly/3WwTGTC.

27. See "Settler Attacks Are Escalating in the West Bank," Doctors of the World, April 12, 2024, https://bit.ly/4gjwS0O.

28. See Megan K. Stack, "For Palestinians, the Future Is Being Bulldozed," *New York Times*, December 9, 2023, https://bit.ly/3CqT5fA.

29. See "A Boy in Gaza Was Killed in an Israeli Airstrike. His Father Held Him and Wouldn't Let Go," AP News, July 11, 2024, https://bit.ly/3WB0rnz.

30. See James G. Paharik, *The Long Journey: In Search of Justice and Peace in Jerusalem* (Collegeville: Liturgical Press, 2009), 91-96.

31. Daniel Estrin, "Israelis and Palestinians Held a Joint Memorial for All Victims of the Ongoing War," NPR, May 14, 2024, https://bit.ly/4gb6Cpj.

32. Liat Atzili, "Choosing Rebirth over Revenge after My Release from Gaza," *New York Times*, February 1, 2024, https://bit.ly/3POzSr4.

33. Patrick Kingsley et al., "How Hamas is Fighting in Gaza," *New York Times*, July 13, 2024, https://bit.ly/3PNzyJp.

34. Jeremy Diamond, "Israel Says Its Operation in Rafah Is 'Limited.' Fighting There Has Left Parts of it Unrecognizable," CNN, July 7, 2024, https://bit.ly/3E4aH19.

35. Abu Saif Atef, "My Gaza House Felt like a Castle. Now It Is Rubble," *Washington Post*, December 12, 2023, https://bit.ly/4g7Qwgc.

36. "'Domicide' Must Be Recognized as an International Crime: UN Expert," Office of the High Commissioner, United Nations Human Rights, October 28, 2022, https://bit.ly/4OOtw1i.

37. Lisa Zengarini, "Holy Land Justice and Peace Decries Weaponization of 'Just War,'" *Vatican News*, February 7, 2024, https://bit.ly/3PNXZ9s.

38. Brammhi Balarajan, "US Interfaith Communities Draw on Decades-Long Bonds to Navigate Israel-Hamas War," CNN, November 22, 2023, https://bit.ly/3WBEIfo.

Part Three
I Will Not Be Silent

On May 31, 2024, leaders of the US Senate and House of Representatives sent Israel's prime minister Benjamin Netanyahu an invitation to address a joint meeting of Congress. The invitation said: "To build on our enduring relationship and to highlight America's solidarity with Israel, we invite you to share the Israeli government's vision for defending democracy, combating terror, and establishing a just and lasting peace in the region."[1]

Controversy swirled around the invitation, initiated by Republicans to apply uncomfortable pressure on Democrats—including Democratic Senate majority leader Chuck Schumer, the highest-ranking elected Jewish official in US history, who had previously stated that Netanyahu's leadership was an obstacle to peace.[2]

Thousands of protesters—some of them attempting to block Netanyahu's route to the Capitol—met the prime minister on July 24, 2024, when he addressed Congress in a defiant and divisive speech boycotted by scores of Democrats.[3] Netanyahu depicted the war as a "clash between barbarism and civilization."[4] No military in history, he claimed, had ever done more than Israel's to prevent harm to civilians. "For Israel," Netanyahu insisted, "every civilian death is a tragedy. For Hamas, it's a strategy."

The following day, Netanyahu met with Kamala Harris, the vice president of the United States and soon to be the Democratic presidential nominee who would unsuccessfully run against Donald Trump in November 2024. Harris, whose multifaceted religious identity reflects influences from the Black Christian tradition, had not attended Netanyahu's speech, but she knew what he had said. Her remarks during their meeting were as significant as his had been from the day before.

Harris called Hamas "a brutal terrorist organization," which had "triggered" the Israel-Hamas war.[5] However, she broke Netanyahu's silence about the war's devastation. Her remarks following the meeting with Netanyahu emphasized that she had spoken to him about "the death of far too many innocent civilians." In addition to lamenting the hunger ravaging millions of Palestinians, Harris's statement continued:

What has happened in Gaza over the past nine months is devastating—the images of dead children and desperate, hungry people fleeing for safety, sometimes displaced for the second, third, or fourth time. We cannot look away in the face of these tragedies. We cannot allow ourselves to become numb to the suffering. And I will not remain silent.

For Netanyahu and Harris, silence was not an option. Neither is silence an option for the authors of the chapters in Part III of *Stress Test*. The ways in which they break silence, moreover, are crucial for Christian-Jewish relations during the Israel-Hamas war and its aftermath. That is because these authors underscore what those relations must and must not do if realistic hopes for a just peace between Israelis and Palestinians are to remain in the dismal wreckage that will linger and fester long after the war ends.

Michael G. Azar warns that Christian-Jewish relations risk losing credibility unless they rid themselves of "historic and persistent anti-Palestinianism." He argues "that a book like this one is fundamentally flawed—especially when other contributors have sometimes shared views that promote and legitimate violence against Palestinians." Such views, he says, are unacceptable. "The Israel-Hamas war demands that Christian-Jewish relations' historic and immoral tendency to ignore or oppose the Palestinian plight must change." Azar has written his chapter "with hope for such change."

Peter Pettit explores issues within his Evangelical Lutheran Church in America (ELCA) to show how important it is for Christian-Jewish relations to meet a decisive challenge: Criticizing the most extreme elements of both Israeli and Palestinian governments in protest against the Israel-Hamas war but doing that ethical work without canceling respect for the Israeli or Palestinian people.

Sarah Pinnock studies how injustice and suffering are falsely and immorally "justified" by ideologies and theologies, nations and religions that defend their aims and interests in ways reminiscent of Netanyahu's 2024 speech to Congress. Weary of the unending cycles of violence, pain, and death that such rationales so dangerously legitimate, she finds hope in the examples of bilateral Israeli-Palestinian organizations that "show how recognizing mutual suffering resulting from ongoing violence may increase empathy between different factions."

John K. Roth wonders whether it can make sense to call himself a "pro-Palestinian Zionist" as the Israeli-Hamas war resists closure and may even expand in the Middle East. But affirmation of that identity, he urges, is a necessary condition to keep hope alive not only for Christian-Jewish relations but also for the future of the Israeli and Palestinian people.

"I will not be silent"—that is the response that the writers of these four chapters want from their readers. Like their fellow contributors to *Stress Test,* these four authors hope for frank debate and dialogue about what they have said. They hope, too, that such debate and dialogue can support and amplify what we owe to each other, reviving, sustaining, and advancing the Christian-Jewish relations that are urgently needed in the wake of the Israel-Hamas war.

Notes

1. See Caitlin Yilek, "Congressional Leaders Invite Israel's Netanyahu to Address U.S. Lawmakers," CBS News, May 31, 2024, https://bit.ly/4joPOhD.

2. See "Majority Leader Schumer Calls on Israeli Government to Hold Elections," March 14, 2024, https://bit.ly/4juONVa.

3. See Ashraf Khalil and Alanna Durkin Richer, "Thousands Fill Washington's Streets to Protest Israel's War in Gaza during Netanyahu's Visit," AP News, July 24, 2024, https://bit.ly/4OowS9K.

4. For the full text of Netanyahu's speech, see "PM Netanyahu's Address to a Joint Meeting of the US Congress," Prime Minister's Office, July 25, 2024, https://bit.ly/40w9TKf.

5. For the full text of Harris's statement, including the quotations that follow, see "Full Remarks: Vice President Kamala Harris Speaks after Meeting with Netanyahu," CNN video, posted July 25, 2024, by WAAY 31 News, YouTube, https://bit.ly/40z1p4Z.

9
Admitting the Sins of Christian-Jewish Relations

Michael G. Azar

In the aftermath of the Nakba of 1948, when the State of Israel was created and hundreds of thousands of Palestinians were forced from their homes, the entirely arbitrary borders of the "Gaza Strip" were invented and imposed. By October 2023, 70 percent of the 2.1 million people in this strip of land were still Nakba refugees. Now, as I write these words in late July 2024, the Israel-Hamas war has displaced almost the entire population yet again. Each week, hundreds of names are added to the lists of the dead—now numbering almost 40,000 since the war began. Countless others join the myriad already injured and maimed; still more become parentless and childless. Centuries-old Palestinian families have been entirely erased from civil registries. There are no clear missing-person statistics, but the number likely reaches further into the tens of thousands. Many surviving in Gaza live in squalor with nowhere to go, but they do so with a hope that they are in "safe zones"—a notion that the ongoing Israeli bombardment time and again proves false. Famine sets in; mass graves continue to reveal themselves. The despair of violence is rivaled only by the despair wrought by denied hopes for a ceasefire. The Nakba continues.

Amid this reality, one cannot help but think that a book like this one is fundamentally flawed—especially when other contributors have sometimes shared views that promote and legitimate violence against Palestinians.[1] Can reflections on the relationship between the Israel-Hamas war and Christian-Jewish relations be anything more than a deflection from the real need for an immediate ceasefire and for Israel to allow humanitarian aid finally to flow unhindered? I am not sure they can.

Nevertheless, even if the most violent aspects of the war someday draw to a close and Gazans are allowed to leave their tragically flammable tents and other shelters to rebuild the places that had been their homes (at least, since 1948), and Israelis from the Gazan and Lebanese frontiers are allowed to leave their temporary housing in hotel rooms and shared apartments and return to their border communities, Christian-Jewish relations will go on. The Christian-Jewish relationship is necessary and important. It has already fundamentally shaped the Holy Land, although it has typically done so by dismissing, discrediting, or displacing the ancient and venerable families of the Holy Land itself. The Israel-Hamas war demands that Christian-Jewish relations' historic and immoral tendency to ignore or oppose the Palestinian plight must change. This imperative is especially important for Christians and Jews who interact with one another in the West—the historic home of Christian-Jewish relations, where most of the world's power and money (but not population) are found. I have written this chapter with hope for such change.

Before October 2023: The Combustibility of Palestine's Reality and Christian-Jewish Relations' Denial

The last time I visited the Holy Land before October 2023 was in the preceding January. I did so while teaching "Christianity in the Middle East," a University of Scranton course through which I have regularly introduced students to the Christian communities of the Holy Land. In January 2023, as many times previously, my American students and I spent almost all our time with the communities that most "pilgrimages" do not at all see, and with whom very few participants in Christian-Jewish relations typically interact: the Palestinian communities of East Jerusalem and the West Bank.

In the West Bank, the students witnessed firsthand the ever-increasing oppression that Israeli military occupation brings. They saw neighborhoods routinely subjected to military "training exercises" for seemingly no other reason than intimidation. They visited streets where school children had been arrested without any notification sent to their parents. Jewish settlers confronted the students. One morning, the students serendipitously shared breakfast with a group of pilgrims and the parish priest from Holy Family Catholic Church in Gaza City.. The priest had been given special permission to visit Bethlehem during the Christmas season. My students and I heard about life in the rest of Palestine, about the troubles facing the tiny Christian minority in the Hamas-ruled region, as Gaza's people endured the worsening humanitarian situation caused by the unholy alliance between Hamas's corruption and Israel's blockade.[2]

When my students asked what hope could exist in such a precarious situation, I told them about the peace movements, especially among Israelis—the notable few with both the will and ability to make major changes. But, I noted, the unfortunate reality was that, despite efforts among peace groups, significant change historically had rarely come without major acts of violence preceding it. Those voices calling for peace and nonviolent resistance, like the Palestinian Christian groups and representatives we encountered, were noticeably losing credibility as the Israeli occupation and blockade hardened and the ideologies of groups such as the Islamic State (ISIS) continued to fill the void that hopelessness creates. Palestinian land continued to be lost; Palestinians continued to live under increasingly harsh Israeli control. The Israeli government clearly favored increased annexation, greater oppression, and division among Palestinians by supporting the Hamas government.[3] Amid this environment, the tension was palpable; hope was weakening. As a Catholic nun put it one evening, this reality had ensured that life was doused with gasoline. Together we feared that someone would soon provide a spark.

As the spring of 2023 wore on and Israel's far-right government solidified its position, increased settler violence and forced displacement further besieged Palestinians in East Jerusalem and the West Bank.[4] But, to my knowledge, major institutions and participants in Christian-Jewish relations outside of the Holy Land said little about these worsening conditions. Even as Christians in Israel increasingly spoke out against the threats, harassment, and arbitrary restrictions they were facing under the current Israeli government, the silence of Christian-Jewish relations abroad was deafening.[5] Respected voices whom I encountered in the dialogue even offered counterclaims. The Christian population in Israel, some said, was growing, and Jerusalem's Christian leaders, who had raised alarm about ongoing hostilities from Israel's Jewish majority, had simply fallen victim to "political manipulation."[6] I had long been familiar with Christian-Jewish relations' historic tendency to decentralize or outright ignore those local Christian voices that did not fulfill a preconceived narrative of Christian life under Israeli sovereignty, and here I saw it continue. Christian-Jewish relations had long and laudably taught the Christian world of the consequences of denying a people a voice of their own—the consequences of speaking for a people without speaking to and with them. And yet, here we were. Apparently, we had not learned our lesson. Or we had only learned it unidirectionally.

But still, no spark.

As summer 2023 unfolded, the Israeli government continued with its plans to annex the West Bank.[7] Trusting in the barrier that they had drawn around the Gaza Strip, replete as it was with cameras, remote-controlled weapons, and other features, Israeli authorities diverted military resources from the Gaza border to the West Bank, including to the vicinity of Hawara, where settlers had perpetrated an anti-Palestinian pogrom the previous February.[8] Was this increased military presence in the West Bank intended to prevent settler violence or to encourage it? The answer depended on where you might find yourself on any particular day and with whom.

The Ruthless Spark

On October 7, 2023, Hamas and like-minded groups from Gaza waged a coordinated attack inside Israel. No one, including the Israeli military who had been aware of Hamas's plans in advance (even the estimated number of hostages they were aiming for), seemed to realize Hamas was capable of this assault.[9] Few expected the attack's brutality. But when the first news reports began to describe the scale of the attack, the world quickly realized that it was unprecedented. No attack in Israel had been as "successful" (though one shudders even to use such a word). Nor had atrocities, including sexual violence and beheadings, so marked any previous attack.

Numerous Christians in Christian-Jewish relations circles rallied in support of the State of Israel, lamenting the Israeli losses and expressing sympathy and concern especially for Jewish colleagues. These expressions were neither surprising nor unreasonable; the historic sympathies of Christians who had fought for Christian-Jewish rapprochement in the past several decades had long been on the side of the Jewish State. Far more Christians in Christian-Jewish relations were closer to Jewish friends than they were to Palestinians, let alone to Palestinians in Gaza.

Amid this sea of sympathy and support, indeed partly because of it, I had other fears—personal and professional—that I was told, more than once, were unreasonable and ill-timed. While many of my Christian-Jewish relations colleagues spoke of little beyond Hamas's "pure evil" and the Israeli need for "self-defense," I feared the war that their views would justify and exacerbate. I feared the unlimited military action that their one-sided response would promote. Knowing the history of the region and its conflicts, having witnessed the Israeli military's regular operations in the West Bank, I feared that Israel would react with unprecedented force that would brutally destroy Gaza and the lives of innumerable civilians, the vast majority of whom were not yet born or old enough to vote when Hamas came to power in 2007.

I was not surprised that Israel's leaders vowed to destroy the perpetrators, to wipe them out completely—to blot them out, as it were, like the biblical Amalekites.[10] But in the end, for better or for worse, I was convinced that Hamas would survive and unavoidably remain a negotiating partner. Why did I think this? For a simple reason: a similar scenario had happened before.

In the early 1980s, five years before Hamas was founded, Israel brutally besieged Beirut. The ostensible reason was to destroy the Palestine Liberation Organization (PLO), designated at the time as a "terrorist" organization. Edward Said aptly assessed the siege of Beirut in words that eerily anticipated Israel's current actions and the world's failures now:

> The Israelis had not only laid siege to the city; they had cut off water and electricity, and had forbidden the flow of medicines and food across the siege lines. A city that numbered about 750,000 people. And this in full view of the world! The proclaimed purpose of this was to destroy the PLO which, General Sharon said at the time, was threatening Israel. . . . The Israeli army, navy and air force conducted continuous bombardments of the city, on some days over 150 sorties. At that point I was at the United Nations, anxiously following the debate in the Security Council. A resolution was put forward, in which the Security Council urged Israel to open the siege lines to permit, for humanitarian purposes, the passage of medicines and other essential things for the besieged inhabitants of Beirut. What was the fate of that resolution? It was vetoed by the United States. On what grounds, you might well ask? Why would anybody want to veto a resolution that spoke of medicines going across a line? The argument presented then was that the resolution was not "even-handed."[11]

Far from being destroyed by Israel's collective punishment of Beirut, the PLO survived and eventually morphed into the Palestinian Authority (PA), now Israel's governing and security partner in the West Bank (at least at the time of this writing in the summer of 2024, although the PA's future is not bright).

Israeli military force did not succeed, at least not as intended, against the PLO. Nor did it succeed against Hezbollah (a group formed in response to Israel's 1982 invasion of Lebanon) in 2006, when a similar scenario replayed on the world stage. I therefore cannot believe it will succeed against Hamas now. Crimes against humanity, collective punishment, the starvation and deaths of thousands—the realities of the genocidal rhetoric coming from the Israeli administration[12]—can never contribute to Israel's "security," though it is the latter that is summoned frequently in attempts to justify the current and immensely destructive war.

Reactions in the Halls of Christian-Jewish Relations

Knowing this history, and shaped as I am by Orthodox Christian spiritual teachings, I was somewhat comforted by the reaction of at least a few Christian leaders in early October who condemned any and all violence surrounding the 10/7 event. The Ecumenical Patriarch of Constantinople, for example, issued a statement on October 8 that included the following words: "Amid anger and destruction, amid evil and bitterness, human beings are easily tempted to think and to act violently. While many deem violence as a necessary means of dispute resolution, we can never see it as part of God's good creation, nor can we ever approve the use of violence to pursue peace."[13] The day preceding, as the extent of the violence of October 7 was beginning to set in, the Patriarchs and Heads of the Churches in Jerusalem expressed similar sentiments: "Our faith, which is founded on the teachings of Jesus Christ, compels us to advocate for the cessation of all violent and military activities that bring harm to both Palestinian and Israeli civilians. We unequivocally condemn any acts that target civilians, regardless of their nationality, ethnicity, or faith. . . . It is our fervent hope and prayer that all parties involved will heed this call for an immediate cessation of violence."[14]

Though this later statement was penned by Christians and based explicitly on the teachings of Jesus, the State of Israel immediately condemned it for "immoral linguistic ambiguity," and several Christians and Jews in the halls of Christian-Jewish relations echoed similar refrains.[15] Some decried the statement as "shockingly weak," "vacuous," "pathetic and devoid of any moral leadership," betraying a "lack of moral clarity" and failing to "support" the Jewish community in the way that Christians should.[16] In the days and weeks following the October 7 attack, some Jewish participants in Christian-Jewish relations discussions labeled calls for a ceasefire "delusional" and emphasized the sense of abandonment they felt from their Christian partners in dialogue.[17] They condemned Christians who had "minimized" Hamas's massacre "by decrying violence 'on both sides,' woefully failing to recognize the moral distinction between those who butcher and those who are butchered, between intentional carnage and self-defence against that carnage."[18]

Israeli authorities described their Palestinian enemies as "human animals," vowed to act "accordingly" by cutting off fuel, food, water, and electricity for two million people, and dropped 6,000 bombs in the first six days of the war—with "maximum damage," not precise civilian-protecting accuracy, as the stated goal.[19] Meanwhile, statements from Christian-Jewish relations dialogue groups and institutes condemned the brutal violence against Israelis on October 7 and expressed sympathies for

Jews affected worldwide but said little about the dehumanizing depictions of Palestinians and the increasing destruction of Gaza (and the West Bank, for that matter) in the days that followed.[20] They argued, instead, that "responsibility" for the deaths of "innocent people" and the "current escalation of violence" rested "solely with Hamas" (as a German Jewish-Christian working group stated) or that it was exclusively "Hamas" who was bringing "suffering" on the "civilian population of Gaza" (as an international group of biblical scholars claimed).[21]

Even when I personally recommended that those institutions of Christian-Jewish relations which had issued statements in support of Israel now consider a statement calling for humanitarian aid, the release of captives, and an end to the violence, I was met with few voices of support. The war, I was told instead, was "justified" or at least "worth it." Palestinian deaths would be "unfortunate" or "regrettable" but, apparently, acceptable. All too many in the Christian-Jewish relations community continued their long-standing tendency to ignore or decentralize the concerns and realities of the Holy Land's Christians and other Palestinians. Participants in Christian-Jewish relations had yet to confront the field's historic and long-standing anti-Palestinianism.

Christian-Jewish Relations' History of Anti-Palestinianism

Contemporary Christian-Jewish relations began at an "Emergency Conference on Antisemitism" convened by sixty-three Christians and Jews from twelve nations in Seelisberg, Switzerland, from July 30 to August 5, 1947. The meeting sought to reform traditional anti-Jewish Western Christian teaching in hopes of correcting and preventing the sort of Christian complacency and complicity that so destructively enabled and supported the unparalleled crimes against Jews perpetrated by Nazi Germany. The Seelisberg participants proposed various theological, governmental, and social responses to antisemitism. On August 5, 1947, they issued the "Ten Points of Seelisberg."[22] Condemning, for example, "the superstitious notion that the Jewish people are reprobate, accursed, reserved for a destiny of suffering," the "Ten Points" criticized and deplored misguided beliefs and pernicious doctrines that they believed underpinned anti-Judaism and Christian antisemitism.

Records also show that the Seelisberg deliberations called for compensation for properties and goods lost in Europe and encouraged greater cooperation with the United Nations (particularly UNESCO). They also insisted that "Jews, particularly European Jews," be allowed to immigrate to Palestine, whose doors, they lamented, had been "closed."[23]

Clearly directed against the British Mandate authorities at the time, the meeting simply expressed a general principle based on humanitarian grounds: "No civilized person would deny to those who years ago were taken away from their homes against their will, the right to relief and to recuperation and the right to build up their own lives afresh."[24]

The oversight here is as ironic as it is total, if not outright racist: The people already living in the land which the Western Christians and Jews of Seelisberg wished to open for the surviving Jews of Europe did not appear on the Seelisberg radar at all. This sentiment would directly contribute to the impending war between Jews and Arabs in Palestine and, especially, the Nakba to come, in which hundreds of thousands of Palestinian Arabs, including entire Christian communities, would be forced out of their homes, never to return. Some would be placed in sealed neighborhoods under military rule. Others were massacred. The sentiment of Seelisberg may have helped to resolve problems in Europe, but it exacerbated and created problems in Palestine.

Perhaps Seelisberg should not be blamed. It was, after all, an "emergency" meeting, and emergency plans are not always the most well thought out, however good the intentions might be.[25] It is difficult to tell Christians and Jews who were reacting to Nazi Germany's unprecedented campaign of systematized extermination that they should react differently. Perhaps they could not anticipate what was to come. Or perhaps they truly believed the decades-old lie espoused by so many previously who had promoted Jewish migration: that Palestine was a "land without a people for a people without a land."

Unfortunately, as Christian-Jewish relations developed over the next few decades, the problems only worsened. As a new generation of Palestinians was raised in refugee camps outside of Israel, and those within the Jewish State emerged from two decades under martial law, Christian-Jewish relations flourished during and after Vatican II (1962–65). Even as Israel's military occupation of new lands seized from Jordan, Egypt, and Syria in the aftermath of the 1967 Arab-Israeli war prompted ecumenical organizations to raise concerns about the plight of Palestinians, the sentiment within Christian-Jewish relations frequently focused elsewhere, speaking out in support of the Israeli government and against what it designated acts of "terror." Some Christian-Jewish relations pioneers promoted overtly racist and collectivizing attitudes against Arabs, portraying them as a fundamentally violent people bent on the destruction of both Israel and Jews and promoting the myth that Palestinians who had left the land now part of the State of Israel had done so voluntarily (and hence were not refugees).[26] The Holy Land's Christian leaders who raised concerns about Israel's military and expansion plans were dismissed by venerable scholars in the field, such as John Oesterreicher, as peddlers of "propaganda" and "alarmists" wrongly using the name of Christ.[27] Other founders of Christian-Jewish relations in the United States, such as A. Roy Eckardt, told Christians that, "in contemporary terms," Jesus would have been "an Israeli," and it was therefore "in an Israeli munitions factory" that one would find true Christian witness.[28]

A few years ago, I wrote an article that brought to light some of these collectivizing and racist attitudes in the formative years of post-Vatican II Christian-Jewish relations.[29] Many of the responses demonstrated that those ways of thinking remained alive and well even if they were less overt than before. Especially in Western Europe and the United States, I found that the Christian-Jewish relations community still harbored anti-Palestinian sentiments. This anti-Palestinianism was not necessarily expressed in open hostility—although I have witnessed that too—but in the often quiet sense that the violence done to Palestinians was primarily their own fault, that their concerns for security were secondary or peripheral to the primary focus on the Jewish connection to and presence in the Holy Land. For Christian-Jewish relations, the State of Israel is central. The State of Palestine that it occupies is not.

The Christians of Gaza and Christian-Jewish Relations' Anti-Palestinianism

In 2005, Israel moved its troops from inside the Gaza Strip to the surrounding land and sea borders. At the time, Christians in that region numbered about 5,000, and, by the fall of 2023, they had declined to about 1,000. In the first eight months of the current war, Christians have suffered no differently than others in Gaza, but the effect has been proportionally worse. At least thirty Christians, 3 percent of a tiny minority in Gaza, have been killed (by late February 2024) by Israeli air strikes, Israeli snipers, or lack of access to medical care.[30] Holy Family Catholic Church and St. Porphyrios Greek Orthodox Church, both in Gaza City, have continued to shelter about 1,000 people between them (mostly, but not all, Christians). Christians in Gaza, as well as their hierarchical authorities elsewhere— from the Pope of Rome to the Greek Orthodox Patriarch of Jerusalem— have directly, repeatedly, and unequivocally called for a complete ceasefire and more humanitarian aid. The lives of their people hang in the balance.

Given the scale of Hamas's attack and Christian-Jewish relations' historic antipathy toward Palestinians, I was not surprised that little was said of the Christians of Gaza in the aftermath of October 7, even as the world witnessed the devastation wrought by Israel's relentless military campaign, reliant as it was on AI (artificial intelligence)—including a system sinisterly called "The Gospel"—for its choice of thousands of structural and human targets.[31] So, through contacts with Christians in Gaza, I began writing a series of emails to a national listserv of Christian-Jewish relations leaders and organizations. I later published some of these writings.[32] Some of the emails led to an invitation to contribute a chapter to this book.

The responses I received were telling. Some were outright hostile. Others were positive, but almost always in private, thanking me for offering a "unique," "different," "necessary," and even "brave" perspective.[33] While such messages were much appreciated, they also unwittingly revealed Christian-Jewish relations' long-standing anti-Palestinianism: for me simply to bring to light the realities of life and death for Christians in Gaza could be "unique" and "brave" only because the field itself had long turned blind eyes to basic realities in the Holy Land. Imagine if I had called for a free Palestine.

Despite my efforts and those of others, some major Christian-Jewish relations participants have continued to work viciously to undermine, discredit, and silence Christians in Palestine and their sympathizers elsewhere. Audacious and myopic, such virulent silencing of suffering to legitimate war is disturbing and shocking but not surprising given Christian-Jewish relations' tendencies in the past. I have personally witnessed other contributors to Christian-Jewish relations suggesting that Gaza may need to be firebombed like Dresden or circulating the perspective that Israel's military should force Christians out of Gaza for their own good.[34] In writing against Christian calls for a ceasefire, one Jewish participant in Christian-Jewish relations made the bold (in my view, racist) move to speak on behalf of Christians in Gaza, denying their voice entirely, explaining to them—contrary to their own, explicit expressions these past many months—that Israel's war against Hamas was necessary and in their best interests.[35] Another respected scholar in the history of Christian-Jewish interaction chose the season of the Christian Passover (Easter)—the most significant of Christian feasts—to write a piece that drove a wedge between the historical Jesus and the Christians of Gaza and to put forward misleading historical claims about the history of Palestine's name.[36]

Michael G. Azar

Overcoming Christian-Jewish Relations' Anti-Palestinian History

To emphasize Palestinian suffering historically and during the Israel-Hamas war is not an act of "moral equivalency" but a simple act of decency. It recognizes that the pain of one must never be used to excuse or deny the pain of another. It is an attempt to resist Christian-Jewish relations' historic and persistent anti-Palestinianism. This anti-Palestinianism appears in frequent speech about what Israel means to Jews, especially in the wake of the Holocaust, but in silence about the ongoing Nakba. It appears in expressed support for the State of Israel's security and right to exist, but in silence over the State of Palestine's right to exist freely and securely. It can be heard not only in vocal laments over Israeli deaths, kidnappings, and sexual assaults, but also in silence about Palestinian deaths, kidnappings, and sexual assaults. It appears in frequent concerns about antisemitism that ignore or promote hostility toward Palestinians. It appears in praise for the achievements of the Seelisberg Conference while ignoring or perpetuating the latter's oversights and violent mistakes.

Founded in the shadow of widespread Christian acquiescence to the Nazi regime, the field of Christian-Jewish relations has potential to move the world beyond past hatreds. Yet, despite its many laudable achievements for Christian-Jewish rapprochement, the history of Christian-Jewish relations has often been replete with triumphalist, racist, and orientalist sentiments toward Arabs in general and Palestinians specifically. These historic sentiments have contributed to the horrific loss of Palestinian lives during the Israel-Hamas war. If Christian-Jewish relations are to survive in the future, if they are to retain any credibility for long-standing concerns about displaced peoples and resistance to racist rhetoric and the genocidal violence it engenders, then Christian-Jewish relations must overcome their past. It must show greater concern for the historic Christian and other Palestinian families of the Holy Land, in addition to the Jewish families so often closer to the center of Christian-Jewish relations, than it has hitherto offered. It must overcome its historically myopic approach to the Holy Land, its historic disconnect from the realities that concern Palestinians and Israelis alike and equally. Unless Christian-Jewish relations reframes its approach to both the State of Palestine and the State of Israel by which it is occupied, the field risks losing its credibility and making its historic achievements irrelevant.

Questions for Dialogue

1. What historical reasons initially led Christian-Jewish relations to focus primarily on Jews and Jewish history in the Holy Land rather than on other peoples and their histories? Were those reasons valid? If so, do they still apply?

2. What are some historic and contemporary examples of anti-Palestinianism in Christian-Jewish relations? What steps should be taken to remove anti-Palestinianism from Christian-Jewish relations?

3. What are the real-world effects of Christian-Jewish relations' failure to deal with anti-Palestinianism?

4. Are there theological reasons for Christians to support Jewish nationalism (i.e., Zionism) any more or less than other forms of nationalism, especially Palestinian nationalism?

Further Resources

Khoury, Rafiq, and Rainer Zimmer-Winkel, eds. *Christian Theology in the Palestinian Context*. Berlin: AphorismA, 2019.

Kildani, Hanna. *Modern Christianity in the Holy Land*. Translated by George Musleh. Bloomington, IN: AuthorHouse, 2010.

Perni, Yasmine. *The Stones Cry Out: Voices of Palestinian Christians*. Video Documentary. 2013. Posted March 18, 2024. Journeyman Pictures, YouTube. https://bit.ly/3CiL2S9.

Ramon, Amnon. *Christians and Christianity in the Jewish State: Israeli Policy Toward the Churches and Christian Communities (1948–2018)*. Translated by Shaul Vardi. Jerusalem: Jerusalem Institute for Policy Research and the Rossing Center for Education and Dialogue, 2021.

The Rossing Center for Education and Dialogue." Attacks on Christians in Israel and East Jerusalem. 2023 Annual Report. https://bit.ly/4jDruIF https://bit.ly/4jDruIF.

Notes

1. The views to which I here refer were either (1) told to me directly in personal or group settings; (2) promoted openly on the national listserv of the Council of Centers on Jewish-Christian Relations; or (3) expressed in a variety of public opinion pieces (whether in print or interviews). While I cite some examples of the latter below, I do not have permission to mention specific names from the first two sources. So, I must keep them anonymous.

2. See the United Nations Office for the Coordination of Humanitarian Affairs, "Gaza Strip: The Humanitarian Impact of 15 Years of the Blockade—June 2022," June 30, 2022, https://bit.ly/3CeZGtA.

3. Jeet Heer, "Why Netanyahu Bolstered Hamas," *Nation*, December 11, 2023, https://bit.ly/3E7fy1R.

4. United Nations Office for the Coordination of Humanitarian Affairs, "About 4,000 Palestinians Displaced in the West Bank in 2023," February 21, 2024 Report, https://bit.ly/40zCCxw.

5. Natan Odenheimer, "'The Escalation is Frightening': Jerusalem Christians Fear for Their Future," *+972 Magazine*, July 14, 2023, https://bit.ly/4ggFvt9.

6. As previously, several anecdotes to which I refer in this essay come from personal or group conversations, in person or by email, for which I am not at liberty to reveal names.

7. Michael Sfard, "Israel is Officially Annexing the West Bank," *Foreign Policy,* June 6, 2023, https://bit.ly/4hvFR04.

8. On these points, see Gershom Gorenberg, "How West Bank Settlements Led to the Conflict in Gaza," *American Prospect*, October 20, 2023, https://bit.ly/3WBGzRo, and Emanuel Fabian, "2 Commando Companies Said Diverted from Gaza Border to West Bank Days before Oct. 7," *Times of Israel*, December 5, 2023, https://bit.ly/4js9VeB.

9. Grace Eliza Goodwin, "Israeli Military Knew How Hamas Planned to Take Hostages Weeks before October 7: Report," *Business Insider*, June 17, 2024, https://bit.ly/4OopKu0.

10. "Netanyahu's References to Violent Biblical Passages Raise Alarm among Critics," *Morning Edition*, NPR, November 7, 2023, https://bit.ly/3Wzxjgv.

11. Edward Said, "Peace and the Middle East," *Journal of Communication Inquiry* 16, no. 1 (1992): 9, https://doi.org/10.1177/019685999201600101.

12. On this point, see, for example, Emma Graham-Harrison and Quique Kierszenbaum, "Israeli Public Figures Accuse Judiciary of Ignoring Incitement to Genocide in Gaza," *Guardian*, January 3, 2024, https://bit.ly/4gcRaZV.

13. For the full statement, see "Statement by His All-Holiness Ecumenical Patriarch Bartholomew in Light of the Tragic Events in the Middle East (Sunday, October 8th, 2023)," https://bit.ly/3PPOQNH.

14. For the full statement, see "The Patriarchs and Heads of Churches in Jerusalem Unite in a Call for Peace and Justice Amidst Unfolding Violence,"

October 7, 2023, https://bit.ly/3WCzKyP. Ecumenical Christian bodies such as the World Council of Churches (WCC) also issued comparable statements. See, for example, "WCC Urgently Appeals for Immediate Ceasefire in Israel and Palestine," October 7, 2023, https://bit.ly/4gjAjoe.

15. Carol Glatz, "Israel Condemns Jerusalem Christian Churches over 'Immoral Linguistic Ambiguity' in Statement on Hamas Attack," *Catholic News Service*, October 9, 2023, https://bit.ly/3POD3iu. See also, more broadly, John L. Allen Jr., "In Gaza War, Israel v. Christian Leaders May Be Preview of Israel v. Vatican," *Crux*, October 15, 2023, https://bit.ly/3PR0sjy.

16. These comments were either shared with me privately or on the national listserv of the Council of Centers on Jewish-Christian Relations (CCJR). In both cases, I am obliged, as previously, to keep the speakers anonymous.

17. Noam Marans, "To Christian Leaders: Your Jewish Neighbors Need You," Blog for *Times of Israel*, November 11, 2023, https://bit.ly/42vy3Hq.

18. Toronto Board of Rabbis, "An Open Letter to Canadian Faith Leaders," October 13, 2023, https://bit.ly/4jxw9Mj.

19. On these points, see Emanuel Fabian, "Defense Minister Announces 'Complete Siege' of Gaza: No Power, Food or Fuel," *The Times of Israel*, October 9, 2023, https://bit.ly/4aOYKJj; Omar Abdel-Baqui, "Israeli Air Force Says It Has Dropped 6,000 Bombs on Gaza," *Wall Street Journal*, October 14, 2023, https://bit.ly/4gm5bVm; and Bethan McKernan and Quique Kierszenbaum, "'We're Focused on Maximum Damage': Ground Offensive into Gaza Seems Imminent," *Guardian*, October 10, 2023, https://bit.ly/4jAjjgv.

20. See, for example, the October 2023 statement from Boston College's Center for Christian-Jewish Learning, https://bit.ly/4azjTqL.

21. For these statements, see "Solidarität mit den Opfern und Frieden für den Nahen Osten!," October 13, 2023, https://bit.ly/3Cs4QCr, and "Statement of the International Organization for the Study of the Old Testament (IOSOT) on the Terrorism Attacks of October 7, 2023," October 20, 2023, https://bit.ly/3WBHP74.

22. The International Council of Christians and Jews, "The Ten Points of Seelisberg," https://bit.ly/4guA4ad.

23. International Council of Christians and Jews, ed., *Reports and Recommendations of the Emergency Conference on Antisemitism [Seelisberg, 1947]*, (International Council of Christians and Jews: Geneva, 1947), 8 (Commission 1.6) and 21 (Resolution 4). See also Christian Rutishauser, "The 1947 Seelisberg Conference: The Foundation of Jewish-Christian Dialogue," *Studies in Christian-Jewish Relations* 2, no. 2 (2007): 34–53, https://bit.ly/4jvSJF6.

24. Reports and Recommendations, 21 (Resolution 4).

25. See further Michael G. Azar, "75 Years after Seelisberg—Reflection," International Council of Christians and Jews, April 2022, https://bit.ly/3Wyr8ta.

26. On this myth, see Rafi Nets-Zehngut, "Origins of the Palestinian Refugee Problem: Changes in the Historical Memory of Israelis/Jews 1949-2004," *Journal of Peace Research* 48 (2011): 235-48. On the "pioneers" of CJR—including A.

Roy Eckardt, Alice Eckardt, Franklin Littell, and others—and their anti-Arabism, see Michael G. Azar, "'Supersessionism': The Political Origin of a Theological Neologism," *Studies in Christian-Jewish Relations* 16:1 (2021), 1–25, https://bit.ly/3Cs5pMz.

27. As quoted in "Judeo-Christian Studies Director Accuses Jordanian Bishops," *NC News Service*, April 22, 1971. See Azar, "'Supersessionism,'" 23–24.

28. As quoted in "See Christ in Israeli Bombs," *National Catholic Reporter*, February 4, 1970. See Azar, "'Supersessionism,'" 21. For a similar point, see A. Roy Eckardt, *Your People, My People: The Meeting of Jews and Christians* (New York: Quadrangle, 1974), 181–82.

29. Azar, "Supersessionism."

30. Maayan Jaffe-Hoffman, "Since Start of Israel-Hamas War, 3% of Gaza's Christians Dead," *Jerusalem Post*, February 17, 2024, https://bit.ly/4h8njCZ.

31. Yuval Abraham, "'A Mass Assassination Factory': Inside Israel's Calculated Bombing of Gaza," *+972 Magazine*, November 30, 2023, https://bit.ly/4hrtl1q, and Yuval Abraham, "'Lavender': The AI Machine Directing Israel's Bombing Spree in Gaza," *+972 Magazine*, April 3, 2024, https://bit.ly/3CnmEi5.

32. See, for example, Michael G. Azar, "Orthodox Christians in Gaza City," *Public Orthodoxy*, November 13, 2023, https://bit.ly/40qkVR4.

33. As previously, I must keep the sources of these comments anonymous.

34. On the former, see the moderator's comments in "Christ Jesus the Jew in Wake of October 7th," Haus am Dom, Frankfurt, Germany, February 13, 2024, https://bit.ly/42sM7kI, and for the latter, see the following, deeply racist and ignorant "open letter" which was forwarded to me by another author in this book: Joel C. Rosenberg, "VERY URGENT: Israeli Leaders, Please Evacuate Palestinian Christians out of Gaza and into the West Bank Immediately—These Christians Face Genocide by Hamas If They Are Forced to Move South," *All Israel News*, November 17, 2023, https://bit.ly/3PScF7q.

35. Eugene Korn, "An Immediate Cease-Fire in Gaza Will Not Bring Peace to the Holy Land," *America*, May 1, 2024, https://bit.ly/3E6BcDo.

36. Paula Fredriksen, "This Easter, Let's Not Try to Pretend Jesus Was a 'Palestinian Jew,'" *Washington Post*, March 28, 2024, https://bit.ly/40LSBd7. Contrary to the popular claims repeated in this article, there is little historical reason to assume that the Roman Empire's choice to change the name of the land of Jesus to "Syria-Palestina" was a "deliberate way to 'de-Judaize' the territory" (though such was the case with the renaming of "Jerusalem" as "Aelia Capitolina"). See, for example, David Jacobson, "When Palestine Meant Israel," *Biblical Archaeological Review* (May-June 2001): 42–47, https://bit.ly/3Cm5wt8.

10
Stresses of the Israel-Hamas War: Interfaith and Intrafaith

Peter A. Pettit

Since my first awareness of the Hamas attack against Israel on October 7, 2023, my perspective on the conflict has evolved through several phases. That is not to say that my perspective on the initial attack itself has changed. Quite the contrary: the brutal and indiscriminate assault on mostly civilian residents of southern Israel and participants in the Nova music festival remains unconscionable, indefensible, immoral, and heinous. No account of the Arab-Israeli-Palestinian conflict can justify the horrors perpetrated by Hamas that day. No "understanding" of Palestinian frustration and displacement should be allowed to mitigate the repulsiveness of the torture, maiming, slaughter, rape, and kidnapping that occurred.

The attack, however, did take place within a historical context. That context is significant in the first perspective that emerged from the raw emotional impact of the early reports. Given the brutality of the Hamas attack, its underlying charter commitment to eliminating the State of Israel, and the evident failure of Israeli prime minister Benjamin Netanyahu's coalition government to protect the residents of the country from attack, I wondered whether a salutary outcome might be two-fold. First, Israel would decimate Hamas, leaving it powerless to attack Israel or to lead Gaza. Second, Israel would depose Netanyahu and seek a government that would reset the process to establish a stable, jointly recognized, and mutually respected two-state solution for the Israeli-Palestinian conflict.

In formulating that fantasy, I drew on presuppositions born of my experience both studying and working in Israel with Jews and Palestinians, learning and teaching about the ancient and modern history of the region, collaborating in Christian-Jewish and wider interfaith conferences and curricular projects, and developing resource materials on Lutheran-Jewish relations for the Evangelical Lutheran Church in America. Those presuppositions included the legitimacy of both Jewish and Palestinian nationalisms based on each community's historical attachment to the same geographical region as homeland. I saw the conflict as a product of the occupying Ottoman Empire's defeat and dismemberment at the end of World War I, giving both communities hope that the time had arrived for their modern sovereignty in the land. Following the failure of the surrounding Arab states to thwart the establishment of the State of Israel in the 1948–49 war and despite internal conflicts in both communities and the meddling of outside forces, a reasonable centrist position had emerged within each community that envisioned two states for two people. The 1936 Peel Commission report had suggested it; the 1947 United Nations Partition Plan had affirmed it; eventually, the Oslo process in the 1990s mapped a timeline and process for it.

The long decade from late 1995 into early 2006, bracketed by the assassination of the Israeli prime minister, Yitzhak Rabin, and the election victory of Hamas in the Palestinian Authority's Legislative Council, had opened a serious challenge to the centrist position. The leadership that emerged in both communities was extremist. During Netanyahu's time as prime minister, the Israeli government has shifted increasingly toward more extreme rejectionist positions regarding Palestinian autonomy. Netanyahu has sustained his coalition by accommodating rejectionist parties. Meanwhile, Hamas has stayed true to its charter commitment to eliminate the State of Israel and promised to continue to pursue that goal even as it reeled under the Israeli counterattack after 10/7. Hence, I imagined, were this war to become a mutually disqualifying conflict between Netanyahu and Hamas, the centrist vision might emerge again with renewed vigor and promise.

Fragmentation and Polarization

Fairly quickly, the illusion shattered. There is no consensus regarding the conflict and its outcome. The responses of churches and governments that may have initially backed Israel's right of self-defense and determination to recover the hostages taken by Hamas were swiftly overwhelmed by horror at the daily media images of the havoc and destruction Israel was wreaking on Gaza. Within the diaspora Jewish community, voices arose to challenge the justifications of the Netanyahu government and the Israel Defense Forces for the extent of the campaign in Gaza. Divisions developed between those who would prioritize locating and rescuing the hostages and those giving priority to utterly defeating Hamas. Long-time advocates for Israel and for the Palestinian community each collected their respective sets of evidence and talking points to reinforce their positions, while others sought to analyze the events of the attack and war more dispassionately. People in all these groups were often speaking in rhetorical worlds different from one another.

One consequence of this fragmentation and polarization was a chilling effect that settled on nearly all discussion of the conflict and the war. Suddenly, many found it difficult to anticipate what the attitudes and emotions of colleagues might be and therefore what sort of reception one's ideas or feelings might garner. Even those who had for years worked together in interfaith settings, both civic and religious, felt wary about discussing the Israel-Hamas war. Trust, built over years—sometimes decades—began to erode. In some cases, a single word or phrase shattered it completely.

These dynamics in professional relationships and friendships continue to be exacerbated by two broader phenomena. The dramatic escalation of criticism of Israel into broadly antisemitic and genocidal tropes has reminded many Jews of the language used during the Third Reich and experiences of antisemitic violence across centuries. The fact that the 10/7 attack was widely described as the worst single-day attack on Jews since the Holocaust has only sharpened that evocation. It is no longer clear in any given exchange what the object of the discussion has become or what the range of the discussion's implications will be. "The worst" is back on the horizon for Jews in a way few could recall in their lifetime.

At the same time, the current media environment and political rhetoric make it difficult to ascertain the accuracy of reporting. Every source is considered biased, at least by someone. The nature of war is that local reporting can only capture partial images, while larger frameworks are carefully guarded by censors. A 24/7 news cycle and the demand for eyeballs and clicks require that outlets and platforms report what they have available, often with the simple and uninformative disclaimer, "This has not been independently verified." On matters of casualty statistics, the extent of infrastructure damage, the nature and exigencies of urban warfare, the existence or degree of famine, and more, we all choose our sources and live with uncertainty, whether or not we admit that reality. In sum, however, the situation does not support meaningful dialogue or encourage trustworthy interactions.

Issues and Tissues

These factors brought another evolution in my perspective. I realized that there is a time for issues and a time for tissues. Most of my engagement with Christian-Jewish and wider interfaith relations has focused on issues of scriptural interpretation, historical legacies, social and psychological factors, and geopolitical dynamics. All of those are very much a part of the present moment, but the urgency of the war and its attendant crises render them secondary. Indeed, when they are explored nowadays, that work often serves polemical interests and is no longer integrated into the critical frameworks that govern prudent analysis.

Understandably, many people need allies, support, encouragement, commiseration, empathy, and understanding more than they need a better analysis or argument for dissecting the conflict. It does not matter how I assess the relative weight of victim numbers from Gaza or generational emotional burdens in Israel—I can bring tissues to join the tears and offer comfort to those who are in grief over both tragedies. Often in interfaith relations an organic experience of empathy can transcend the deepest doctrinal divides. For a time, such empathy with the raw pain and grief occasioned by felt suffering of every kind may be the most profound interfaith resource we can offer.

Revisiting Long-term Issues

Nevertheless, and at some greater remove from the immediacy of 10/7, at least two long-standing and far-reaching issues within Christian-Jewish relations do take on greater urgency in the context and wake of the Israel-Hamas war. One is the Christian theological assessment of the land promises in Jewish scripture and their relevance to the modern State of Israel. Another is the deep embeddedness of both antisemitism and Orientalism—the latter including negative stereotypes about Muslims in the Middle East—in Western culture and its impact on Western engagement with the governments and peoples on the front lines of the conflict.

The promises of God to biblical Israel consistently include a promise to give the people a land in which they will be able to live out their individual and collective identities as God's people. So firmly is that promise fixed in biblical Israel's understanding of the covenant that exile from the land is understood as a result of the people's failure in faithful living. Whether as outright punishment or as discipline intended to bring repentance and restore faithfulness, separation from the land is imposed by God as a mirror image of the people's separation from God and God's Torah. Restoration to the land is experienced or hoped for as evidence of God's faithfulness to the promises and to Israel.

These dynamics have afforded ample interpretive space for thinking about the land, Zionism as a nationalist homeland movement, and the State of Israel. That space includes Christian as well as Jewish interpretations. The New Testament's scenario in the Book of Revelation, for example, sees the restoration of the Jews to their homeland as a necessary step in the establishment of God's ultimate kingdom under the lordship of Jesus Christ. Christian essentialist interpretations that give exclusive priority to

Jewish claims without regard to Palestinian heritage in the land seem to contradict the equally biblical understanding that all the nations of the world will be blessed in and by Israel. On the other hand, Christian moralist interpretations that judge the State of Israel as unfaithful and therefore forfeiting any claim to the biblical land promises seem to contradict the repeated biblical promises of restoration, despite repeated moral failure, as well as the Christian assertion that no individual, let alone people or nation, can use reputedly perfect moral rectitude to lay claim to any of God's promises.

In my view, interpretive movement is needed to emphasize that God's promise to Israel shows God's intention for every people in the world to have a place to live out its God-given identity in peace and with sovereignty.[1] The significant variation in the boundaries of Israel's promised land as charted in different promises and in reports of the land's extent adds the principle that humans within specific historical circumstances must draw the lines and establish the governments that will fulfill God's intention for all peoples across the whole earth. The competing homeland claims and the more aggressive assertions of the most radical versions of those claims by both Jews and Palestinians in the present circumstance make this issue more urgent.

One thing I have learned and will continue to give consideration is a colleague's observation that Christianity since the Holocaust has broadly taken stock of its anti-Jewish heritage but has not as adequately taken stock of its complicity in and heritage of colonialism. To be sure, the millennia-long homeland connection of Jews to the land makes the case of Israel and Palestine different from the typical colonial scenario, in which a people who have no prior connection to the land arrive to claim it for themselves. Pilgrims in America and Boers in South Africa never spoke of "coming home" to those new lands. Yet colonialism does play a role in Israel's story in at least two ways.

First, Christian millennialist hopes in the eighteenth and nineteenth centuries were significant in the development of the British government's support of a Jewish homeland, momentously articulated in the 1917 Balfour Declaration.[2] Similar sentiments among Christian Zionists influenced the United States government's recognition of the State of Israel in 1948 and affected US international relations decisions throughout the past century.[3] Second, the framework of international geopolitics that undergirded the formation of the League of Nations and the United Nations is itself implicated in Western colonialist legacies. The role of these organizations in establishing the 1922 Palestine Mandate and in setting forth the 1947 Partition Plan cannot be assessed apart from those legacies.

These factors do not in themselves delegitimize Israel's claim to existence or brand it as a "settler colonialist" enterprise that should be dismantled. The Jewish people do have an authentic heritage in the land from which they were violently separated by the Roman Empire and kept in exile by subsequent Christian, Muslim, and secular governments. The homeland sensibility of Jews for the land deserves and demands respect, just as the homeland sensibility of Palestinian Arabs does as well. The Israel-Hamas war has led me to realize that Christian theologies about promised land, in whatever form, must also take account of the dynamics of (Christian) colonialism that have helped to shape the world's engagement with homeland sensibilities of diverse kinds. That project is still under development in my own thinking.

The second long-standing and far-reaching issue within Christian-Jewish relations challenges our precision, honesty, and integrity in criticism. Few people disagree that the tilt toward rejectionism in the Israeli government, including policies and practices in the West Bank as well as the prosecution of the Israel-Hamas war, constitutes a problem. Israeli protests against the Netanyahu coalition before and after 10/7 testify to that. At the same time, few people disagree about the genocidal commitments of Hamas and the inhumane, despicable character of its attack on Israel and even of its disregard for the Palestinian people of Gaza. Both regimes have earned the criticism they receive; both violate norms and values held among Christians, Jews, Muslims, and humanists of many stripes.

The challenge lies in distilling the legitimate criticism to leave aside vestiges and tropes of the antisemitism and Orientalism that are insinuated into Western culture.[4] As we rise to the challenge of criticizing the most extreme elements of both the Israeli and Palestinian governments in protest against the Israel-Hamas war, how do we diligently steer clear of the triggers that propel critiques of policy or practice toward bigoted cancellation of respect for the Israeli or Palestinian people?

What we say is difficult enough to manage; what is heard is even more challenging. Absent the implicit trust that is the fruit of long personal experience with another person, people who have experienced abuse rely on their survival-mode skills to understand the world around them. The abuses of antisemitism and Orientalism have conjured a wise wariness among those who have suffered them, including a keen sensitivity to coded language and innuendo. Awareness of the codes and images that carry embedded bigotry can help us to avoid being misunderstood. Only the good, long, hard work of building trustworthy relationships can afford us forbearance when our words have the potential to wound.

A Particular Issue in a Lutheran Frame

The potential for wounding in contexts of Christian-Jewish relations has become more acute in the advocacy and rhetoric of mainline Protestant denominations regarding the Israel-Hamas war.[5] At the national meetings of the Episcopal Church and the Presbyterian Church (USA) in 2024, significant debate took place around proposals that are highly critical of Israel and its actions in the Israel-Hamas war.[6] Christian Zionism, a diverse movement that supports the State of Israel, basing its outlooks on biblical interpretations, has come under vigorous critique among mainline Christians who disagree with Christian Zionist support for Israel in the Israel-Hamas war. Concerns exist that historical Jewish Zionism will too easily be tarred with the same brush. Anti-Zionist Jewish organizations such as Jewish Voice for Peace and IfNotNow often collaborate with their Protestant counterparts, who proffer the endorsement of the Jewish groups as evidence that they are not antisemitic.[7] Such are the pain and threat felt in other segments of the Jewish community, though, that the Anti-Defamation League—not without internal controversy—has included both groups in its database documenting rising antisemitism during the current war.[8]

Within the Evangelical Lutheran Church in America (ELCA), the wounding with words first took on organizational significance in 2005, when the Churchwide Strategy for Engagement in Israel and Palestine was adopted with "Peace Not Walls" as its campaign theme. The strategy and campaign were developed during the Second Intifada (2000–2005), when Israel erected its security barrier to protect civilians from Palestinian attacks originating just across the Green Line, the border separating pre-1967 Israel from the Occupied Palestinian Territory. For many Israeli Jews, "the wall" was a necessary and effective deterrent to terror. It became necessary, in their eyes, because the Palestinian president, Yasser Arafat, had walked out of the final-stage peace negotiations at Camp David in 2000 and instigated a new wave of violence. For the ELCA to adopt "Peace Not Walls" as its campaign slogan seemed clearly to side with a Palestinian view of the conflict and to reverse the dynamic of Palestinian responsibility for the failure of the Oslo peace process.

The ELCA's "Peace Not Walls" campaign was developed by the (then) Division for Global Mission (DGM) and Division for Church in Society, in collaboration with the leadership of the Evangelical Lutheran Church in Jordan and the Holy Land (ELCJHL). Two consultations were held, in 2004 and 2005, at which representatives of the two churches, with the personal leadership of their presiding bishops, reviewed the proposed strategy and refined its language. Among several dozen participants, two represented the ELCA's Consultative Panel on Lutheran-Jewish Relations.

In addition to offering a presentation on the perspective of the panel regarding the Arab-Israeli-Palestinian conflict and participating in the deliberations of both consultations, they provided detailed commentary on the final draft of the strategy within five days of its distribution. The DGM staff indicated that there was inadequate time to engage with that commentary before submitting the draft to the DGM board for consideration.

The strategy as adopted by the 2005 ELCA Churchwide Assembly included no plan for engagement in Israel except as Israelis might join individually in activities of the ELCA and ELCJHL. A prior declaration of the ELCA to the Jewish community asserting the church's "urgent desire to live out our faith with love and respect for the Jewish people"[9] was blunted awkwardly in the final paragraph of the strategy document, where we read that "the ELCA recommits itself to . . . living out its faith in Jesus Christ with love and respect for all people—Jewish, Christian, and Muslim."[10] The awkwardness and effort to avoid specifying the church's commitment to the Jewish community are evident in the fact that the reworded statement falsely identifies "all people" as only those in the Abrahamic traditions.

Although the strategy did include several references to interfaith dialogue and action, as well as a desired outcome of "the enrichment of the ELCA strategy for engagement in the Holy Land through deepening of interfaith relations,"[11] the materials produced by the strategy in subsequent years have included no Jewish perspectives that diverge from that of the ELCJHL. The broader context and other perspectives about the conflict were explicitly bypassed when the strategy stated, "Advocacy would be focused on issues emerging out of the ELCA's *accompaniment* with the Evangelical Lutheran Church in Jordan and the Holy Land and Lutheran World Federation, which illustrate the larger issues of justice and peace in the region."[12]

The Priority of Accompaniment

Accompaniment is the critical factor in this approach. The accompaniment model for global engagement by North American and European churches developed as a salutary effort to shift from a pattern of "missionaries 'taking' the gospel to every corner as pearl merchants . . . [to] hunting for treasures, discovering God's presence and revelation already present."[13] This change emphasizes "a walking together that practices interdependence and mutuality. . . . The conversation is no longer between a giver and a receiver, but between churches, all of which have gifts to give and to receive."[14] After centuries of missional models that were "institutional structures . . . dominated by the North and West," accompaniment emerged "to nurture interdependent relationships of mutual trust and respect."[15] In a spirit of implicit contrition and pronounced humility, the churches of Europe and North America acknowledged the need to listen more closely to the churches with whom they are in partnership elsewhere in the world, to learn from their experience, and to follow their lead as partners in mission in their locales. The accompaniment model emerged as "a paradigm for the future" in the 1999 foundational strategic document, "Global Mission in the Twenty-first Century: A Vision of Evangelical Faithfulness in God's Mission."[16]

Much could be said about GMTC regarding Christian-Jewish and wider interfaith relations. A fair summary might note that there is minimal, if any, recognition that the work of God in and through other communities of faith could contribute to a fuller understanding of Christian mission. Interfaith dialogue is countenanced as valuable for "mutual understanding and respect between the ELCA and people of diverse faiths," but discernment of mission and of God's gracious activity is restricted to the ELCA and its global and ecumenical Christian partners.[17]

Listening to partner churches absent any framework for other faith communities' witness to God's work to shape our understanding of the gospel has limited the strategic perspective that the ELCA allows itself. "Peace Not Walls" developed as a megaphone for the ELCJHL within the ELCA. This result was explicitly anticipated in the strategy: "The ELCA will intensify its use of the public media . . . to 'tell the story,' amplifying the voices of companions in the region"; and, "arranging strategic visits from the ELCJHL to the ELCA, especially in connection with major Lutheran meetings and networks, would build relationships, express companionship, and increase the ELCA's capacity to do advocacy."[18] Leading Palestinian Lutheran pastors, Palestinian Lutheran youth dance groups, Palestinian Lutheran musicians, and Palestinian Lutheran artists have all been featured guests and contributors at churchwide and synodical assemblies, churchwide youth gatherings, and, of course, global mission events.

Dynamics of Radical Accompaniment

In 2022, after nearly two decades of the strategy's work, the implementing body of "Peace Not Walls" in the ELCA, the Middle East and North Africa (MENA) area desk of Service and Justice, initiated a review process of the campaign. It was prompted by an awareness that "today much is different" from what it was at the outset of the campaign.[19] The "signs of hopeful possibility" that were noted in 2005 as stimulating the church's sense of urgency to develop a strategy "have largely vanished."[20] While the process developed new "signs of hopeful possibility" to motivate the evolution of the strategy moving forward, the tone was set by a litany of oppression charged against Israel. Without any reference to Palestinian agency, governance, factionalism, violence, or failure, the urgency of the Israeli-Palestinian situation was attributed to the "perpetual humanitarian, political, economic and ecological crisis" in Palestine and Israel.[21]

A review team of ten members appointed by MENA may account for the exclusively anti-Israeli characterization of the situation, reflecting the overwhelming influence of the ELCJHL in developing the review. Beyond the report's identification of 30 percent of the team as ELCJHL members and 50 percent Palestinian, two additional members of the team have close family ties to the Palestinian community. One is married to a Palestinian and the other grew up in East Jerusalem in the family of a long-time Lutheran World Federation program director. No one outside the ELCJHL and the ELCA circle implementing "Peace Not Walls" was included on the team.

The review process included an online feedback form soliciting input from "PNW-related ELCA stakeholders." It garnered "nearly 80 responses from the following constituencies: current and former ELCA staff, ELCA bishops, ALAMEH members, PNW network members, former YAGM volunteers, and former PNW young adult trip leaders and participants."[22] The report itself notes, as one of the "contextual factors" to be kept in mind in analyzing the survey, that "the scope of the perspectives received was limited to ELCA-related networks and, in most cases, to people who are already engaged with PNW in some way—though a few respondents were ecumenical colleagues and people active in Palestine/Israel issues but disaffiliated from PNW and/or the ELCA."[23] It also states: "Throughout, the review team endeavored to keep in mind the need to center the voices and perspectives of Palestinian partners in discerning ways forward."[24]

One measure of the degree to which the review and report identify with Palestinian perspectives is the recommendation to change the banner of the campaign from "Peace Not Walls" to *Sumud*. This Arabic word is defined as "perseverance and steadfastness" and identified as "a lived strategy of 'resistance through existence'" and "a contextual theological principle."[25] The Sumud website identifies Sumud as "the ELCA Churches [*sic*] response to occupation and injustice in Palestine and Israel," adding that the term *Sumud* "is widely used by Palestinian theologians and others to signify Palestinian resistance to the Israeli occupation of Palestinian lands and people."[26] The report recommends that "ELCA Service and Justice, through SUMUD and in partnership with the Office of the Presiding Bishop, will initiate a review of [the 2005 strategy document] to: . . . develop a new or significantly revised strategy for engagement with the goal of bringing this strategy forward through the channels most appropriate and necessary for adoption."[27] Preemptively, it would seem, the new campaign banner was implemented throughout the network and the ELCA website within months of the report's release and prior to any action adopting the report's recommendations.

The Stress of Accompaniment

Within days after 10/7, the ELCA released the report of the "Peace Not Walls" review team. The church changed the name of the campaign before the end of October and began to rebrand its website immediately. Thus, what might have been conceived initially as a responsible, best-practices periodic program review has become a stress point within the ELCA and in Lutheran-Jewish relations.

The ELCA homepage has a banner with a scrolling, three-panel header. The panel on display at first landing is "Resources for the Crisis in the Holy Land."[28] Clicking on "Learn More" leads to a page listing dozens of resources from the ELCA, the ELCJHL, Jerusalem Christian religious leaders, the World Council of Churches and Lutheran World Federation, Churches for Middle East Peace, Church World Service, the Red Cross, the United Nations, and others. Nowhere is there a link to any Israeli or Jewish source.

Among the ELCA resources is the church's 1995 social statement, "For Peace in God's World."[29] That statement asserts that "through faithfulness in its life and activities as a community for peace, the Church in the power of the Holy Spirit becomes a presence for peace that disturbs, reconciles, serves, and deliberates."[30] "For Peace in God's World" builds on the earlier, 1991 foundational ELCA statement, "The Church in Society: A Lutheran Perspective," which indicates that the church seeks "to learn from ... all people, in order to have the best possible information and understanding of today's world, . . . to analyze social and environmental issues critically," and "to engage those of diverse perspectives, classes, genders, ages, races, and cultures in the deliberation process so that each of our limited horizons might be expanded and the witness of the body of Christ in the world enhanced."[31] One must wonder how the church is to achieve such high ideals of engagement in the absence of evidence or perspective from significant players in this conflict.

The ELCA has voiced its "urgent desire to live out our faith in Jesus Christ with love and respect for the Jewish people,"[32] and the "Peace Not Walls" review claimed that its recommendations "follow the justice principle of 'nothing about us without us.'"[33] Where are love and respect when church resources for understanding a war initiated by the deadliest single-day attack on the Jewish people since the Holocaust include nothing from Jewish colleagues? How is the justice principle enacted justly when so much is said and implied about Israel without any participation by Israelis or Jews?

The Israel-Hamas war reveals and deepens stress tests in the church's effort simultaneously to accompany the Palestinian Lutheran community and to maintain constructive, respectful, even loving relationships with the Jewish people. Achieving that goal is possible, but the way in which the ELCA has implemented accompaniment renders it exceedingly difficult. The church has said that the ELCJHL "is the primary relationship through which the ELCA sees the situation in Palestine and Israel."[34] More careful discernment could make a distinction between the understanding of mission needs and circumstances within another church's field and the assessment of geopolitics in a conflict involving that church's people with their perceived enemy.

The accompaniment model calls for full partnership, mutual respect, and dialogue—not for either church to surrender to the other its calling to discern ethics and the gospel from its own situation. Just as the Lutheran Church feels stress in relating to Jews when the government of the Jewish state engages in actions that are inimical to the church's values, so within that church there is stress when one part of the body assesses the dynamics of a war differently from the part that is on the front lines. In both cases, navigating the stress depends on the trust and respect that can only grow with time and experience, and also on the capacity of both parties to hear and honor the truths that are discerned within each other's circumstances.

Questions for Dialogue

1. How might the idea of shifting from "issues to tissues" during a crisis like the Israel-Hamas war help to sustain interfaith relationships through times when those with diverse backgrounds, experiences, and faith perspectives may find themselves responding in very different ways?

2. What is your understanding of God's relationship to the lands that people call their homelands, and what are the underpinnings of that understanding?

3. Where would you draw the line between (1) legitimate criticism of Israeli policy and antisemitism and (2) legitimate criticism of Palestinian policy and Orientalist or anti-Muslim bigotry?

4. How can one church sustain a partnership with another while disagreeing about the geopolitical dynamics in which the other is embroiled?

5. What relative weight should a church give to the geopolitical perspectives of another church and to those of secular or other religious groups?

Further Resources

Evangelical Lutheran Church in America. "Preaching and Teaching 'With Love and Respect for the Jewish People.'" September 2022. https://bit.ly/4hBsDyF.

Halevi, Yossi Klein. *Letters to My Palestinian Neighbor*. New York: HarperCollins, 2018.

Lutheran World Federation Council. "Statement on the Crisis in Gaza, the Occupied Palestinian Territories, and Israel." June 2024. https://bit.ly/4hfxOEC.

Pettit, Peter A. "On Not Choosing Sides: The Peacemaking Challenge in Israel/Palestine." *Christian Century* 131, no. 16 (August 6, 2014): 10–11.

Pettit, Peter A. "What's Behind the Hamas-Israel War?" October 17, 2023. Posted November 2, 2023. St. Paul Quad Cities, YouTube. https://bit.ly/4hdGvPP.

Shalom Hartman Institute. *For Heaven's Sake*. Podcast. https://bit.ly/40S0GwZ.

Notes

1. I find biblical support for this outlook when considering the table of nations in Genesis 10 in conjunction with prophetic insights such as Amos 9:7: "Are you not like the Cushites to me, O people of Israel? says the Lord. Did I not bring Israel up from the land of Egypt and the Philistines from Caphtor and the Arameans from Kir?" For my own development of this interpretive movement see "A New Christian Zionism?" *Christian Century* 134, no. 18 (August 30, 2017): 20–25.

2. On these points see, Shalom Goldman, *Zeal for Zion* (Chapel Hill: University of North Carolina Press, 2009); Robert O. Smith, *More Desired Than Our Owne Salvation: The Roots of Christian Zionism* (Oxford: Oxford University Press, 2013).

3. See Caitlin Carenen, *The Fervent Embrace: Liberal Protestants, Evangelicals, and Israel* (New York: New York University Press, 2012); Stephen Spector, *Evangelicals and Israel: The Story of American Christian Zionism* (Oxford: Oxford University Press, 2009).

4. Two studies are especially significant on this point. See David Nirenberg, *Anti-Judaism: The Western Tradition* (New York: Norton, 2013); Edward W. Said, *Orientalism* (New York: Pantheon, 1978).

5. These denominations include the American Baptist Convention, the Disciples of Christ, the Episcopal Church, the Evangelical Lutheran Church, the Presbyterian Church (USA), the United Church of Christ, and the United Methodist Church.

6. See David Paulsen, "Resolutions on Israeli 'Apartheid' Top Agenda of General Convention International Policy Committee," Episcopal News Service, April 17, 2024, https://bit.ly/3Qbqqi1. Episcopal resolutions to condemn Israel as an apartheid state did not pass in 2024. See Michael Gryboski, "Episcopal Church Bishops Reject Resolution Declaring Israel an 'Apartheid' State," *Christian Post*, June 25, 2024, https://bit.ly/4auG8Ot. For Presbyterian discussions, see Eric Lederman, "PC (USA) Engagement with Israel/Palestine at the 226th General Assembly," *Presbyterian Outlook*, July 1, 2024, https://bit.ly/4h0PpQJ.

7. Visit www.jewishvoiceforpeace.org and www.ifnotnowmovement.org for further information about these Jewish groups.

8. See "Who Are the Primary Groups Behind the U.S. Anti-Israel Rallies," Anti-Defamation League, November 8, 2023, https://bit.ly/3PPqeob.

9. "Declaration of the Evangelical Lutheran Church in America to the Jewish Community," 1994, https://bit.ly/3PXyna7.

10. "Churchwide Strategy for Engagement in Israel and Palestine," 2005 Pre-Assembly Report, Section V, 54 (hereafter "Strategy").

11. "Strategy," 52.

12. "Strategy," 53. Italics added.

13. The Staff of the Division for Global Mission of the Evangelical Lutheran Church in America, "The Accompaniment Model of Mission," *Word & World* 25, no. 2 (Spring 2005): 204.

14. "The Accompaniment Model of Mission," 204.

15. Mark Thomsen, "Accompaniment: Interdependence Rather than Dominion," *Word & World* 25, no. 2 (Spring 2005): 208.

16. Division for Global Mission, "Global Mission in the 21st Century: A Vision of Evangelical Faithfulness in God's Mission," Evangelical Lutheran Church in America (ELCA), 1999. This document, hereafter abbreviated GMTC, is available through the office of the Service and Justice home area of the ELCA, currently led by Pastor Khader El-Yateem (773-380-2645; 8765 W Higgins Rd, Chicago IL 60631).

17. GMTC, 30.

18. "Strategy," 54, 2.

19. "ELCA Peace Not Walls: Accompaniment, Awareness-raising and Advocacy for Palestine and Israel—2022-2023 Review Summary and Recommendations," October 2023, 3 (hereafter "Review"), https://bit.ly/4aBJrDE.

20. "Review," 3.

21. "Review," 4.

22. "Review," 21; ALAMEH is the Association of Lutherans of Middle Eastern Heritage; YAGM is the Young Adults in Global Mission program, which places young adults as volunteers in partner churches around the world.

23. "Review," 21.

24. "Review," 9.

25. "Review," 5, 9.

26. See https://bit.ly/3EjbRWJ.

27. "Review," 32.

28. See https://www.elca.org/.

29. For the text of "For Peace in God's World," see https://bit.ly/42vArOo.

30. "For Peace in God's World," 4.

31. For the text of "The Church in Society: A Lutheran Perspective," see https://bit.ly/4jHZPGS. For the quoted statements, see 6 and 8.

32. See footnote 9 above.

33. "Review," 5.

34. "This Is: SUMUD (formerly *Peace Not Walls*)," *Living Lutheran* (April 12, 2024), https://bit.ly/4h8c6Tf.

11
Holocaust Remembrance, Theodicy, and Christian Zionism

Sarah K. Pinnock

Hamas's attack against Israel on October 7, 2023, was the worst mass murder of Jews since the Holocaust. Surely that attack was evil. Israel's retaliation resulted in a war that has inflicted a huge death toll on Palestinian civilians. That death toll can also be called evil.

For Israelis and Jews worldwide, 10/7 deepened fears about antisemitism and safety. For Palestinians in Gaza—Muslims and Christians—10/7 and its aftermath brought immense suffering and insecurity. These already divisive differences between Israelis and Palestinians are even more conflict-ridden when, as so often happens, a focus on one side seems to diminish and disrespect the other.

My research deals with the concept and the problem of *evil*. It concentrates particularly on post-Holocaust Jewish and Christian reflection that is sometimes called *theodicy*. Such thinking wrestles with a key question: Is evil's destructive presence compatible with or explainable by the existence of God, especially if God is thought to be good and just? My studies include the writings of Holocaust survivors, theologians, and philosophers who call into question theodicy justifications of evil as part of God's plan.

I approach the problem of evil as a Christian. My father was a Baptist theologian who taught in seminaries in the US and Canada, and I grew up as an evangelical. As an adult, I attended mainline Protestant churches, and I began to explore Buddhist meditation in graduate school. For more than twenty-five years, I have taught comparative religion to undergraduate students at Trinity University, a Presbyterian-founded liberal arts college in San Antonio, Texas. Interweaving my personal and academic viewpoints, this *Stress Test* chapter uses a Holocaust-and-theodicy lens to focus my response to the Israel-Hamas war.

Auschwitz and Bearing Witness to Suffering

Auschwitz, a Holocaust site emblematic of evil, has been central to my involvement in Christian-Jewish relations and dialogue. Over the years, I have made six visits to the Auschwitz-Birkenau death camp in Oświęcim, Poland. For several years (interrupted by the COVID-19 pandemic), I have joined an annual pilgrimage with peacemakers from multiple religious traditions. Led by the Jewish Zen teacher Bernie Glassman, these Auschwitz gatherings, which started in 1996, bring together Buddhists, Christians, and Jews who share rituals from their traditions.

Glassman established three guiding tenets for encountering Auschwitz: (1) not knowing, not holding fixed views or assumptions; (2) bearing witness, attending to suffering and seeing the other as oneself; and (3) taking action that cares for "everyone and everything."[1] As a participant, I have met with Holocaust survivors and second-generation descendants, Germans with inherited National Socialist legacies, Israelis, Arabs, Lakota tribe members, Zen practitioners, atheists, and people of many nationalities who remember together the trauma of mass suffering at Auschwitz.

The identification with victims affects me strongly, especially when I sit silently in the death camp at the railroad ramp where Jews were unloaded and sent to gas chambers. But as a Christian of European descent, I know that my identity has more in common with bystanders and perpetrators than with victims of injustice and violence. In responses to evil, I notice that identification with victims is a common focus. Indeed, my entry into Holocaust reflection was through the narratives of Jewish survivors. Since 10/7, I observe that my students are more likely to focus on Palestinian deaths rather than Israeli deaths, and the most vocal and visible response by students is actively pro-Palestinian. One reason, I believe, is because of the asymmetry of the Israel-Hamas war.[2] The students see a well-equipped Israeli military using sophisticated weaponry supported by the US. That power retaliates against Hamas, whose fighters are embedded in a civilian population under siege and trapped in small areas. Hamas terrorism began the war, but subsequent Israeli destruction creates sympathy for Palestinian civilians in Gaza, who are largely defenseless.

Yom HaShoah 2024

In considering what has changed in Christian-Jewish relations since 10/7, Holocaust remembrance events in San Antonio, Washington DC, and Jerusalem provide significant case studies, because they show how the Israel-Hamas war intersects with Holocaust memory. These events also display how responses to 10/7 take on features of what I call "theodicy logic," which has political as well as religious implications.

May 6, 2024, was Holocaust Remembrance Day. On that Monday, I attended the San Antonio Yom HaShoah Holocaust Remembrance gathering at Temple Beth-El. I was familiar with the ceremony, which honored Holocaust survivors from the local community and their descendants with candle lighting and readings, closing with the Kaddish prayer in Hebrew. This annual gathering is organized by local Jewish congregations and sponsored by the Jewish Federation and the Holocaust Museum of San Antonio. The 2024 memorial program included two special guests, author Joshua M. Greene and Ivan Wilzig who spoke about Siggi Wilzig, Ivan's father and the subject of *Unstoppable*, Greene's biography about him.[3] The elder Wilzig, a Holocaust survivor, immigrated to the US from Eastern Europe and became an entrepreneur in banking and oil. Ivan's humorous stories about his father's business escapades brought some levity to Yom HaShoah. It also illustrated the flourishing of Jewish refugees in the United States, including the descendants of Holocaust survivors in San Antonio.

October 7 was on my mind as I entered Temple Beth El, and I wondered how the Israel-Hamas war might be addressed. Introductory remarks mentioned the 10/7 Hamas attack and linked remembrance of Holocaust victims with the Israeli victims who were either killed or taken hostage in Gaza. The service expressed the gravity of Hamas's threat to Israel and the resulting unease and insecurity experienced by Jews. But for me, as a non-Jewish participant at Yom HaShoah, as candles were lighted, I somehow wanted to bring the Palestinian families killed in Gaza into the space of remembrance, although I knew that would seem incongruous to many participants.

Connections between 10/7 and the Holocaust were also highlighted in speeches delivered at the Annual Days of Remembrance Ceremony, convened by the US Holocaust Memorial Museum on May 7, 2024. President Joe Biden stressed the urgency to "bear witness to the perils of indifference, the complicity of silence."[4] He underscored that "the terrorist group Hamas unleashed the deadliest day of the Jewish people since the Holocaust," with more than 1,200 killed and over 250 taken hostage in Gaza. He advised vigilance against antisemitism, the ancient hatred of Jews, which continues today with "slogans calling for the annihilation of Israel," leading some Jews to hide their identity to avoid harassment. Biden expressed "ironclad" support for Israel as a Jewish state. He quoted the late Jewish congressman and Holocaust survivor Tom Lantos, who said: "The veneer of civilization is paper thin. We are its guardians, and we can never rest." Biden concluded that we must rise against hate and recognize our common humanity.

What struck me about the US president's Holocaust Remembrance Day speech was how it justified Israel's war against Hamas. The US not only endorses the fight against Hamas but also provides vast military support to the Israel Defense Forces (IDF). Like Israel, moreover, the US has a history of decisive retaliation against terrorism from Arab regimes. After the September 11, 2001, al-Qaeda attacks on New York City and Washington, DC, the US launched wars in Iraq and Afghanistan to eliminate al-Qaeda and to kill Osama bin Laden. I understand the priority of national security, and I benefit from its protection of citizens. Israel, it seems to me, is acting as the US would in comparable circumstances.

For both nations, a version of "theodicy logic" legitimates massive war as a just response to the evil of terrorism. That is, Israel and the US embody justice and goodness. Attacks against them are evil. Plans to defend what is just and good necessitate not only recognizing evil but destroying it to vindicate the side that is right. Theodicy logic may or may not reference God and divine plans. The defense of justice and goodness, understood in terms of national sovereignty and national interest, is enough to keep such logic at play. Defense of one nation's sovereignty and interest easily leads to the conviction that destruction of the other's is morally imperative.

Seven months after 10/7, the Israel-Hamas war also figured prominently in Israeli Holocaust remembrance. Yom HaShoah began the eight Days of Awe, which culminated with Yom Ha'atzmaut (Independence Day) on May 14. At the opening ceremony for Holocaust Martyrs' and Heroes' Remembrance Day at Yad Vashem, the speeches by Israel's president and prime minister showed how closely the Holocaust relates to the current conflict.

President Isaac Herzog declared that "October 7 was not a Holocaust because today we have the State of Israel and the Israel Defense Forces." Israel's strength safeguards against another Holocaust. Herzog spoke of "faith in the righteousness of our path" as encouraging the strength to stand firm and fight for a better future. The legacy of Holocaust survivors is resilience, pride, and hope. "The eternal people," insisted Herzog, "is here—forever."[5] The State of Israel is the answer to the Holocaust. Inspired by Holocaust remembrance, its defense legitimates the IDF's action.

In his speech, Prime Minister Benjamin Netanyahu named the evil of both the Nazis and Hamas as genocide. Forces of evil, or "monsters," seek not only to kill but to abuse and torture and take pride in it. He mentioned Hamas as in league with Iran, waging war to destroy Israel. He denied claims that Israel is committing genocide and dismissed the International Criminal Court and the United Nations for judging Israel and its leaders. He underscored that no nation came to the rescue of Jews during the Holocaust. If necessary, Netanyahu insisted, Israel will stand alone to "defeat our genocidal enemies."[6] Such genocide rhetoric is powerful. It assists justification for Israel's war to destroy Hamas, even at the cost of huge civilian casualties in Gaza.

Parallel Remembrance

Yom HaShoah observances in May 2024 crystallized three crucial insights. First, the Hamas attack and the Holocaust are paired together in American and Israeli remembrance. Second, the response to the killing of Jews is "Never again"—indeed "Never again is now"—and increased national security for Israel. Those commitments are taken to justify Israel's war against Hamas. Third, Palestinians are not mourned as victims in the Israel-Hamas war and have no place in Holocaust remembrance. As the war continues, there is no appropriate setting for remembering the Israeli and Palestinian victims together. Doing so could create a problematic moral equivalence between the Hamas attack and the Israeli counterattack and neglect the historical context.

After 10/7, I am torn. I feel solidarity with both Jews and Palestinians. But most Americans are divided; they see only one side as blameworthy in the war. Furthermore, I am uneasy about associating the Holocaust with the Hamas attack on Israelis, especially if that association is used to justify an extreme militaristic response by Israel that will not cease until Hamas is destroyed. During the Holocaust, Jews were civilians, persecuted and murdered by Nazi Germany. Today, the State of Israel is an impressively formidable military power. Violence by Hamas against Israelis cannot be disassociated from the political situation in Israel and the Occupied Palestinian Territory. As the Jewish scholar Shaul Magid puts it, "by framing Palestinian violence against the occupation as inherently antisemitic, we invalidate violent resistance to oppression caused by the Jewish state."[7] I cite that judgment not to condone violence, but to see conflict intensified by political injustice where Palestinians in Gaza are subordinate to Israeli power and under Israeli legal restrictions as residents of Israel and the West Bank.

Some pro-Israel accounts stress that Hamas's attack on 10/7 amounts to an existential threat to Israel, one akin to the Holocaust's existential threat to the Jewish people. Such thinking found expression in Joe Biden's insistence that "there is no equivalence—none—between Israel and Hamas. We will always stand with Israel against threats to its security."[8] This position affirms Christian-Jewish alliances. But at the same time, it condones thousands of deaths and ignores war crimes and crimes against humanity identified by the International Criminal Court, such as the invasion of Rafah in May 2024, which displaced over a million Palestinians who had taken refuge there.[9] Positions like the one Biden took in his statement on May 20, 2024, legitimate the deaths of Palestinians as a means to Israel's security.

Theodicy's Justification of Evil

Responses to war display theodicy logic when the suffering of one group is instrumentalized. The term *theodicy* was coined in 1710 by the German philosopher Gottfried Wilhelm Leibniz. He used it to refer to intellectual explanations for evil as necessary for a greater future good. Following Leibniz, theodicy involves defending the belief that God is good and just, and it also defends the view that evil—natural disasters or humanity's willful inhumanity—are parts of God's providential plan and its fulfillment.[10]

The Holocaust raises theodicy questions such as: Why did God permit genocide against the European Jews? Was it punishment for sin or a test of faith? Surely, those who died were not the most sinful or in need of testing. Is God almighty or absent? Would God ever abandon the biblical covenant with the descendants of Abraham? As Zachary Braiterman has shown, many Jewish survivors of the Holocaust, as well as philosophers and theologians, refused to accept God as responsible for the Holocaust, and they reject theodicy.[11] Nevertheless, theodicy logic is at work in responses to the October 7 attack. The Israel-Hamas war is justified as necessary for the higher aim and the good of Israel's security.

The Holocaust theologian Irving Greenberg once offered a striking and challenging "working principle." "No statement, theological or otherwise," he said, "should be made that would not be credible in the presence of the burning children."[12] Most Jewish and Christian Holocaust theologians agree that mourning is the appropriate response to the deaths of Jewish children in the Shoah. No explanatory reasons could justify such deaths. Holocaust survivor and philosopher Emmanuel Levinas encapsulated his objections to theodicy in an essay called "Useless Suffering," where he states that "the justification of the neighbor's pain is certainly the source of all immorality."[13] Following Levinas, suffering—not intended by God—like that in the Holocaust or in the Israel-Hamas war is unjustified. Analyses and policies that claim it is justified should be unconscionable.

The Catholic theologian Johann Baptist Metz believes that theological statements should be checked by the litmus test of the Holocaust, and as a German he recognizes that Christian individuals and churches largely failed to speak out against National Socialism.[14] He underscores that the moral response to suffering is to offer compassion and aid, not theodicy.

The Anglican theologian Naim Ateek, a Palestinian who lives in Jerusalem, echoes Irving Greenberg. In his 2014 essay "For the Sake of the Burning Children of Gaza," Ateek laments the children and families killed in Gaza a decade ago, but his mourning seems even more needed in 2024 and beyond. Amid his grief, Ateek argues that the right to "defend" Israel becomes a justification for aggression. Such justification displays theodicy's instrumental logic. His 2014 question seems even more urgent ten years on: "Is the war Israel is conducting credible in light of these children, held captive and unable to leave Gaza, killed for the crime of being born on the wrong side of an arbitrary border?"[15] With more than 10,000 Palestinian children dead in Gaza six months after 10/7, Greenberg's statement holds true. It is not credible to make theodicy justifications for their deaths.

More controversy rightly swirls around theodicy when Christians use it to justify the Holocaust. In Christian-Jewish dialogue, a historic encounter took place when the American Jewish philosopher Richard Rubenstein visited Berlin in 1961 and met with Heinrich Grüber, the Dean of the Evangelical Protestant Church in postwar Germany, a clergyman well known for his wartime opposition to National Socialism. Grüber warmly welcomed Rubenstein in a spirit of Christian-Jewish reconciliation. As they talked, Grüber emphasized the significance of the Jewish people, underscoring his views about the Jews' destiny and role in salvation history. But Rubenstein was shocked to hear Grüber claim that the Holocaust must be part of God's providential plan. Grüber's theodicy propelled Rubenstein's anti-theodicy views in key writings such as *After Auschwitz*.[16]

Rubenstein found allies among German Christian theologians who also rejected Grüber's problematic theodicy. They found it incredible that, somehow, God would allow the Jews to be slaughtered as part of a divine plan that, in effect, legitimated what the Nazis did in the Holocaust. Dorothee Soelle, for example, rejected Grüber's theodicy and its conception of a "sadistic God" who makes people suffer and punishes non-believers for the sake of a plan.[17] Rejections of Grüber's theodicy have political implications too. They caution against the-end-justifies-the-means arguments that seek to legitimate violence and war as necessities for pursuing national interests and state security.

Christian Zionism and Theodicy

In general, Christian support for the modern State of Israel contains implicit theodicy justifications. Prior to the British Mandate (1920–48) and the UN plan to partition Palestine into Jewish and Arab states in May 1948, Protestant missionary organizations, particularly in the United Kingdom, assisted Jews in returning to Palestine. Among Christians, there was widespread cultural understanding that the Bible supported the return of Jews to the Holy Land.[18] In 1917, Britain's Balfour Declaration promised the creation of a Jewish nation to be a home for refugees fleeing pogroms in Russia and antisemitism elsewhere. Christian beliefs about the Jews returning to Israel encouraged the United Nations' decision to divide Palestine into two states in 1948.

Christian Zionism rests on beliefs about divine providence that include a special role for the people of Israel, even the State of Israel, to fulfill God's plan. But that outlook encompasses a problematic destiny for Jewish existence. While appearing friendly to the Jewish people and the State of Israel, Christian Zionism usually includes the conviction that the Jews cannot achieve salvation apart from accepting Jesus Christ.

Even when Christian Zionism recognizes that its outlook rests on Christianity's superseding Judaism and takes steps to mitigate the discrimination, if not antisemitism, that is implicit in that outlook, the Christian Zionist view interprets Jewish existence and the State of Israel as the means to Christian ends. The Christian Zionist support for the State of Israel can be enthusiastic, even militaristic, but that support cannot be ultimate. It is the means to the end of God's essentially Christian plan.

Christian Zionism projects onto Jews a status that remains "mythical" socially and politically.[19] Support for Israel by Christian theologians may seem like one way to overcome anti-Jewish Christian attitudes of the past. Yet Israel as a modern state and the fate of the Jews may receive problematic attention, both moral praise and blame, in continuation of the symbolic role Jews inhabit in Christian cultural imagination.

Apocalyptic Christian Zionism

Amid the Israel-Hamas war, intense support for the State of Israel comes from evangelical and nondenominational churches that are politically right-wing and firmly in Donald Trump's MAGA Republican tribe. In my own city, San Antonio, Texas, Pastor John Hagee founded Christians United for Israel (CUFI) in 2006. Hagee is a prolific author with an online ministry based in Cornerstone Church, which has 17,000 members. CUFI organizes large gatherings and conducts political lobbying in Washington, DC. Hagee has invited prominent Israeli politicians, including Benjamin Netanyahu, to speak at the Cornerstone Church's annual Night to Honor

Israel, an event that has taken place for more than forty years. After 10/7, Hagee spoke at the March for Israel in Washington, DC (November 14, 2023), which was organized by the Jewish Federations of North America.[20] The march called for release of the hostages taken by Hamas, an end to antisemitism, and support for Israel's self-defense against terrorism. It was held at a time when many pro-Palestinian demonstrations were occurring across the US.

Theodicy is at the center of Hagee's support for Israel. He believes that God's plan for history included the Holocaust as a necessary precursor to the State of Israel. Furthermore, in his 2006 book, *Jerusalem Countdown*, Hagee claims that Jewish settlers must move into the West Bank to restore the biblical boundaries of the Land of Israel. Palestinian displacement may be a necessary, justified means to that end. According to Hagee, war on the State of Israel is a fulfillment of prophecy in Ezekiel 38, which he believes includes attacks by Russia, Iran, and other Muslim countries. These attacks will culminate in a nuclear war.[21] The final battles of Armageddon will take place in Israel followed by the second coming of Jesus Christ and the judgment of nations. According to Hagee, Israel will be soaked in blood, but he holds out hope that the Jews, the people of Israel, will be saved by the Messiah.[22]

On April 8, 2024, Hagee posted a video message entitled "The War on Israel."[23] He expressed unwavering support for Israel's war against Gaza and declared that to leave Hamas in power is to lose the war. Hagee champions the State of Israel and calls on Christians to repent of antisemitism, but he is anti-Muslim and anti-Catholic. Supporting Donald Trump's 2024 reelection as US president, he vehemently criticizes Democrats who seek a ceasefire in the Israel-Hamas war or limits on American heavy-weapon supplies for Israel.

Christian Zionism rests on theological claims about the chosen people of Israel and the land of the Bible, and fundamentalist churches include Israel in prophecies about apocalyptic end times. Jewish history, including the State of Israel and its future, are incorporated into the narratives of Christian Zionism in theodicy-logic ways that instrumentalize Jewish history, including atrocities it may contain, as the means that support God's alleged plan for the Christian salvation of human history.

In this scheme of theodicy, Christian Zionism removes Jewish self-determination. For instance, Hagee's support for Israel places limits on Jewish autonomy since, according to his beliefs, it would be wrong for Israel to give up any part of the Holy Land if the government wished to do so for the sake of peace with Palestinians. Jews are role-players in a fundamentally Christian conception of history. Netanyahu and his wartime followers are part of that cast.

The Future of Israel and Palestine

At some yet-to-be-determined point, the Israel-Hamas war will end. For self-governance by Jews and Palestinians, I believe that any just territorial settlement requires two states or two autonomous sections within one state. Unfortunately, partition barriers, Jewish settlement occupation in the West Bank, and the devastation in Gaza make envisioning and enacting either resolution immensely difficult if not unrealistic.

In 2017, I traveled to Israel and the West Bank. I saw the situation on the ground. From Jerusalem, I passed through government checkpoints and barriers. I observed restrictions on Palestinians. I saw their land appropriated and fortified by Israeli settlers. Walls stood everywhere—barriers protecting the perimeter of Israel, surrounding refugee camps, and separating Jewish settlements and Palestinian lands. As living conditions have worsened continually since the 1967 Six-Day War and the Palestinian economy has deteriorated since the first *intifada* in 1987, terrorism and retaliation have grown.

The domination of Gaza and the occupation of West Bank generate strong Palestinian resistance. In the Palestinian village of Bil'in, west of Ramallah, I attended a Friday demonstration that has been ongoing since 2005. It started as a protest against the separation barrier that took Palestinian farmland, and in fact, after a legal case, the Israeli Supreme Court decided in 2007 to reroute the wall. Since then, the weekly protest continues with local Palestinians joined by visiting activists marching to the barrier wall as a symbolic statement against the occupation.[24] When I attended in March 2017, demonstrators lit a fire adjacent to an iron gate overlooked by Israeli guards. I was informed that tear gas had been used on protesters. Through this gate, as in other areas of the West Bank, there may be Israeli raids on Bil'in and other villages, usually conducted at night. Seeing this situation up close showed me how deep the divisions are, and how security will be essential, whether there is a one- or two-state solution.

I place hope in grassroots efforts to overcome mistrust and violence among communities. In 2014, at a Holocaust colloquium, I learned firsthand about the Parents Circle – Families Forum (PCFF) founded in 1995 as an organization dedicated to dialogue and reconciliation.[25] I had the opportunity to talk with Robi Damelin, and Bassam and Salwa Aramin, who are public figures and leaders. As a mother, Robi spoke about her 28-year-old son David who was serving in the Israeli army reserves when he was shot by a Palestinian sniper in 2002. Then Bassam, with his wife at his side, told us about his 10-year-old daughter Abir who was shot by Israeli border police outside her school in 2007. The PCFF and the activism of those bereaved parents have received worldwide recognition as advocates for peace. Pope Frances invited Bassam Aramin and Jewish co-leader Rami Elhanan to meet with him at the Vatican in March 2024, affirming the Catholic Church's hope for peace despite the Israel-Hamas war.

In Israel, a few days after Prime Minister Netanyahu spoke at Yom HaShoah in May 2024, the Parents Circle and Combatants for Peace (CFP) held their annual gathering on May 12. The theme was the "next generation" and the stories of children "whose only crime was being born Palestinian or Israeli." These organizations, co-led by Israelis who served in the military and Palestinians who have participated in the struggle for freedom, had leadership balanced between Israelis and Palestinians to explore mutual safety and justice and to humanize the other.[26] I learned that the Parents Circle organizes a gathering for adults called the Parallel Narrative Experience, which takes groups of Israelis and Palestinians to locations such as the ruins of the Arab village of Lifta and the Yad Vashem Holocaust Memorial in Jerusalem. As they visit locations of historical trauma, these groups remind me of the Zen Peacemakers and the Bearing Witness retreats in Auschwitz, which bring together those who identify with victims, bystanders, and perpetrators.

Auschwitz and Dialogue

As a Holocaust scholar, I have visited Auschwitz to bear witness and remember the victims of genocide. As a Christian who practices Buddhism, I have prayed and meditated in the camp. I believe that inhabiting places of loss can lead to connections with the pain of others. The retreat's founder, Bernie Glassman, puts it this way:

> At Auschwitz, before we could bear witness to what happened there many years ago, we had to bear witness to each other and the differences among us. As we did that, an intimacy arose naturally and spontaneously. As we listened to each other, we began to take care of one another. At the same time, an intimacy arose between ourselves and Auschwitz. The names we chanted became our own. The barbed wire became softer with time. Love came back to us from ruined barracks that before we couldn't bear to enter.[27]

The sharing of suffering is not meant to equate the Holocaust with something else. Being together in Auschwitz shows the diversity of people's experiences and histories. Glassman views the purpose of the Auschwitz gathering as akin to *tikkun olam* in the Jewish tradition: putting broken pieces back together, making things whole.[28]

A leader in the Auschwitz gathering recommended that I read "What Is Love Asking from Us? Reflections on Gaza and the Bodhisattva Path," an essay by the Buddhist teacher Tara Brach.[29] I discovered that Brach has led meditation gatherings for Israelis and Palestinians since 10/7. In those gatherings, she addresses the demonizing and dehumanizing of others, which leads to violence. As a meditation teacher trained in clinical psychology, Brach observes that those traumatized by violence may not be able to see others as sharing the same desires to be safe, free, and at ease. She proposes that we should cultivate compassion for all involved in the Israel-Hamas war and extend such radical acceptance to other conflicts.[30]

This empathetic approach resonates with the Parents Circle where bereaved Israeli and Palestinian parents share their experiences. As an American Christian, listening to Jewish and Israeli voices is essential, but I also want to include Palestinian experiences about the aftermath of 10/7. It is difficult to hear narratives and feel tension between conflicting positions. Holocaust scholar Björn Krondorfer has developed the concept of "unsettling empathy" to describe difficult participant experiences during workshops between Jews and Germans and between Israelis and Palestinians as well. He finds that resistance and frustration often occur as groups divided by conflicts come together to speak about what has happened.[31] I agree with him. Listening to traumatic memories is difficult. Nor does it work to idealize empathy or peacemaking. Both are hard, unsettling work. The aftermath of 10/7 involves irreconcilable interpretations of history, and conversations can break down or never even begin. I identify this tension with the "not knowing" of the Auschwitz gathering, bearing witness to evil without theodicy justifications.

In Between

After 10/7, I feel caught in between. Yom HaShoah is key for Christian relations with Jews, and I have experienced Holocaust victims being remembered alongside Jewish victims of Hamas attacks. I must also find ways to remember Palestinian families victimized and killed in Gaza during the Israel-Hamas war.

At the meditation gatherings in Auschwitz, participants share the Jewish Kaddish, the Catholic Way of the Cross, and Buddhist rituals for hungry souls. Such religious practices memorialize and express compassion for those who suffered and died. Extending from the

Holocaust, such interfaith rituals potentially could include Israeli and Palestinian victims of the Israel-Hamas war.

Evil and dangerous attempts to justify it preoccupy me. Christian Zionism uses theodicy to legitimate conflict as the Jewish people return to the biblical kingdom of Israel, supposedly to fulfill God's plan. Theodicy's logic is also at work in the Israel-Hamas war. Unavoidably, that logic polarizes and inflames situations and hinders resolutions. In the US, I see either/or divisions between concern about Israeli victims of terrorism and Palestinian victims of war. I find hope in bilateral Israeli-Palestinian organizations, such as the Parents Circle and Combatants for Peace. These groups show how recognizing mutual suffering resulting from ongoing violence may increase empathy between different factions. They give me hope that it will be possible to remember the victims of the Israel-Hamas war compassionately, which means with no room for theodicy.

Questions for Dialogue

1. Is it possible *not* to "take sides" in response to 10/7?

2. Does empathy for both Israelis and Palestinians evade the need to wrestle with the causes of terrorism or war?

3. How can Christians make objections to Israeli government policies without hindering dialogue?

4. When people listen to narratives of loss without making theodicy justifications, politically or religiously, what is the impact of this witnessing?

Further Resources

Cohn-Sherbok, Dan. *The Politics of Apocalypse: The History and Influence of Christian Zionism.* Oxford: Oneworld, 2006.

Glassman, Bernie. *Bearing Witness: A Zen Master's Lessons in Making Peace.* New York: Random House, 1998.

Haynes, Stephen R. *Reluctant Witnesses: Jews and the Christian Imagination.* Louisville: Westminster John Knox, 1995.

Krondorfer, Björn. *Unsettling Empathy: Working with Groups in Conflict.* New York: Rowman & Littlefield International, 2020.

Magid, Shaul. *The Necessity of Exile: Essays from a Distance.* Brooklyn: Ayin Press, 2023.

Notes

1. Bernie Glassman, *Bearing Witness: A Zen Master's Lesson in Making Peace* (New York: Random House, 1998), 84; and "The Three Tenets," https://bit.ly/42FYtpN.

2. As of late May 2024, reliable estimates indicated that more than 36,000 Palestinians had been killed since October 7, compared to approximately 1,200 Israelis killed by Hamas or taken hostage. See "Gaza Offensive to Last at Least until Year's End, Israeli Official Says," *New York Times*, May 29, 2024, https://bit.ly/4jtDRqO.

3. See Joshua M. Greene, *Unstoppable: Siggi B. Wilzig's Astonishing Journey from Auschwitz Survivor and Penniless Immigrant to Wall Street Legend* (Los Angeles: Insight, 2014).

4. See "President Joe Biden Delivers Remarks at U.S. Holocaust Memorial Days of Remembrance Ceremony," posted May 7, 2024, WFAA-ABC, YouTube, https://bit.ly/4jDgsDu.

5. Israeli President Isaac Herzog, speech on May 5, 2024, https://bit.ly/4hyqOTj.

6. Israeli Prime Minister Benjamin Netanyahu, speech on May 5, 2024, https://bit.ly/4hd5EdI.

7. Shaul Magid, *The Necessity of Exile: Essays from a Distance* (Brooklyn: Ayin Press, 2023), 197.

8. "Biden Criticizes International Criminal Court's Request for Arrest Warrants Against Israeli Leaders," posted May 21, 2024, The London Standard, YouTube, https://bit.ly/42BjMsM.

9. For instance, the International Court of Justice (ICJ) at the UN ordered Israel to stop the attack on Rafah. Israel did not. Subsequently, the ICJ charged that Israel had committed war crimes and crimes against humanity. See Rob Schmitz and Daniel Estrin, "The Top U.N. Court Has Ordered Israel to Stop Its Rafah Military Operation," NPR, May 24, 2004, https://bit.ly/4ayD83y.

10. For more on these points, see Sarah K. Pinnock, *Beyond Theodicy: Jewish and Christian Continental Thinkers Respond to the Holocaust* (Albany: SUNY Press, 2002).

11. See Zachary Braiterman, *(God) After Auschwitz: Tradition and Change in Post-Holocaust Jewish Thought* (Princeton: Princeton University Press, 1998).

12. Irving Greenberg, "Cloud of Smoke, Pillar of Fire," in *Auschwitz: Beginning of a New Era?* ed. Eva Fleischner (New York: Ktav, 1977), 23.

13. Emmanuel Levinas, "Useless Suffering," in *The Provocation of Levinas: Rethinking the Other*, ed. Robert Bernasconi and David Wood (New York: Routledge, 1988), 163.

14. Johann Baptist Metz, *The Emergent Church: The Future of Christianity in a Post-Bourgeois World* (New York: Crossroad, 1981), 19.

15. Naim Ateek, "For the Sake of the Burning Children of Gaza," *Palestine Chronicle*, August 1, 2014, https://bit.ly/4aCt09Q. See also Naim Ateek, *Justice*

and Only Justice: A Palestinian Theology of Liberation (Maryknoll, NY: Orbis, 1989).

16. See, for example, Richard L. Rubenstein, *After Auschwitz: History, Theology, and Contemporary Judaism*, 2nd ed. (Baltimore: Johns Hopkins University Press, 1992).

17. Dorothee Soelle, *Suffering*, trans. Everett R. Kalin (Minneapolis: Fortress, 1975), 24.

18. See Daniel Cohn-Sherbok, *The Politics of Apocalypse: The History and Influence of Christian Zionism* (Oxford: Oneworld, 2006), 189.

19. Stephen R. Haynes, *Reluctant Witnesses: Jews and the Christian Imagination* (Louisville: Westminster John Knox, 1995), 63.

20. For information provided about the November 14, 2023, March for Israel, see https://www.marchforisrael.org/.

21. John Hagee, *Jerusalem Countdown* (Lake Mary, FL: FrontLine, 2006), 106.

22. Hagee, *Jerusalem Countdown,* 189.

23. See https://bit.ly/3PTS7LU.

24. See Michael Schutz, "The Democratizing Qualities of the Palestinian Village Bil'in's Civil Resistance Campaign," *Journal of Political Power* 16, no. 2 (2023): 254–75, https://doi.org/10.1080/2158379X.2023.2251107.

25. For more information about PCFF, see www.theparentscircle.org.

26. For more information about Combatants for Peace, see cfpeace.org/about-en/.

27. Glassman, *Bearing Witness*, 88.

28. Glassman, *Bearing Witness*, 41.

29. Brach's article, dated May 11, 2024, is accessible here: https://bit.ly/4hsAyyi.

30. See Tara Brach, *Radical Compassion* (New York: Viking, 2019).

31. Björn Krondorfer, *Unsettling Empathy: Working with Groups in Conflict* (New York: Rowman & Littlefield International, 2020), 100.

12
Making the Best of What We Have

John K. Roth

An American philosopher, I am also a Protestant Christian who affirms two principles that govern this chapter. First, *sin*—the willful disrespect of what is right, good, and just—pervades human existence. It inflames the violence people inflict on one another, including the Holocaust, the Hamas attack on Israel, and the dropping of hundreds of 2,000-pound American/Israeli bombs on civilian Palestinians in Gaza.

Second, dust to dust, ashes to ashes—every nation-state will perish. Political rhetoric tries to reassure us that "our country" will exist and hopefully thrive forever. Such promises resonate because much of what people—Americans, Israelis, Palestinians—hold dear does depend on the national life of which we are a part. But nations come and go, usually the victims of conflict produced by the very particularity that nations prize. Although nationhood and nationality are destined for oblivion, the nature and time of their demise are not known in advance. Making the best of what we have is our lot instead.

For more than fifty years, I have studied, written, and taught about the Holocaust and other mass atrocity crimes. Early on, that life-changing commitment showed me how tragically my Christian tradition led to Nazi Germany's genocide against the Jewish people. Christianity did not cause the Holocaust, but it was a necessary condition for that disaster. No Christianity = No Holocaust—that is the devastating linkage. It compels me to do what I can to mend Christian-Jewish relations.

That task became more fraught and urgent on 10/7—October 7, 2023—when Hamas's invasion of Israel from the Gaza Strip killed more Jews than on any single day since the Holocaust. From an American perspective, that traumatic day has been likened to 9/11 and Pearl Harbor combined. The crushing Israeli response has turned Gaza into wasteland, killing tens of thousands of defenseless Palestinians, ruining the future for those who survive. These observations are not to say, however, that Hamas lacks support from Palestinians. Reliable polling in September 2024 showed that about 36 percent of Palestinians in Gaza and the West Bank prefer Hamas to govern them. According to pollster Khalil Shikaki, a majority holds that "violence or armed struggle is the most effective step for ending the Israeli occupation."[1]

Several weeks earlier, measures of public opinion in the United States showed 48 percent of Americans disapproving of Israel's military actions in Gaza, with 42 percent approving, a change from March 2024, when 55 percent disapproved and 36 percent approved. Prior to that, in November 2023, American approval of Israel's actions stood at 50 percent.[2] Comparable polling in Israel found 39 percent of Israelis overall saying that Israel's military response against Hamas in Gaza has been about right, 34 percent stating it had not gone far enough, and 19 percent holding that it had gone too far.[3] Divisions on these matters understandably run deep between Jewish and Arab Israelis. The data in such snapshots of public opinion will remain in flux, but they continue to show that the brutal Israel-Hamas war is immensely divisive.

If my post-10/7 contributions to Christian-Jewish relations are to bridge divisiveness and be significantly constructive, I must stress-test my identity by probing what it means to call myself—as I currently do—a pro-Palestinian Zionist. That stance entails three affirmations: (1) Israel has the right to exist and defend itself as a Jewish democratic state; (2) the Israeli carnage against Palestinians in Gaza must stop, and that region must be rebuilt; (3) a just two-state solution to the Israeli-Palestinian conflict is paramount, and the United States has important responsibilities to help achieve that goal.

My Zionism

I take Zionism to mean self-determination and statehood for the Jewish people in Israel, their ancestral homeland.[4] Especially in the context of the Israel-Hamas war, my pro-Palestinian Zionism raises persistent questions. What, for example, are the sources, textures, and limits of my Zionism? My Christian forebears—Scots-Irish Quakers and German Christian pacifists from Alsace-Lorraine—crossed the Atlantic to the United States in the mid-nineteenth century. My family tree contains no Holocaust victims or survivors, but family historians think it may include old Jewish branches.

Born in the late Michigan summer of 1940, I have few firsthand recollections of World War II and none of the Holocaust. As a child, I knew no living Jews, but biblical people—Abraham and Moses, Rachel and Ruth, David and Jonathan, Joseph and Mary, Jesus and his followers—were vivid to me from the Bible stories that my parents read to me many nights before I fell asleep. I knew about the Ten

Commandments and the idea that we should love our neighbors as ourselves long before I had heard of Auschwitz or the Gaza Strip, crimes against humanity, and genocide. Biblical narratives—the people and teachings they contain—made deep and lasting impressions upon me.

After the State of Israel was proclaimed on May 14, 1948, my boyhood continued in southern Indiana. Sometimes it took me to an Ohio River hamlet named Bethlehem and to a church called Hebron. Eventually, I learned that the United States, my country, was a place that early Christian settlers imagined to be "God's New Israel," their trans-Atlantic crossings like a biblical exodus from European corruption to a promised land. Many American towns—Salem or Jericho, Canaan or Nazareth, Goshen or Carmel—recalled biblical sites in ancient but also contemporary Israel.

This background, however, was not enough to make me a Zionist. It took the Holocaust, the Nazi genocide that murdered six million European Jews during World War II, to do that. As I became increasingly aware of that catastrophe in the early 1970s, my contempt for antisemitism and racism intensified as I welcomed the existence of a Jewish homeland in Israel.

The State of Israel did not make up for the Holocaust. Nothing could. Nor did I see God's hand at work in the new state's establishment. Instead, I gradually and now increasingly have come to see the huge price that continues to be paid for the State of Israel's existence. During the first Arab-Israeli war (1948–49), for example, at least 700,000 Palestinians were displaced from their homes in what became known as the Nakba (Arabic for *catastrophe*). Palestinian displacement led the United Nations General Assembly to adopt Resolution 194 on December 11, 1948. It states that "refugees wishing to return to their homes and live at peace with their neighbors should be permitted to do so at the earliest practicable date," a provision that bolsters ongoing Palestinian claims to a "right of return," which Israel adamantly rejects.

Despite the Nakba and its reverberations, I still defend Israel's right to exist, recognizing that my commitment—grounded in the abiding conviction that the establishment of the State of Israel was a necessary response to the Holocaust—is fraught in another significant way. Debate swirls around the claim that the State of Israel's existence resulted from Western-supported *settler colonialism*.[5] With approval and assistance especially from Great Britain and the United States, the narrative goes, Jews—before and after the Holocaust—gained control of Palestinian territory, marginalizing and often violently displacing Indigenous Arab people while establishing a state and culture of their own. Critics argue that the settler-colonialist interpretation is misguided, because Zionism was a Jewish nationalist liberation movement seeking to escape Europe's antisemitic and racist domination. Nevertheless, contested through the settler-colonialist interpretation remains, it credibly grasps what the Jewish scholar Dov Waxman underscores:

> Unlike other national liberation movements, or nationalist movements in general, Zionism required the mass relocation and resettlement of Jews to an area (Palestine) that was inhabited by another population (Arabs). In doing so, Zionists had to justify their presence and overcome the resistance of the indigenous population, who saw them as intruders. In this respect, the Zionist project was similar to colonial projects undertaken by European settlers in North America, Australia, New Zealand, Algeria, Brazil, and South Africa. . . . Although they frequently claimed that the "natives" would benefit from their presence since they brought progress and "civilization" to them, in reality the indigenous population ended up being dispossessed of its land, and socially and politically marginalized at best (at worst, they were simply killed off).[6]

Should the settler-colonialist interpretation abolish my defense of the State of Israel? No, but that narrative limits the defense in the same way that my understanding of American history makes me critical of my own country. I have written this chapter in an American house occupying land that once belonged to Native Americans. From the seventeenth into the early twentieth century, American settler colonialism displaced and committed genocide against them from the Atlantic to the Pacific to create the United States.[7]

My country is scarred by greed and violence, haunted by racism and genocide against Indigenous peoples. Nothing can turn the clock back or adequately atone for that sin. And yet the United States contains possibility and hope, commitment and promise that may yet create what the Constitution of the United States calls "a more perfect union," one that moves toward pluralism and inclusiveness, stronger respect for human rights, better liberty, sounder democracy, and firmer justice.[8] Pulled and tugged between the right and wrong, the good and evil of my country's history, I am challenged by unresolvable moral tension, but I stand by my country because it can be better. Such critical hope informs my Zionism, which puts me in substantial agreement with the Palestinian American historian Rashid Khalidi:

While the fundamentally colonial nature of the Palestinian-Israel encounter must be acknowledged, there are now two peoples in Palestine, irrespective of how they came into being, and the conflict between them cannot be resolved as long as the national existence of each is denied by the other. Their mutual acceptance can only be based on complete equality of rights, including national rights, notwithstanding the crucial historical differences between the two. There is no other possibility, barring the unthinkable notion of one people's extermination or expulsion by the other.[9]

In Spite of Despair

I began this chapter on Yom HaShoah, May 6, 2024, a day when the cry of sirens in the State of Israel brought a two-minute silent standstill as the nation remembered the Holocaust. The Yom HaShoah sirens have screamed in Israel for more than sixty-five years, but they shrieked differently in 2024. As never before, they warned: Be vigilant—do not take the State of Israel's existence for granted. As never before, Yom HaShoah's Israeli sirens could also be heard as defiant expressions of resistance and courage affirming that, in spite of the Holocaust, Jewish life remains strong and resilient. As never before, however, the sirens may have sounded an unintentional alarm about the State of Israel's future, especially its standing in the world. Israel's devastating response to the Hamas atrocities of 10/7—including Prime Minister Benjamin Netanyahu and his followers' vow to annihilate Hamas—has created international instability, an immense humanitarian disaster for millions of Palestinians, and for the United States, Israel's major ally, deepening political division as Americans contend with national elections that have put the rule of law and democracy itself at risk.

On May 6, 2024—Yom HaShoah—as hostage-return and ceasefire talks stalled, Israel began a military offensive in and around Rafah, the southernmost city in the Gaza Strip and home to more than a million Palestinians seeking refuge from seven months of war. Determined to eliminate Hamas in Rafah, the Israeli military entered the city on May 14. By the time the Israel Defense Forces allowed journalists to enter Rafah two months later, the city was a wasteland. As the summer of 2024 drew to a close, the Palestinian death toll, including thousands from Rafah and its vicinity, exceeded 40,000.[10]

Few Americans have responded more personally and testified more movingly about the suffering of defenseless Palestinians in Gaza than the surgeon Samer Attar, a professor at Northwestern University School of

Medicine. A veteran of war zone medicine, Attar spent two weeks in bombed-out Gaza. He was one of the first from an international team of doctors to be embedded, cut off from the outside world, in what he calls "apocalyptic" conditions—the worst he has seen—working valiantly against all odds to save mutilated and starving children from amputation or death.[11]

Attar had to step over dead bodies in makeshift, unsterile surgery rooms devoid of anesthesia and life-saving equipment. The health care system in Gaza, said Attar, had "collapsed." The video diaries he kept bear witness to that. He met Palestinians trying to create a future for themselves, but as one man told him, "There is no future."

Many of his patients, Attar believed, could be saved "if they were just about anywhere else in the world." But the necessity of triage meant that saving one life meant someone else would die or be permanently disabled. For conditions to improve, Attar stressed, a ceasefire could not come too soon. It must be accompanied by significant humanitarian and medical aid allowed into Gaza, evacuation of the injured to better medical facilities, and the repair and protection of Gaza's medical infrastructure.

Attar's 13-minute *New York Times* video is at once painful yet indispensable to see and hear. Amid the grisly wounds, the unbearable suffering, and needless death, the Palestinian medics and nurses who helped Attar have carried on in spite of despair. More than that, said Attar, he experienced resilience, kindness, compassion, generosity, and even joy among them.

At the video's end, Attar speaks with a man collecting dirt to build a garden. He wants to grow vegetables for the child he hopes his three-months-pregnant wife will deliver. Attar asks her if she has a message she would like to share. "I wish the war would be over," she says. "And I hope people will survive the war. I hope that we can dream of what will come after the war."

Supplied by the United States, the 2,000-pound, tunnel-busting bombs dropped by Israel reduced much of Gaza to uninhabitable rubble even as American president Joe Biden unconvincingly protested indiscriminate Israeli attacks. On a proportional basis, the Israeli bombardment of the Gaza Strip has arguably been more destructive than the Allies' bombing of Germany in World War II.[12] To make matters worse, spring's arrival in 2024 meant that famine was imminent for Palestinian civilians in Gaza. No resolution of the conflict was visible as Biden's speech at the US Holocaust Memorial Museum's annual Days of Remembrance ceremony lamented Hamas's attack against Israel and deplored antisemitism but was conspicuously silent about Israel's bludgeoning warfare in Gaza.[13]

Concurrently, Israeli streets filled with protesters against Netanyahu—as they did again in September 2024—whose policies are seen as antithetical to the release of Hamas's hostages. Any further political leadership role for Hamas was understandably unacceptable for Israelis, but many of them were convinced that Netanyahu's leadership was bankrupt, his policies far from Israel's best interests.

While the Yom HaShoah sirens screamed in Israel, the United States stood between a rock and a hard place in a pivotal election year. It embraced iron-clad support for Israel but needed to distance itself from the ongoing Israeli decimation of Palestinians. The bottom line is that the United States has not only defended Israel—the right response to Hamas's 10/7 attack—but also been complicit in immense and unjustifiable Palestinian suffering in Gaza and the West Bank. No diplomacy, however skilled, and no amount of humanitarian aid will cleanse Americans' blood-stained hands, at least not completely.

Will despair prevail? Or, in spite of despair, can the hopes of a pregnant Palestinian woman—"I hope people will survive the war. I hope that we can dream of what will come after the war."—still make sense and inspire Christians, Jews, Muslims, and also Americans, Israelis, and Palestinians to make the best of what we have?

The Irony of Israeli History

In 1982, my guiding friend Elie Wiesel arranged for me to teach in Israel. I was the first non-Jewish professor to offer courses on the Holocaust at the University of Haifa. My time in Haifa deepened my commitment to foster good relations between Christians and Jews and did much to make me a post-Holocaust Zionist who affirms the State of Israel's rightful existence and its responsibility to defend itself.

Among my memorable experiences at the university, I recall a conversation with a student as the two of us waited for our buses home one spring evening. Older than my students in the United States, this *Sabra* (native-born Israeli) was different in other ways as well. Although not unusual for Israeli students at the time—army duty necessitated that he and his peers sometimes came to the university in military garb—I was not accustomed to seeing them carrying weapons along with their books. That description fitted my *Sabra* acquaintance perfectly.

The student-solder talked tougher than he seemed. I did not learn his name, but I have not forgotten what he said. Upon learning that I was a visiting professor, a Christian from California, he asked what I taught. I told him about my work in the university's Holocaust studies program.

Thereafter, I mostly listened because the student-soldier was more irritated than impressed. Such courses, he stressed, were of little use to him. He already knew what the Holocaust taught, namely, that weakness is a recipe for disaster. Since the establishment of the State of Israel in 1948, he continued, there had been more than enough struggle to occupy his attention. Concern about the Holocaust seemed unhelpful. How much better it would be, he insisted, to move beyond that sad catastrophe of powerlessness and to concentrate instead on the lessons of Israel's strength, its determined and successful self-defense in a post-Holocaust world. Our bus departures cut the conversation short, but the young man's "last word" has remained with me. "If Jews had a possessed a state of their own," he asserted on the run, "there would have been no Holocaust."

I wonder whether the now sixty-something, post-10/7 *Sabra* ever had second thoughts about his "last word" to me in 1982. Certainly I have, because his claim, "If Jews had possessed a state of their own, there would have been no Holocaust," seems no more convincing now than it was then. And yet, the Haifa student-soldier's "last word" still makes its case, which applies to Palestinians as well as to Israelis. Statelessness can mean helplessness and hopelessness. Defenselessness is unsound policy. National power does make one's opponents think twice before tampering with it, and anyone who tampers with Israel's security, or with Jewish well-being, anywhere in the world should not expect to do so with impunity.

My office at the University of Haifa was high up in the Eshkol Tower atop Mount Carmel. Frequently mentioned in the Bible and a favorite haunt of the prophet Elijah, Mount Carmel is a dominant geographical feature of northern Israel. This Israeli landmark is less a single peak than a steep, rocky ridge. Stretching for several miles, at the northwest it drops into the Mediterranean Sea. To the southeast, it ends with a majestic vista of the fertile plain below and of Galilee beyond. My window looked out toward Galilee, but it slanted northeast. My view reached into southern Lebanon.

By late February 1982, it was only a matter of time before the Israeli military would enter Lebanon to clear out the Palestine Liberation Organization (PLO) installations that threatened Israel's settlements along the northern border. I was reminded of that possibility daily, as sonic booms from Israeli jets on their missions shook the office tower where I worked.

In early June, when Operation Peace for Galilee began, my family and I were sightseeing in Jerusalem. Our bus ride back to Haifa was slower than usual because the road was clogged by troop transports and tanks heading north. In the days that followed, however, the view from my office window was much the same as it had been before. As far as I could see from Mount Carmel, the world was beautiful, tranquil, peaceful. But that impression was a surrealistic deception. War raged only thirty miles away. The jets came more frequently, their dashes north counterpointed by the chugging of helicopters bearing casualties south to the hospital in Haifa. Less than a hundred miles distant, Beirut would soon fall under siege. Sabra and Shatila awaited their addition to the world's places of mass atrocity crimes.

Israel's early incursions into southern Lebanon in the summer of 1982 were widely understood and even found acceptable largely because determination to defend one's own citizens and territory against armed violence is a virtue indispensable for any nation that intends to survive. But the reach of the Israeli incursion exceeded its grasp. Striking farther and farther north and putting Beirut under siege, Israel eventually dispersed the PLO's chief military presence from the region. But those successes also drove Israel into the mass graves of Sabra and Shatila. In those places near Beirut, hundreds of Palestinian and Lebanese civilians were slaughtered, often raped as well, by Christian militias aligned with Israel, while Israeli forces under defense minister Ariel Sharon facilitated the mayhem. Israel besmirched its character in the late summer of 1982 because of its determination to cleanse Lebanon of PLO threats.

More than forty years on, 1982 is but one reminder that the Israeli-Palestinian conflict is old, bloody, atrocity-laden, and again expanding into Lebanon as well as Gaza. Unfortunately, the current and spreading Israel-Hamas war is much worse than any previous aspects of that struggle. In the summer of 1982, Israel demonstrated that it unquestionably possessed the best equipped, most efficiently trained armed forces in the Middle East. In 2024, Israel's military is even stronger. It can unleash massive destruction while its vaunted Iron Dome defends Israel from air attacks. This strength, however, diminishes international support for Israel, which is increasingly isolated and even out of favor in much of the United States, especially among young people whose support for the US-Israel alliance cannot be taken for granted.

Antisemitism got a huge boost from Sabra and Shatila forty years ago. It has been even more resurgent during the current Israel-Hamas war. It is foolish to think that antisemitism will be curbed if only Israel is less militant. But there is no question that Israel's destructive war in Gaza inflames and intensifies antisemitism. No amount of deploring antisemitism, not even massive infusions of Holocaust education or Christian corrections of ancient teachings of contempt about Jews and

Judaism, will stanch the incitement of antisemitism provoked by the overreach of Benjamin Netanyahu's military campaign in Gaza. Neither will Netanyahu's removal from political power and a permanent ceasefire in Gaza be enough, but those steps are necessary to start turning the antisemitic tide.

Hamas's 10/7 attack on Israel was evil—period, full stop. Israel was on the right side when it defended itself. But in doing so, it chose to embrace further evil by unleashing violence that no credible theory of just war can validate. Tragedy abounds in the current Israel-Hamas war. It is compounded by *irony*. A resolute opponent of antisemitism and supporter of Israel, the American Christian theologian Reinhold Niebuhr underscored that the defining marks of irony in sinful history are found in the human propensity to overlook what can be seen if one looks, to act without taking account of consequences that can be anticipated if one is awake and aware. On one occasion, he described ironic situations as follows:

> If virtue becomes vice through some hidden defect in the virtue; if strength becomes weakness because of the vanity to which strength may prompt the mighty man or nation; if security is transmuted into insecurity because too much reliance is placed upon it; if wisdom becomes folly because it does not know its own limits—in all such cases the situation is ironic.[14]

Niebuhr's description depicts the irony of Israeli history as the Israel-Hamas war drags on without much hope for a favorable resolution. Doing what is right—defending itself—Israel, under Netanyahu, does much that is wrong. Displaying military strength, at least doing so too much, Israel shows its weakness. Seeking security in the devastation of Gaza and the misguided belief that Hamas can be stamped out, Israel creates more insecurity. Thinking they know best, Netanyahu and his right-wing partners produce lethal folly that endangers not only Israel but also the Middle East and even the world.

The only way out of dangerous and deadly ironic circumstances, Niebuhr rightly believed, was for people to acknowledge the predicament and to change their ways accordingly. Folly, however, can be so entrenched that moving beyond the ironies of sinful history—Israeli, Palestinian, American—is far easier said than done.

An Important Step

Honest responses to key questions that Carol Rittner and I asked our *Stress Test* contributors to address are an important step to dispel illusions that produce ironic situations embedded in the Israel-Hamas war and to sustain constructive Christian-Jewish relations. Those questions include: (1) To what extent does Israel have a right to defend itself? (2) Do Palestinians have a right to a state of their own? (3) Have Hamas or Israel committed war crimes, crimes against humanity, or even genocide? (4) What should happen when the war ends?

First, at least in principle, the world comprises sovereign states with secure borders that enjoy freedom from coercion and invasion. Their existence entails a right to self-defense. Israel has that right, which legitimated action against Hamas after it invaded Israel. Hamas was not only raping, pillaging, terrorizing, and murdering individual Israelis but also putting Israel's existence at risk. Credible ethical standards, however, require limits on a nation's right to self-defense. Those limits reject the argument that a state has the right to defend itself "by any means necessary." Nor do those limits accept that "the end justifies the means" or that "might makes right." Furthermore, credible ethical standards do not play self-serving games that crown the Israeli military as the most moral in the world, a claim that goes too far to legitimate whatever that army decides to do.

Israel retaliated against Hamas and vowed to destroy it. The illusion that Hamas can be destroyed has led Israel to violate the right to self-defense because that right cannot credibly legitimate the carnage that Israel has inflicted on defenseless Palestinians, many of them children, during the gruesome military campaign in Gaza. Insistence that such massive civilian casualties are collateral damage, the unfortunate cost of unavoidable urban warfare that necessitates destruction of the lethal Hamas tunnel network in Gaza, has no ethically justifiable standing. What Israel has done in Gaza sullies the concept of a right to national self-defense. No one—Israeli or American, Jewish or Christian—should take pride in that result.

Second, just as the Jewish people have a right to self-determination and statehood, so do the Palestinian people. In mid-2024, the journalist Kim Hjelmgaard reported, Palestine has a flag, a national anthem, diplomats, and its own international dialing code. "In fact," he added, "three-quarters of the world's 195 countries—143 UN member states plus the Vatican and Western Sahara—say it's a state."[15] The State of Israel has much more because it has a permanent population, a defined territory, a government, and the capacity to enter into relations with other states—conditions that imply independence and must be met for the realistic existence of a nation-state.[16] Presently, Palestine has no effective independence from Israel, which occupies the West Bank and Gaza, the territory fundamental for an authentic Palestinian state.

Israel faces what may be an intractable dilemma. An independent Palestinian state, let alone one controlled by Hamas, is anathema to Netanyahu and to many Israelis. But the status quo, or anything approximating it, keeps Israel and the world too much at risk. If Israel is willing, allies exist, first and foremost the United States, who could pave the way for a two-state solution in which both Israel and Palestine have a future of peace, justice, and economic prosperity. Israel and Israelis may remain unwilling to take the risks that must be taken to achieve a viable two-state solution. But the motto of Theodor Herzl, one father of the modern Zionism that led to the State of Israel, warrants remembering: "If you will it, it is no dream."

Palestinians deserve more than "paper statehood." They deserve a homeland with safe and secure borders, a state that, in turn, respects the borders and security of its neighbors. For that outcome to prevail, Palestinians must reject Hamas's misguided charter claims. The original Hamas charter (1988) called for total destruction of Israel as a necessary condition for the liberation of Palestine. What appeared to be a more moderate revision of the charter (2017) still affirmed not only Hamas's "long-standing goal of establishing a sovereign, Islamist Palestinian state that extends, according to Article 2, from the Jordan River to the Mediterranean Sea and from the Lebanese border to the Israeli city of Eilat" but also an "inalienable" right of return for Palestinian refugees displaced by the wars of 1948 and 1967.[17] Ethical realism scraps those conditions.

Better prospects exist. On May 9, 2024, owing to Israel's overreaching response to the Hamas attack on 10/7, the United Nations General Assembly overwhelmingly resolved that "the State of Palestine is qualified for membership in the United Nations." My country, the United States, discouragingly voted against this resolution, but I enthusiastically support it. Long-standing Israeli hostility to a Palestinian state is behind Netanyahu's cynical, pre-10/7 behind-the-scenes support for Hamas, his war in Gaza, and his administration's expansion of Jewish settlements in the West Bank.[18] Yet the Palestinian right to statehood has growing support that will not die. Israeli resistance only strengthens the leverage of this right.

Third, atrocity crimes enumerated in international law have worsened the Israel-Hamas war. Hamas committed crimes against humanity—murder, torture, sexualized violence, enforced disappearance, to identify a few—when it attacked civilians in Israel on October 7, 2023. Israel has repeatedly committed war crimes through massive military assaults that have laid waste to Gaza and its Palestinian civilian population, despite claims that it only seeks to destroy Hamas. These crimes include inflicting starvation and famine on Palestinians in Gaza. Netanyahu and his war cabinet are responsible for a horrendous humanitarian crisis that has no end in sight. Regarding ethnic cleansing, which lacks standing as a specific crime under international law, it is a close call whether Israel has used force or intimidation by one ethnic or religious group to remove another ethnic or religious group from certain geographic areas. This close-call status applies to genocide as well.

Ironically, Hamas is a genocidal movement that has not enacted genocide. Given its history with the Holocaust, Israel deplores genocide, and yet its actions in Gaza are close enough to intentional destruction "in whole or in part [of] a national, ethnical, racial or religious group, as such" that the International Court of Justice has found it "plausible" that Israel has committed acts that violate the 1948 Convention on the Prevention and Punishment of the Crime of Genocide. The question of genocide remains unsettled, and time will tell what the verdict should be. However, unless Christian-Jewish relations reckon with these grim realities, they will lack credibility.

Fourth, not only in May 2024 but also as the first anniversary of 10/7 came and went, the end of the Israel-Hamas war remained in suspense, partly because of expanded conflict between Israel and Hezbollah. But "the day after" will arrive, and daunting work must begin. It will take years to make Gaza humanely habitable. A generation of Palestinian children has lost health and education, while Israelis have to deal with pariah status as antisemitism afflicts Jews and takes its toll on life's quality wherever it is found. Crippled, not destroyed, Hamas must not be allowed to regain political power over Gaza and the Palestinian people. In consultation with Israel, but not under its domination, a democratic political infrastructure must be created by and for the Palestinian people, a task that needs to include support from Arab countries, the United States, and the United Nations.

Before October 7, 2023, the idea of a two-state solution for the Israeli-Palestinian conflict had become a nonstarter. Ironically, it took a brutal war to revive that idea, not as a lofty ideal but as a concrete necessity if the Middle East is not to be a tinderbox that ignites more than regional destruction. Complicit as Americans have been in Gaza's destruction, we have a leading responsibility to rebuild conditions in Gaza and the West Bank and to promote a two-state response to the Israeli-Palestinian conflict, which the world cannot allow to continue as it has done for decades. This cause may be forlorn, but it will be given up with immense peril.

While battling antisemitism, Christians must do all we can to relieve Palestinian suffering and to encourage Israel to take the risks of building two just and peaceful states—one Palestinian, the other Israeli—with secure borders and stable economies. It is entirely possible that none of these hopes may be realized. But amid the rubble, in spite of the carnage, no matter how badly events have gone, opportunity remains to pursue better ways. If Christian-Jewish relations can advance in these directions, their validity will be improved, and that will help to mend the world.

A New Kind of "We"

The Jewish philosopher Sarah Kofman survived the Holocaust in Paris as a child, hidden in the home of a Christian widow named Mémé.[19] Kofman's father, a rabbi named Berek, was murdered at Auschwitz. She called that event "my absolute."[20] She meant, I believe, that her father's Auschwitz death was wrong—period, full stop. What's more, no one should die that way, the victim of us-versus-them thinking and acting, which mock words such as "human" and "humanity."

Lethally embodied in the SS, the vast organization that implemented the Holocaust, Nazism utterly rejected the idea of an inclusively shared humanity. Kofman's despising of that ideology led her to make a decisive point—in my judgment no Holocaust insight is more important—"No community is possible with the SS."[21] To that imperative she added that a "new kind of 'we'" must be found.[22] She had only modest convictions about progress toward that goal. But absent the will to make the best of what we have, the human condition will go from bad to worse.

The stress test I face as a pro-Palestinian Zionist, the challenge confronting Christian-Jewish relations amid the current Israel-Hamas war and its aftermath, is this: With whom can I and must I have community and with whom can I and must I not?

My pro-Palestinian Zionism means that no community is possible with Hamas—unless Hamas profoundly changes its anti-Zionist position. My pro-Palestinian Zionism also means that no community is possible with Benjamin Netanyahu and his right-wing government unless they make changes that seem unlikely at best. Nor can I find community with Americans—Christians or Jews—who keep bending the knee to Netanyahu and his crimes-against-humanity policies, or with advocates of Palestinian nationalism who seek control, even metaphorically, "from the river to the sea."

Instead, I must make community with those—especially fellow Americans—who work to end the war, support replacing Netanyahu and his ilk with more inclusive Israeli leadership, relieve Palestinian suffering, rebuild Gaza, and pursue a just two-state initiative that has a chance, even if only a modest one, for success. My pro-Palestinian Zionism may make it impossible to have community with some Christians and some Jews—personally and organizationally—but I know that friends and allies exist and that the best future for Christian-Jewish relations depends on my standing in solidarity with them and expanding that much-needed community as much as possible. Making the best of what we have requires me—and others, I hope—to move in those directions.

Questions for Dialogue

1. Why is the Israel-Hamas war a stress test for Christian-Jewish relations?

2. Are you a Zionist? Are you a pro-Palestinian Zionist? How did you arrive there?

3. Does the Israel-Hamas war make Americans complicit in war crimes and crimes against humanity?

4. Working together, what should Christians and Jews keep doing, stop doing, and start doing in response to the Israel-Hamas war and its aftermath?

Further Resources

Grob, Leonard, and John K. Roth, eds. *Encountering the Stranger: A Jewish-Christian-Muslim Trialogue.* Seattle: University of Washington Press, 2012.

Roth, John K. *The Failures of Ethics: Confronting the Holocaust, Genocide, and Other Mass Atrocities.* Oxford: Oxford University Press, 2015.

Rubens, Heather Miller. "We Must Have Courage to Dialogue." *National Catholic Reporter*, September 25, 2024. https://bit.ly/42KFRFo.

In addition, online searches can connect readers with sources that I have found helpful. (1) Ezra Klein's podcasts on the Israel-Hamas war consistently offer insightful perspectives. (2) Commentaries on the Israeli-Palestinian conflict by Richard Haass, Nicholas Kristof, and Fareed Zakaria are reliably informative. (3) Independent, nonprofit news organizations such as *The Intercept* (https://theintercept.com/) and

Truthout (https://truthout.org/) offer challenging reporting and provocative opinion.

Notes

1. See Itay Stern, "A Pollster Sheds Light on Palestinian Attitudes Toward the U.S., Israel and Hamas," NPR, July 26, 2024, https://bit.ly/3Wtf3Fl.

2. See Megan Brennan, "Disapproval of Israeli Action in Gaza Eases Slightly," Gallup News, July 10, 2024, https://bit.ly/4gd0tcq.

3. See Laura Silver and Maria Smerkovich, "Israeli Views of the Israel-Hamas War," Pew Research Center, May 30, 2024, https://bit.ly/4axHI1U.

4. Michael Stanislawski, *Zionism: A Very Short Introduction* (New York: Oxford University Press, 2017) provides a compact and reliable study. Important critical perspectives on Zionism include Shaul Magid, *The Necessity of Exile: Essays from a Distance* (Brooklyn, NY: Ayin, 2023).

5. Helpful discussions of the concept of settler colonialism, specifically as applied to the State of Israel, include: Rashid Khalidi, *The Hundred Years' War on Palestine: A History of Settler Colonialism and Resistance, 1917–2017* (New York: Picador, 2021); Adam Kirsch, *On Settler Colonialism: Ideology, Violence, and Justice* (New York: W. W Norton, 2024); Simon Sebag Montefiore, "The Decolonization Narrative is Dangerous and False," *Atlantic*, October 27, 2023, https://bit.ly/4hszIl8; Derek J. Penslar, *Zionism: An Emotional State* (New Brunswick, NJ: Rutgers University Press, 2023); Jennifer Schuessler, "What Is 'Settler Colonialism'?" *New York Times*, January 22, 2024, https://bit.ly/4gfs3pt; Dov Waxman, *The Israeli-Palestinian Conflict: What Everyone Needs to Know* (New York: Oxford University Press, 2019). For an insightful inquiry about the Holocaust as a necessary condition for the creation of the State of Israel, see Evyatar Friesel, "The Holocaust: Factor in the Birth of Israel?" Yad Vashem, https://bit.ly/4giU4fQ. This article is excerpted from Israel Gutman, ed., *Major Changes Within the Jewish People in the Wake of the Holocaust* (Jerusalem: Yad Vashem, 1996), 519–44.

6. Waxman, *The Israeli-Palestinian Conflict*, 42–43.

7. The most poignant and powerful book I know on this topic is Ned Blackhawk's prize-winning *The Rediscovery of America: Natives Peoples and the Unmaking of U.S. History* (New Haven, CT: Yale University Press, 2023).

8. On these points, see Leonard Grob and John K. Roth, *Warnings: The Holocaust, Ukraine, and Endangered American Democracy* (Eugene, OR: Cascade, 2023).

9. Khalidi, *The Hundred Years' War on Palestine*, 246.

10. On these points, see Julia Frankel, "Israel Confirms Its Forces Are in Central Rafah in Expanding Offensive in the Southern Gaza City," AP News, May 31, 2024, https://bit.ly/42vKcvM.

11. See Samer Attar, with video by Alexander Stockton and Amanda Su, "Two Weeks Inside Gaza's Ruined Hospitals," *New York Times*, May 21, 2024, https://bit.ly/42z8lBT.

12. See Julia Frankel, "Israel's Military Campaign in Gaza Seen as Among the Most Destructive in Recent History, Experts Say," AP News, January 11, 2024, https://bit.ly/3WxbIoZ.

13. See "President Joe Biden Delivers Remarks at U.S. Holocaust Memorial Days of Remembrance Ceremony," posted May 7, 2024, WFAA-ABC, YouTube, https://bit.ly/4jDgsDu.

14. Reinhold Niebuhr, *The Irony of American History* (New York: Charles Scribner's Sons, 1952), viii.

15. Kim Hjelmgaard, "Palestine Has a Flag, an Anthem and Even Its Own Dialing Code," *USA Today*, May 29, 2024, 6A. For the online version of this article, see https://bit.ly/4h0RtrX.

16. See, for example, the Montevideo Convention 1933, which is often cited when international conditions for and understandings of statehood are at play, https://bit.ly/4hxBLoe.

17. Bruce Hoffman, "Understanding Hamas's Genocidal Ideology," *Atlantic*, October 10, 2023, https://bit.ly/4h7jjTy.

18. See Mark Mazetti and Ronen Bergman, "'Buying Quiet': Inside the Israeli Plan That Propped Up Hamas," *New York Times*, December 10, 2023, https://bit.ly/3WyAzZy.

19. For Kofman's account of her life with her Christian rescuer, see Sarah Kofman, *Rue Ordener, Rue Labat*, trans. Ann Smock (Lincoln: University of Nebraska Press, 1996).

20. Sarah Kofman, *Smothered Words*, trans. Madeleine Dobie (Evanston, IL: Northwestern University Press, 2001), 9.

21. Kofman, *Smothered Words*, 70. See also John K. Roth, *Sources of Holocaust Insight: Learning and Teaching about the Genocide* (Eugene, OR: Cascade, 2020), 140–54.

22. Kofman, *Smothered Words*, 73.

Epilogue
An Enormous Effort

Carol Rittner and John K. Roth

As this book went to press during the autumn of 2024, the first anniversary of the 10/7 Hamas attack on Israel came and went. More than a year after that disaster, too little is better in the Middle East. The belligerence of Israeli prime minister Benjamin Netanyahu and his right-wing enablers has made the State of Israel less stable and the Palestinian people more destitute. Burrowed beneath cities and crucial infrastructure in the Gaza Strip, Hamas's tunnel network—estimated to extend 350 to 450 miles within a territory that is only twenty-five miles at its longest point—kept Palestinians captive to Israeli attacks that are determined to destroy Hamas, something which can only be achieved by obliterating the tunnel system.[1] Most of the Gaza Strip has been reduced to uninhabitable rubble.

Meanwhile, land-grabbing Jewish settlers in the Occupied Palestinian Territory have stolen West Bank homes from Palestinians. Calls for a two-state solution to the Israeli-Palestinian conflict grow louder, but this goal seems little more than wishcasting as most Israelis and Palestinian militants do not support it. The bellicose nationalism of Netanyahu and his followers threatens to turn the West Bank into a second Gaza. Instead of a two-state solution, the future may hold what some are calling a one-state "non-solution" that would result de facto in Israeli military control reaching "from the river to the sea." What's more, along the Israel-Lebanon border, conflict between Iran-backed Hezbollah and the Israel Defense Forces ignited a regional war with more Gaza-like devastation and worldwide aftershocks. Israel cannot bomb and kill its way to the security it needs. Winning the wars could mean losing the peace.

Stress Test seeks to be an exception to the proposition that little is better regarding the Israel-Hamas war as 2024 moves into 2025 and beyond. Whether the book warrants that judgment, however, depends on how well it withstands scrutiny. Editors rarely write critical reviews of their books, but that is what this Epilogue must be, as a key question remains: Does this book pass the stress test that the Israel-Hamas war and its reverberations create for Christian-Jewish relations? Five events from August 2024 help frame and contextualize our response.

1. In Chicago, on Thursday, August 22, US Vice President Kamala Harris accepted the Democratic Party's nomination for the American presidency. The raucous crowd quieted toward the end of her forty-minute speech when she spoke briefly about a divisive matter: the Israel-Hamas war. Emphasizing that she was working with President Joe Biden "to get a hostage deal and a ceasefire deal done," she also stressed that she would "always ensure Israel has the ability to defend itself, because the people of Israel must never again face the horror that a terrorist organization called Hamas caused on Oct. 7, including unspeakable sexual violence and the massacre of young people at a music festival." She also underscored that "the scale of suffering [in Gaza] is heartbreaking," adding that "President Biden and I are working to end this war, such that Israel is secure, the hostages are released, the suffering in Gaza ends and the Palestinian people can realize their right to dignity, security, freedom and self-determination."[2]

    Harris tried to thread the proverbial needle, doing so as prudently as politically possible. She condemned Hamas, supported Israel, and offered hopes for Israelis and Palestinians. As for the heartbreaking scale of suffering in Gaza, her speech offered no explicit mention of who was causing it or what would be needed to end the Israeli atrocities that are made possible, at least in part, by military support funded by American taxpayers. Rightly, Hamas was not spared, but accountability was otherwise difficult to locate in her remarks.

2. On August 21, the day before Harris's acceptance speech, the journalists Vivian Yee and Bilal Shbair specified that the heartbreaking scale of suffering in Gaza includes Palestinian orphans—"so many orphans in such chaos," Yee and Shbair wrote, "that no agency or aid group can count them."[3] Their article flagged that some attempts to do so have been made, a step that could lead readers to "Unaccompanied and Separated Children in Gaza," a June 2024 report from the respected and reliable International Rescue Committee.[4] Ten months into the Israel-Hamas war, the International

Rescue Committee reported that "more than 39,000 Palestinians have been killed, and at least 50 percent of the identified fatalities are reportedly women and children. Another 91,000 have been injured. . . . Between 15,000 and 19,000 children are estimated to have been orphaned."

Multiplying the misery and hopelessness, Israel's military has destroyed or damaged more than 80 percent of Gaza's schools, prompting analysts to use the term "scholasticide," which connotes the systematic demolition of education.[5] It is good and right to affirm that Israel should be secure and hostages released, that Palestinians should be able to realize their right to dignity, security, freedom, and self-determination. Yet such words are little more than promissory notes, scarcely worth the paper on which they are written, unless people—including Christians and Jews—are willing to play a part in the challenging work of rebuilding needed to make progress toward realizing these goals.

3. On August 11, Andrew Silow-Carroll, a journalist for the Jewish Telegraphic Agency (JTA) interviewed the influential Rabbi Irving "Yitz" Greenberg to help launch *The Triumph of Life: A Narrative Theology of Judaism*, the long-awaited capstone of Greenberg's distinguished career. Alluding to the biblical imagery in Isaiah 42:6, Greenberg told Silow-Carroll, "I believe Israel has been a light unto the nations." But he qualified that judgment by adding, "at the moment its reputation is not showing much light."[6] Greenberg had the Israel-Hamas war at the forefront of his mind. He finished *The Triumph of Life* as the war laid waste to Palestinian life in Gaza. Nevertheless, Greenberg describes the Israel Defense Forces (IDF) as "the most moral army in the world."[7]

Fifty years earlier, Greenberg stated a "working principle": "No statement, theological or otherwise, should be made that would not be credible in the presence of the burning children."[8] Nothing Greenberg has written is more forceful, telling, and demanding than that. If moral grading of armies makes sense, which is dubious, Greenberg's principle unmasks the dangerous hollowness of his IDF assessment. Fortunately, *The Triumph of Life* contains more accurate judgments and far better hopes. Rightly acknowledging that the Israeli counterattack after 10/7 has "devastated much of Gaza," Greenberg predicted that "Israel will persist and end Hamas's power." Israel, moreover, will "change leadership, and strive to create a more ethical, inclusive society." Greenberg added, "I even believe in a long-term process in which militant Palestinians turn from undermining the Jewish state toward more democratic, societally constructive, autonomous self-rule." If that path is taken, he believes, Israeli trust of Palestinians can grow, and a door can open for "a Palestinian state that could live in peace with Israel."[9]

Three of Greenberg's predictions are credible, at least mostly. Israel will survive the war, but with a badly tarnished international reputation. Hamas's power will be curbed but likely not ended, because Hamas is an ideology, not merely a political party, and the Israel-Hamas war will have radicalized Palestinians in ways that do not encourage reconciliation with Israel. Leadership will change in Israel. Netanyahu may face judicial proceedings that could lead to imprisonment. But it is less certain—though not impossible—that Israel's determination to be a Jewish state will "create a more ethical, inclusive society." As for the rest—hopes for new trust between Palestinians and Israelis and a two-state solution—little supportive evidence exists. It will be a long time, if ever, until anything approximating a triumph of life will emerge from the Israel-Hamas war.

4. On August 23, the day after the Democratic Convention concluded, Richard Haass, who was president of the Council on Foreign Relations from 2003 to 2023, made a short statement about the Israel-Hamas war in "Unconventional," the day's entry for *Home and Away*, his Substack commentary. His words implicitly questioned Greenberg's optimism. "The United States," said Haass, "continues to raise expectations for a ceasefire in Gaza that neither Israel nor Hamas seem to want. The war will likely go on (albeit at a lower level of intensity) for months or even years. No plan for governing Gaza or building an alternative to Hamas is evident. . . . Meanwhile, what is heating up is violence between Israel and Hezbollah in the north and between settlers (and on occasion the IDF) and Palestinians in the West Bank."[10]

Haass's bleak scenario seems far more likely than hopeful, Israel-as-light-to-the-nations forecasts about the triumph of life. A ceasefire may take place. Hamas hostages, the few who remain alive and the remains of those who are not, may be recovered. But the Israel-Hamas war—and oppressive conditions for Palestinians in the West Bank—are, at least for the foreseeable future, synonymous with failure, loss, and misery.

5. On August 31, the Israeli military announced that the bodies of six hostages taken in the 10/7 attack had been recovered from a Hamas tunnel under the city of Rafah in the Gaza Strip. An Israeli autopsy revealed that all six had been shot in the head. The murdered dead included Ori Danino, age twenty-five, Alex Lobanov, age thirty-three, Almog Sarusi, age twenty-seven, Carmel Gat, age forty, Eden Yerushalmi, age twenty-four, and Hersh Goldberg-Polin, age twenty-three, a California-born Israeli-American, whose parents, Rachel Goldberg and Jon Polin, pleaded for his life at the Democratic National Convention in Chicago on August 21.

The Israel-Hamas war is, in essence, two wars in one, fought both above and below ground. The Hamas tunnel network not only prolongs the war but blurs accountability for its devastation. In its efforts to neutralize Hamas—which requires dismantling its extensive tunnel network—the Israeli military is often blamed for the deaths of defenseless Palestinians. But the leaders of Hamas have masterminded the snaking tunnels beneath the Gaza Strip. They know that their strategies have made innocent Palestinians pawns of war—human shields—in a ruthless struggle to suppress Israeli control of Gaza.

Who should be held accountable in and for the Israel-Hamas war? Necessary and unavoidable, that question reaches far and wide, probing the state of Christian-Jewish relations. Responses to it will show how much pressure, tension, wear-and-tear they can withstand and how resilient and constructive Christian-Jewish relations can be in unsettling and unsettled circumstances fraught with difficulties that will not soon be resolved.

Stress Test enlisted American Christian writers to speak courageously about Christian-Jewish relations in 2024 and beyond. The aim was to probe beyond polite diplomacy to confront the carnage unleashed by the Hamas attack on October 7, 2023, and to assess the State of Israel's devastating response. That demanding work also requires Christians to

Epilogue

respond to the anger, frustration, and grief gripping people—especially youth and young adults—as they confront the violence, including rape, hostage-taking, starvation and, arguably, ethnic cleansing, which fuels more driven upheaval. The health and future of Christian-Jewish relations depend, in significant ways, on how well American Christians meet these challenges, on how well they follow this book's governing epigraph, Saint Paul's admonition in Ephesians 4:25: "Putting away falsehood, let all of us speak the truth to our neighbors, for we are members of one another." Using this Epilogue's five-part August 2024 framework, how well does this book withstand scrutiny? What are its strengths and weaknesses? Where does it succeed or fall short? Here are five clusters containing points on both sides of the ledger.

- Like Kamala Harris, Christian-Jewish relations must thread the needle of fairness. The 10/7 Hamas attack has done lasting harm to Israel. The Israeli response has done the same to Palestinians. Christians need to acknowledge the suffering and loss; they should try to advance healing and rebuilding, peace and justice. *Stress Test* emphasizes these points and supports those causes.

- When the journalists Vivian Yee and Bilal Shbair wrote about Palestinian orphans—"so many orphans in such chaos"—they insisted, at least by implication, that American Christians need to focus on the agonizing particularities of the Israel-Hamas war. Unless that demanding work is done, dialogue about healing and rebuilding, peace and justice, will remain general and abstract. As *Stress Test* tries to avoid that shortcoming, the reminder remains: Never lose sight of the suffering, dying, and bereaved people—especially children—caught in the Israel-Hamas war and its aftermath.

- Irving Greenberg thinks that Israel will change leadership and find its way to be "a more ethical, inclusive society." *Stress Test* strongly affirms that Benjamin Netanyahu and his right-wing followers are responsible for much of the devastation of the Israel-Hamas war. American Christians need to support Jews who seek different and better leadership for Israel. The book does not detail how to best support that coalition, but this concern should be high on the Christian-Jewish agenda.

- The curmudgeonly Richard Haass likely thinks that Christian-Jewish relations have little to contribute to a hopeful resolution of the Israel-Hamas war. *Stress Test* suggests that he may be right. None of the book's contributors are experts in international relations. Its authors are scholars who hold no diplomatic credentials or powers. In addition, they know that the influence of Christianity and Judaism in the United States is declining.[11] But also, they understand that, while good Christian-Jewish relations have limited power to effect global change, constructive opportunities do exist. *Stress Test* identifies some of the most important.

Christian-Jewish dialogue can bring diverse people together, especially in local communities. It can strengthen both traditions by sharing and multiplying their ethical commitments, including protest and resistance against antisemitism. Christian-Jewish coalitions, moreover, can be enhanced if their work includes Muslims, excludes anti-Palestinianism, and insists on a two-state solution to the Israeli-Palestinian conflict. Christian-Jewish relations will also be strengthened by rethinking how the Holocaust should—and should not—be pivotal within them. The Holocaust recedes into the past but must not be forgotten. As generational changes take place in an increasingly globalized world, that catastrophe is not top of mind for all, but it deserves a place in everyone's moral education about the differences between right and wrong, justice and injustice. That role entails diligence in Christian-Jewish relations to avoid instrumentalizing the Holocaust to legitimate war that destroys defenseless civilians. If memory of the Holocaust does not stir concern for the vulnerable, it fails. Making a start in responding to such concerns, *Stress Test* suggests how much more work must be done.

- The contributors to *Stress Test* disagree about how best to respond to the question of who is and should be held accountable in and for the Israel-Hamas war. Far from being a weakness, this diversity highlights the complexity of assigning and assessing accountability. Yes, Benjamin Netanyahu and his nationalist compatriots must be held accountable. Yes, Hamas leaders must be held accountable. American decision-makers are also culpable. The list goes on and on. Participants in the work of Christian-Jewish relations need to evaluate our accountability as well. Even if we cannot decisively control events, we must ask: What should we keep doing? What should we stop doing? What should we start doing? And regarding those three queries, are we doing the best we can? *Stress Test* does not fully answer those questions. That is true in part because the accountability concerns the future as well as the present and the past.

One more event, this taking place in the summer of 2024, deserves notice. On August 20, Cardinal Pierbattista Pizzaballa, patriarch of Jerusalem, spoke in Rimini, Italy. "In crisis" were the words he used to describe dialogue between religious communities in the Holy Land.[12] "Right now," he emphasized, "Christians, Jews, and Muslims cannot meet with one another, at least not publicly. Even at the institutional level it is a struggle to talk to one another."

Eventually, the Israel-Hamas war will end, Pizzaballa affirmed, emphasizing that "to rebuild the trust from these attitudes of distrust, of hate, of deep disdain will be an enormous effort." Efforts to do that work, he underscored, must center not on "elites" but on local, grassroots communities. Pizzaballa urges them to focus less on narratives about themselves and more on lifting "their gaze to see and recognize the other."

The contributors to *Stress Test* stand in solidarity with Cardinal Pizzaballa, their fellow Christian. They know they have not completed the necessary work and they also know they cannot desist from it. So they carry on, encouraging Christian, Jewish, and Muslim friends to join an enormous effort to create hope where little can be found and to make good, in spite of the odds against it, the promise in Psalm 30:5: "Weeping may linger for the night, but joy comes with the morning."

Notes

1. On these points, see, Adam Goldman et al., "'Moving in the Dark': Hamas Documents Show Tunnel Battle Strategy," *New York Times*, September 3, 2024, https://bit.ly/4aA3XUR. See also Adam Goldman et al., "Israel Unearths More of a Subterranean Fortress Under Gaza," *New York Times*, January 16, 2024, https://bit.ly/3E8aha1.

2. For the full text of Harris's speech, see "Full Transcript of Kamala Harris's Democratic Convention Speech," *New York Times*, August 23, 2024, https://bit.ly/3E9bga6.

3. See Vivian Yee and Bilal Shbair, "The War in Gaza Is Making Thousands of Orphans," *New York Times*, August 22, 2024, https://bit.ly/3PNHCKb.

4. The report is accessible at https://bit.ly/40JxhoJ.

5. On these points see, United Nations Office of the High Commissioner for Human Rights, "UN Experts Deeply Concerned Over 'Scholasticide' in Gaza," April 18, 2024, https://bit.ly/3WX3sir.

6. See Andrew Silow-Carroll, "At 91, Rabbi Yitz Greenberg Writes the 'Big Book' His Admirers Had Been Waiting For," Jewish Telegraphic Agency, August 11, 2024, https://bit.ly/3CdWT3P.

7. Irving Greenberg, *The Triumph of Life: A Narrative Theology of Judaism* (Philadelphia: Jewish Publication Society; Lincoln: University of Nebraska Press, 2024), 273.

8. Irving Greenberg, "Cloud of Smoke, Pillar of Fire: Judaism, Christianity, and Modernity after the Holocaust," in *Auschwitz: Beginning of a New Era; Reflections on the Holocaust*, ed. Eva Fleischner (New York: Ktav, 1977), 23.

9. Greenberg, *Triumph of Life*, 285.

10. Richard Haass, "Unconventional (August 223, 2024)," *Home and Away*, Substack, https://bit.ly/42rUxZG.

11. On this point, see Public Policy Research Institute (PPRI), "Religious Change in America," March 27, 2024, https://bit.ly/42nMqxk.

12. See Justin McLellan, "Jerusalem Cardinal: Interreligious Dialogue Currently in 'Crisis,'" National Catholic Reporter, August 22, 2024, https://bit.ly/3PStZt8.

Selected Bibliography

Amnesty International. *'You Feel Like You Are Subhuman': Israel's Genocide Against Palestinians in Gaza.* December 5, 2024. https://bit.ly/4OT3RER.

Ateek, Naim Stifan. *Call and Commitment: A Journey of Faith from Nakba to Palestinian Liberation Theology.* Eugene, OR: Cascade, 2023.

Ateek, Naim Stifan. *A Palestinian Theology of Liberation: The Bible, Justice, and the Palestine Israel Conflict.* Maryknoll: Orbis, 2017.

Baconi, Tareq. *Hamas Contained: The Rise and Pacification of Palestinian Resistance.* Stanford, CA: Stanford University Press, 2018.

Bashir, Bashir, and Amos Goldberg, eds. *The Holocaust and the Nakba: A New Grammar of Trauma and History.* New York: Columbia University Press, 2019.

Beinart, Peter. *Being Jewish After the Destruction of Gaza: A Reckoning.* New York: Knopf, 2025.

Brueggemann, Walter. *Chosen? Reading the Bible Amid the Israeli-Palestinian Conflict.* Louisville, KY: Westminster John Knox, 2015.

Carenen, Caitlin. *The Fervent Embrace: Liberal Protestants, Evangelicals, and Israel.* New York: New York University Press, 2012.

Carter, Jimmy. *Palestine: Peace Not Apartheid.* New York: Simon & Schuster, 2007.

Cohn-Sherbok, Dan. *The Politics of Apocalypse: The History and Influence of Christian Zionism.* Oxford: Oneworld, 2006.

Cook, Steven A. *The End of Ambition: America's Past, Present, and Future in the Middle East.* Oxford: Oxford University Press, 2024.

Cunningham, Philip A., Ruth Langer, and Jesper Svartvik, eds. *Enabling Dialogue about the Land: A Resource Book for Jews and Christians.* New York: Paulist, 2020.

Selected Bibliography

Elgindy, Khaled. *Blind Spot: Americans and the Palestinians, From Balfour to Trump*. Washington, DC: Brookings Institution, 2019.

Ellis, Marc H. *Burning Children: A Jewish View of the War in Gaza*. Eugene, OR: Wipf and Stock, 2017.

Ephron, Dan. *Killing a King: The Assassination of Yitzhak Rabin and the Remaking of Israel*. New York: W. W. Norton, 2016.

Evans, Jimmy, and Mark Hitchcock. *What's Next? Israel-Gaza War: Connecting Today's Headlines to Tomorrow's Prophetic Events*. Austin, TX: Tipping Point Press, 2023.

Frantzman, Seth J. *The October 7 War: Israel's Battle for Security in Gaza*. New York: Post Hill, 2024.

Fredericks, James L., and Tracy Sayuki Tiemeier, eds. *Interreligious Friendship After "Nostra Aetate."* New York: Palgrave Macmillan, 2015.

Glassman, Bernie. *Bearing Witness: A Zen Master's Lessons in Making Peace*. New York: Random House, 1998.

Glover, Jonathan. *Israelis and Palestinians: From the Cycle of Violence to the Conversation of Mankind*. Cambridge, UK: Polity, 2024.

Grob, Leonard, and John K. Roth, eds. *Anguished Hope: Holocaust Scholars Confront the Palestinian-Israeli Conflict*. Grand Rapids, MI: William B. Eerdmans, 2008.

Grob, Leonard, and John K. Roth, eds. *Encountering the Stranger: A Jewish-Christian-Muslim Trialogue*. Seattle: University of Washington Press, 2012.

Gushee, David P. *The Moral Teachings of Jesus: Radical Instruction in the Will of God*. Eugene, OR: Cascade, 2024.

Halevi, Yossi Klein. *Letters to My Palestinian Neighbor*. New York: HarperCollins, 2018.

Haynes, Stephen R. *Reluctant Witnesses: Jews and the Christian Imagination*. Louisville: Westminster John Knox, 1995.

Held, Shai. *Judaism Is About Love: Recovering the Heart of Jewish Life*. New York: Farrar, Straus and Giroux, 2024.

Kessler, Edward, and Neil Wenborn, eds. *A Documentary History of Jewish-Christian Relations: From Antiquity to the Present Day*. Cambridge: Cambridge University Press, 2024.

Khalidi, Rashid. *The Hundred Years' War on Palestine: A History of Settler Colonialism and Resistance, 1917-2017*. New York: Henry Holt, 2020.

Khoury, Rafiq, and Rainer Zimmer-Winkel, eds. *Christian Theology in the Palestinian Context*. Berlin: AphorismA, 2019.

Kildani, Hanna. *Modern Christianity in the Holy Land*. Translated by George Musleh. Bloomington, IN: AuthorHouse, 2010.

Kirsch, Adam. *On Settler Colonialism: Ideology, Violence, and Justice*. New York: W. W. Norton, 2024.

Klar-Chalamish, Carmit, and Noga Berger. *Silent Cry: Sexual Violence Crimes on October 7*. Tel Aviv-Yaffo, Israel: The Association of Rape Crisis Centers in Israel, February 2024.

Krondorfer, Björn. *Unsettling Empathy: Working with Groups in Conflict*. New York: Rowman & Littlefield International, 2020.

Kronish, Ron. *Profiles in Peace: Voices of Peacebuilders in the Midst of the Israeli-Palestinian Conflict*. L.E.A.R.H.N. Peacemaking Publications, 2022.

Leighton, Christopher M. *A Sacred Argument: Dispatches from the Christian, Jewish, and Muslim Encounter*. Eugene, OR: Wipf and Stock, 2024.

Magid, Shaul. *The Necessity of Exile: Essays from a Distance*. Brooklyn: Ayin Press, 2023.

Manekin, Mikhael. *End of Days: Ethics, Tradition, and Power in Israel*. Brookline: Academic Studies, 2023.

McCann, Colum. *Apeirogon*. New York: Random House, 2021.

McCarthy, Eli. *A Just Peace Ethic Primer: Building Sustainable Peace and Breaking Cycles of Violence*. Washington, DC: Georgetown University Press, 2020.

Mead, Walter Russell. *The Arc of a Covenant: The United States, Israel, and the Fate of the Jewish People*. New York: Knopf, 2022.

Mishra, Pankaj. *The World After Gaza: A History*. New York: Penguin, 2025.

Morris, Benny. *Righteous Victims: A History of the Zionist-Arab Conflict, 1881-1998*. New York: Vintage, 2001.

Pappe, Ilan. *The Ethnic Cleansing of Palestine*. Oxford: Oneworld, 2006.

Ramon, Amnon. *Christians and Christianity in the Jewish State: Israeli Policy toward the Churches and Christian Communities (1948–2018)*. Translated by Shaul Vardi. Jerusalem: Jerusalem Institute for Policy Research and the Rossing Center for Education and Dialogue, 2021.

Roy, Sara. *Unsilencing Gaza: Reflections on Resistance*. London: Pluto, 2021.

Said, Edward W. *Orientalism*. New York: Penguin, 2019 (First edition 1978).

Saif, Atef Abu. *Don't Look Left: A Diary of Genocide*. Boston: Beacon, 2024.

Shreiber, Maeera Y. *Holy Envy: Writing in the Jewish Christian Borderzone*. New York: Fordham University Press, 2022.

Shipler, David K. *Arab and Jew: Wounded Spirits in a Promised Land*. New York: Penguin, 2002.

Shitrit, Lihi Ben. *The Gates of Gaza: Critical Voices from Israel on October 7 and the War with Hamas*. Berlin: De Gruyter, 2024.

Shitrit, Lihi Ben. *Righteous Transgressions: Women's Activism on the Israeli and Palestinian Religious Right*. Princeton: Princeton University Press, 2015.

Smith, Robert O. *More Desired than Our Owne Salvation: The Roots of Christian Zionism*. Oxford: Oxford University Press, 2013.

Stanislawski, Michael. *Zionism: A Very Short Introduction*. New York: Oxford University Press, 2017.

Stern-Weiner, Jamie, ed. *Deluge: Gaza and Israel from Crisis to Cataclysm*. New York: OR Books, 2024.

Tapie, Matthew, Alan Brill, and Matthew Levering, eds. *The Challenge of Catholic-Jewish Theological Dialogue*. Washington, DC: Catholic University of America Press, 2024.

Troen, S. Ilan. *Israel/Palestine in World Religions: Whose Promised Land?* New York: Palgrave Macmillan, 2024.

Waxman, Dov. *The Israeli-Palestinian Conflict: What Everyone Needs to Know*. Oxford: Oxford University Press, 2019.

Yaron, Lee. *10/7: 100 Human Stories*. New York: St. Martin's, 2024.

Websites

Aljazeera, https://www.aljazeera.com/tag/israel-palestine-conflict/.

American Jewish Committee, https://www.ajc.org/IsraelHamasWarResources.

Carnegie Endowment for International Peace, https://carnegieendowment.org/?lang=en.

The Council on American-Islamic Relations (CAIR), https://www.cair.com/.

Council of Centers on Jewish-Christian Relations (CCJR), https://ccjr.us/dialogika-resources/themes-in-today-s-dialogue/israel-hamas.

Council on Foreign Relations (CFR Education), https://education.cfr.org/resources-Israel-Hamas-war.

International Crisis Group, https://www.crisisgroup.org/.

Middle East Institute, https://www.mei.edu/.

RAND, https://www.rand.org/latest/israel-hamas-war.html.

The Washington Institute for Near East Policy, https://www.washingtoninstitute.org/.

Editors and Contributors

Editors

Carol Rittner is a Distinguished Professor of Holocaust and Genocide Studies Emerita and the Dr. Marsha Raticoff Grossman Professor of Holocaust Studies Emerita at Stockton University. A frequent visitor to Israel, Rittner has published extensively about the Holocaust, genocide, and Christian-Jewish relations. Her books include *The Holocaust and the Christian World*; *Holocaust Education Today: Confronting Extremism, Hate, and Mass Atrocity Crimes*; and *Pluralizing Dialogue: Insights, Actions, and Implications in Eva Fleischner's "Judaism in German Christian Theology Since 1945."*

John K. Roth is the Edward J. Sexton Professor of Philosophy Emeritus at Claremont McKenna College, where he taught for more than forty years and was the founding director of the Center for the Study of the Holocaust, Genocide, and Human Rights (now the Mgrublian Center for Human Rights). Formerly a visiting professor at the University of Haifa, Israel, he has published hundreds of articles and reviews and authored or edited more than fifty books, including *The Failures of Ethics*; *Sources of Holocaust Insight*; and *Warnings: The Holocaust, Ukraine, and Endangered American Democracy* (with Leonard Grob).

Contributors

Michael G. Azar is Professor of Theology and Religious Studies at the University of Scranton. He is the author of *Exegeting the Jews: The Early Reception of the Johannine "Jews"* as well as articles about Christian responses to the Holocaust and the implications of those responses for the Middle East and the Palestinian people. With expertise on Eastern Christian-Jewish interaction, Azar is a special advisor to the Orthodox Chair of the Orthodox Christian-Jewish dialogue and a member of its planning committee.

Mary C. Boys is the Skinner and McAlpin Professor of Practical Theology at Union Theological Seminary. Her distinguished work in advancing Christian-Jewish relations has been recognized by numerous awards and honorary degrees. Her many books include *Jewish-Christian Dialogue: One Woman's Experience*; *Has God Only One Blessing? Judaism as a Source of Christian Self-Understanding*; *Christians and Jews in Dialogue: Learning in the Presence of the Other* (with Sara S. Lee); and *Redeeming our Sacred Story: The Death of Jesus and Relations between Jews and Christians*.

Philip A. Cunningham is Professor of Theology and Co-Director of the Institute for Jewish-Catholic Relations at Saint Joseph's University. A former president of the International Council of Christians and Jews, he concentrates on biblical studies, religious education, and theologies of Christian-Jewish relations. His books in that field include *Maxims for Mutuality: Principles for Catholic Theology, Education, and Preaching about Jews and Judaism*; *Seeking Shalom: The Journey to Right Relationship between Catholics and Jews*; and *Enabling Dialogue about the Land: A Resource Book for Jews and Christians*.

Massimo Faggioli is Professor of Historical Theology at Villanova University. A columnist for *Commonweal* and *La Croix International*, his journalism includes commentary on the Israel-Hamas war. His recent books are *The Oxford Handbook of Vatican II* and *Global Catholicism: Between Disruption and Encounter*. In addition to serving on the editorial committee of the journal *Concilium*, Faggioli is a member of the steering committee for *Vatican II: Event and Mandate*, a multi-volume, intercontinental commentary about the pivotal Second Vatican Council.

Christopher M. Leighton is the founding director of the Institute for Islamic, Christian, and Jewish Studies in Baltimore, Maryland, where he worked for thirty-three years. A Presbyterian minister who has lived in Israel, he has also served as an adjunct professor at St. Mary's Seminary and University and Johns Hopkins University. His publications include *Talking About Genesis*, the study guide for television journalist Bill Moyers' *Genesis* series and, most recently, *A Sacred Argument: Dispatches from the Christian, Jewish, and Muslim Encounter*.

James G. Paharik is the Director of the National Catholic Center for Holocaust Education at Seton Hill University, where he is also a Professor of Sociology. His areas of research and teaching include Holocaust and genocide studies, as well as the conflict in Israel/Palestine, which is the topic of his book *The Long Journey: In Search of Justice and Peace in*

Jerusalem. His most recent publications include *The Door That Opened and Never Closed: Essays in Honor of Eva Fleischner.*

John T. Pawlikowski is Professor Emeritus of Social Ethics at the Catholic Theological Union (CTU) in Chicago. For decades, he engaged in the direction of CTU's Catholic-Jewish Studies program. In addition to serving as president of the International Council of Christians and Jews and on the board of the United States Holocaust Memorial Museum, Pawlikowski has published many articles and books on Christian-Jewish relations, including *Christ in the Light of the Christian-Jewish Dialogue*; *Jesus and the Theology of Israel*; and *Restating the Catholic Church's Relationship with the Jewish People.*

Peter A. Pettit, the teaching pastor at St. Paul Lutheran Church in Davenport, Iowa, is a former Research Fellow at the Shalom Hartman Institute in Jerusalem, where he was a co-director of the Institute's Theology Conference since its inception in 1984 and co-director of the New Paths: Christians Engaging Israel project. The author of many articles on Christian-Jewish relations, he has held research fellowships at the Hebrew University, American Jewish University, and the Oxford Centre for Hebrew and Jewish Studies.

Sarah K. Pinnock is Professor of Contemporary Religious Thought at Trinity University (Texas), where she has also chaired the religion department. Her research focuses on the problem of evil, the Holocaust and genocide, and death and dying. Her books include *Beyond Theodicy: Jewish and Christian Continental Thinkers Respond to the Holocaust*; *The Theology of Dorothee Soelle*; and *Facing Death: Confronting Mortality in the Holocaust and Ourselves*. In addition to travel in Israel, she has often participated in interfaith journeys to Auschwitz-Birkenau with the Zen Peacemakers.

Elena Procario-Foley is the Brother John G. Driscoll Professor of Jewish-Catholic Studies, Professor of Religious Studies, and Director of the Core Curriculum at Iona University, where she has taught for more than twenty-five years. A former chair of the Council of Centers on Jewish-Christian Relations (CCJR), she also chairs the board of the Manhattan College Holocaust, Genocide, and Interfaith Center. The editor of *Horizons: The Journal of the College Theology Society*, Procario-Foley has also published *Frontiers in Catholic Feminist Theology* and *Righting Relations After the Holocaust and Vatican II: Essays in Honor of John T. Pawlikowski.*

Index

A

Abbas, Mahmoud, 22, 27, 28, 33, 56
academic freedom, 123, 125
Afghanistan, 135, 212
Al Qaeda, 135
Andrés, José, 166
anti-Judaism, 60, 93, 106, 137, 154, 183
anti-Palestinianism, 115, 174, 183, 185, 186, 187, 249
antisemitism, 35, 183, 233
Antisemitism, 35, 183, 233
anti-Zionist, 58, 62, 137, 199, 238
apartheid, 29, 105, 122, 126
Arabs, 17, 76, 153, 184, 187, 198, 210, 228
Arafat, Yasser, 17, 20, 21, 22, 23, 24, 25, 26, 199
Attar, Samer, 229

B

Begin, Menachem, 19
Beirut, 20, 40, 43, 44, 45, 181, 233
Ben-Gurion, David, 15, 16
Ben-Gvir, Itamar, 37, 109
Bethlehem, 16, 17, 25, 27, 139, 151, 178, 227
Bible, 77, 91, 92, 103, 104, 216, 217, 226, 232
border crossers, 147, 153
Borowitz, Eugene, 73
Brach, Tara, 220
Braiterman, Zachary, 214
British Mandate (1920-48), 184, 216
Brueggemann, Walter, 106
Buddhism, 219

C

Camp David, 19, 24, 63, 199
Canada, 209
Catholic Church, 20, 23, 28, 60, 62, 63, 72, 73, 74, 75, 86, 88, 89, 90, 91, 92, 93, 117, 133, 134, 135, 136, 137, 140, 141, 219
Catholic education, 141, 142
Catholicism, 73, 74, 133, 134, 135, 136, 137, 140
Catholic-Jewish dialogue, 63, 139, 141
Catholic-Jewish relations, 73, 134, 135, 141, 146
ceasefire, 15, 18, 31, 32, 33, 34, 35, 37, 38, 41, 42, 43, 48, 49, 50, 80, 117, 120, 121, 126, 138, 146, 169, 177, 182, 185, 186, 217, 229, 230, 234, 244, 246, 247
Christian Zionism, 199, 209, 216, 217, 221
Christianity, 17, 60, 69, 70, 71, 72, 74, 75, 86, 129, 133, 134, 136, 178, 197, 216, 225, 249

Index

Christian-Jewish dialogue, 62, 63, 64, 69, 73, 78, 80, 116, 215, 249
Christians United for Israel (CUFI), 216
Christmas, 19, 49, 139, 178
civilians, 25, 27, 31, 32, 35, 39, 40, 41, 44, 46, 56, 62, 86, 88, 104, 138, 140, 156, 167, 169, 173, 180, 182, 199, 209, 210, 213, 230, 233, 236, 249
Cohen, Roger, 127
colonialism, 81, 122, 123, 127, 197, 198, 227, 228
Columbia University, 115, 116, 121, 128
Council of Centers on Jewish-Christian Relations (CCJR), 50
covenant, 80, 90, 92, 196, 214
crimes against humanity, 36, 38, 47, 58, 61, 62, 181, 214, 227, 235, 236
Cunningham, Philip A., 52, 85

D

Declaration on the Relation of the Church to Non-Christian Religions, 17
deicide, 106, 139
democracy, 92, 102, 173, 228, 229
Deuteronomy, Book of, 103, 109
dialogue, 18, 31, 50, 51, 52, 55, 59, 60, 62, 63, 64, 69, 70, 77, 78, 79, 80, 81, 85, 93, 107, 117, 133, 135, 139, 140, 145, 146, 147, 148, 153, 154, 155, 156, 157, 161, 162, 164, 165, 166, 167, 168, 169, 170, 175, 179, 182, 195, 200, 201, 204, 210, 218, 219, 248, 250
diaspora, 72, 76, 78, 80, 86, 110, 194
disinformation, 85, 86, 140
divestment, 105, 123
Douthat, Ross, 133

E

East Jerusalem, 17, 24, 28, 29, 39, 178, 179, 202
Easter, 186
Eckardt, A. Roy, 185
Egypt, 17, 18, 19, 22, 23, 55, 102, 184
empathy, 116, 122, 162, 163, 165, 167, 174, 196, 220, 221
Episcopal Church, 199
ethnic cleansing, also see genocide, 48, 105, 126, 237, 248
Europe, 15, 125, 127, 128, 134, 135, 136, 138, 183, 184, 185, 201, 211, 228
Eusebius, 71
Evangelical Lutheran Church in America (ELCA), 174, 193, 199, 200, 201, 202, 203, 204
Evangelical Lutheran Church in Jordan and the Holy Land (ELCJHL), 199, 200, 201, 202, 203, 204

F

famine, 33, 59, 119, 177, 195, 230, 237
Fatah, 26, 39
Final Solution, 15, 125
Friedman, Thomas, 120

G

Gallant, Yoav, 31, 36, 43, 47
Gantz, Benny, 38
Gay, Claudine, 115
Gaza City, 31, 39, 40, 41, 115, 185
Gaza Strip, 17, 22, 23, 25, 26, 27, 29, 34, 36, 39, 42, 44, 46, 48, 177, 179, 185, 225, 227, 229, 230, 243, 247
Gaza-Jericho Agreement, 22, 23
Gazans, 33, 36, 121, 122, 166, 177
Genesis, 58, 91, 103

Genesis, Book of, 58, 91, 103
genocide, 32, 36, 37, 46, 47, 48, 49, 61, 62, 69, 101, 105, 106, 123, 125, 126, 127, 128, 135, 163, 164, 212, 214, 219, 225, 227, 228, 235, 237, 248
Gessen, Masha, 121, 138
Glassman, Bernie, 210, 219
Global South, 77, 88, 136
globalization, 77, 140, 141
Globalization, 140
Golan Heights, 17, 18, 23, 29, 40, 48, 107
Goldberg, Michael, 101
Greenberg, Irving, 214, 215, 248
Greene, Joshua M., 211
Gregerman, Adam, 50, 90, 91
Grüber, Heinrich, 215
Gutman, Roy, 56

H

Hagari, Daniel, 120
Hagee, John, 216
Haifa, 45, 231, 232
Halev, Michal, 167
Haniyeh, Ismail, 36, 40, 41
Harris, Kamala, 39, 173, 244, 248
Harvard University, 115
Herzl, Theodor, 71, 89, 236
Herzog, Isaac, 33, 59, 212
Hezbollah, 20, 26, 30, 31, 38, 40, 41, 43, 44, 45, 47, 48, 60, 61, 85, 103, 120, 181, 237, 243, 246
Holocaust, 23, 24, 30, 51, 55, 56, 60, 61, 69, 76, 100, 101, 102, 116, 125, 127, 128, 133, 134, 135, 136, 137, 140, 141, 161, 162, 163, 168, 187, 195, 197, 203, 209, 210, 211, 212, 213, 214, 215, 217, 218, 219, 220, 221, 225, 226, 227, 229, 231, 232, 233, 237, 238,249
Holocaust Remembrance Day, 211, 212

Holy Family Catholic Church, 166, 178, 185
Holy Land, 16, 17, 24, 25, 27, 52, 70, 71, 76, 99, 102, 108, 110, 169, 178, 179, 183, 184, 185, 186, 187, 200, 203, 216, 217, 250
Holy See, 16, 22, 24, 27, 28, 32, 63, 71, 72, 92, 135, 137, 138, 140
hostages, 30, 32, 33, 34, 35, 37, 38, 41, 42, 47, 48, 57, 87, 108, 120, 123, 126, 138, 146, 169, 180, 194, 217, 231, 244, 245, 247
human rights, 69, 104, 164, 168, 228
Human Rights Watch, 29, 49, 59
humanitarian crisis, 31, 108, 138, 229, 237

I

Iftar, 151, 156
International Council of Christians and Jews (ICCJ), 77
International Court of Justice (ICJ), 32, 37, 39, 61, 62, 237
Iona University, 117, 145
Iran, 20, 30, 34, 35, 38, 39, 40, 41, 44, 45, 46, 56, 60, 61, 85, 93, 121, 212, 217, 243
Iraq, 127, 135, 212
Ireland, 37
Irenaeus, 70
irony, 128, 231, 234
Islam, 25, 135, 137, 141, 151
Israel Defense Forces (IDF), 16, 20, 26, 31, 36, 39, 40, 41, 43, 44, 45, 46, 48, 49, 51, 55, 57, 58, 59, 60, 62, 76, 116, 166, 194, 212, 229, 243, 245, 246
Israel, land of, 28, 52, 72, 74, 75, 88, 90, 91, 103, 104, 108, 127, 217
Israel, people of, 90, 216, 217, 244

Index

Israel, State of, 15, 16, 17, 20, 22, 26, 28, 29, 35, 36, 50, 51, 55, 63, 71, 72, 73, 75, 76, 77, 80, 81, 86, 88, 89, 90, 91, 92, 100, 102, 105, 117, 120, 123, 125, 126, 127, 130, 133, 135, 136, 137, 139, 140, 141, 177, 180, 182, 184, 185, 187, 193, 194, 196, 197, 199, 212, 213, 216, 217, 227, 228, 229, 231, 232, 235, 236, 243, 247

Israeli-Palestinian conflict, 15, 24, 33, 43, 50, 51, 52, 55, 56, 78, 80, 92, 127, 142, 146, 163, 164, 165, 167, 193, 200, 226, 233, 237, 243, 249

J

Jenin, 30

Jerusalem, 16, 19, 21, 24, 28, 34, 40, 64, 70, 71, 72, 73, 74, 75, 80, 88, 100, 107, 120, 130, 138, 168, 179, 182, 185, 203, 210, 215, 217, 218, 219, 232, 250

Jesus Christ, 25, 70, 71, 74, 80, 88, 90, 91, 129, 153, 182, 185, 186, 196, 200, 203, 216, 217, 226

Jewish settlements, 20, 23, 30, 105, 141, 218, 236

Jewish students, 106, 115, 128, 145, 148, 149, 150, 153

Jewish Students, 106, 115, 128, 145, 148, 149, 150, 153

Jews, European, 101, 116, 128, 183, 214, 227

Jordan, 17, 21, 23, 55, 73, 102, 120, 139, 184, 200, 236

Judaism, 17, 18, 20, 58, 63, 71, 72, 73, 74, 75, 78, 79, 80, 86, 90, 93, 106, 125, 129, 133, 135, 136, 137, 141, 216, 234, 245, 249

just war theory, 51, 69, 75, 76, 79, 87

Justin Martyr, 70

K

Khalidi, Rashid, 228
Khan Younis, 32, 38, 41
Kofman, Sarah, 238
Kristof, Nicholas, 166
Krondorfer, Björn, 220
Küng, Hans, 64

L

land promises (biblical), 52, 71, 77, 92, 196, 197
League of Nations, 15, 197
Lebanon, 20, 26, 40, 41, 43, 44, 45, 47, 55, 100, 102, 120, 138, 139, 181, 232, 233, 243
Leibniz, Gottfried Wilhelm, 214
Levinas, Emmanuel, 214
Leviticus, 91
Leviticus, Book of, 91, 104

M

Magid, Shaul, 213
Maier, Charles, 134
Marr, Wilhelm, 128
Masson, Robert, 152
Melchior, Michael, 64
Middle East, 18, 21, 23, 29, 40, 55, 77, 78, 80, 85, 92, 93, 99, 105, 109, 119, 120, 127, 130, 149, 157, 174, 178, 196, 201, 203, 233, 234, 237, 243
Midrash, 110
Mishra, Pankaj, 133, 137
misinformation, 140, 162
Morocco, 29, 162
Mubarak, Hosni, 19
Muslim Students, 149, 150, 151
Muslims, 65, 73, 79, 92, 93, 99, 100, 101, 110, 111, 146, 149, 150, 151, 154, 157, 161, 162, 164, 165, 196, 198, 209, 231, 249, 250

N

Nakba, 16, 36, 127, 163, 177, 184, 187, 227
Nazi Germany, 15, 47, 101, 116, 183, 184, 213, 225
Netanyahu, Benjamin, 23, 24, 26, 27, 29, 30, 31, 33, 34, 35, 36, 37, 38, 40, 41, 42, 43, 44, 45, 46, 47, 48, 49, 50, 59, 109, 110, 120, 121, 126, 173, 174, 193, 194, 198, 212, 216, 218, 219, 229, 231, 234, 236, 237, 238, 243, 246, 248, 249
Niebuhr, Reinhold, 234
Nirenberg, David, 106
North America, 77, 78, 100, 105, 162, 200, 217, 228
Norway, 22, 23, 37
Nostra Aetate, 17, 18, 72, 90, 94, 134, 135, 137, 139, 141
Notes on the Correct Way to Present Jews and Judaism in Preaching and Catechesis in the Roman Catholic Church, 72
Nova music festival, 57, 193

O

Occupied Palestinian Territory, 41, 199, 213, 243
Oesterreicher, John, 185
Open Letter to His Holiness, Pope Francis, and to the Faithful of the Catholic Church, 80
Operation Peace for Galilee (1982), 20, 100, 232
Operation Protective Edge (2014), 27
Orientalism, 196, 198
Origen, 71
Oslo Accords, 22, 23, 34
Ottoman Empire, 194

P

Palestine Liberation Organization (PLO), 17, 20, 21, 22, 24, 27, 28, 81, 100, 181, 232, 233
Palestine, State of, 21, 27, 28, 35, 56, 63, 92, 185, 187, 236
Palestinian Authority (PA), 22, 24, 25, 27, 28, 130, 181, 194
Palestinian Students, 141
Parents Circle—Family Forum (PCFF), 218
Passover, 25, 103, 186
Peel Commission, 194
Peres, Shimon, 23, 27
Pettit, Peter, 174
Pinnock, Sarah, 174
Pittsburgh, 162, 165
Pizzaballa, Pierbattista, 73, 250
pluralism, 102, 156, 228
Poland, 128, 210
Pontifical Biblical Commission (PBC), 91
Pope
  Benedict XVI, 60, 73, 89, 141
  Francis I, 27, 28, 31, 32, 47, 74, 75, 76, 79, 80, 87, 88, 90, 92, 93, 133, 134, 135, 136, 138, 139, 141, 147, 149, 150, 155, 157
  John Paul II, 20, 24, 25, 63, 69, 72, 74, 75, 86, 133, 135, 136, 141
  John XXIII, 74
  Paul VI, 17, 18, 19, 71, 135
  Pius X, 60, 71, 88
  Pius XII, 60
prayer, 31, 71, 102, 127, 130, 148, 149, 150, 151, 156, 182, 211
Presbyterian Church (USA), 199
principle of proportionality, 88
propaganda, 49, 57, 58, 109, 123, 140, 185
Protestant, 52, 55, 105, 107, 199, 209, 215, 216, 225
protests, 35, 42, 93, 116, 119, 121, 122, 128, 141, 145, 156, 165, 198

R

Rabin, Yitzhak, 22, 23, 194
racism, 18, 22, 107, 126, 127, 227, 228
Rafah, 35, 36, 37, 42, 168, 214, 229, 247
Rahner, Karl, 73
Ramadan, 33, 34, 151
Ramallah, 25, 33, 218
rape, 56, 57, 58, 59, 108, 193, 248
refugees, 16, 19, 35, 102, 139, 150, 177, 184, 211, 216, 227, 236
right of return, 17, 227, 236
right to self-defense, 116, 122, 140, 235
Rittner, Carol, 15, 51, 55, 234, 243
Roman Empire, 70, 198
Rome, 27, 61, 74, 87, 185
Rome Statute, 61
Rosen, David, 73
Roth, John K., 15, 174, 225, 243
Rubenstein, Richard, 215
Russia, 25, 38, 48, 136, 216, 217

S

Sabra, 20, 231, 232, 233
Sadat, Anwar, 19
safe zone, 37, 177
Said, Edward, 181
San Antonio, 209, 210, 211, 216
Saudi Arabia, 99
Schillebeeckx, Edward, 153
Schumer, Chuck, 33, 110, 173
Second Intifada, 25, 199
Second Vatican Council/Vatican II, 17, 20, 62, 63, 71, 72, 73, 133, 134, 135, 136, 137, 139, 141, 184, 185
Security Council (United Nations), 17, 18, 21, 34, 35, 38, 46, 181
Seelisberg, 183, 184, 187
September 11, 2001 (9/11), 135, 146, 212, 225
Seton Hill University, 161, 166

Settlers, 26, 106, 108, 120, 178, 179, 217, 218, 227, 228, 243, 246
sexual violence, 51, 56, 57, 58, 59, 166, 180, 244
Shabbat, 148, 156
Shafik, Minouche, 115, 116
Sharon, Ariel, 20, 24, 26, 100, 233
Shatila, 20, 233
Shatz, Adam, 136
Shoah, 23, 24, 76, 78, 85, 86, 101, 102, 108, 128, 136, 137, 214
Simchat Torah, 30
sin, 93, 214, 225, 228
Sinai Peninsula, 17, 18, 19
Sinwar, Yahya, 36, 40, 42, 45, 46
Sisterhood of Salaam Shalom, 164, 169
Six-Day War (1967), 17, 218
Smotrich, Bezalel, 109
Social Humility, 148, 150, 155, 157
Soelle, Dorothee, 215
South Africa, 32, 61, 122, 126, 197, 228
Soviet Union, 102
Spain, 21, 37, 162
Staatsräson, 136
starvation, 38, 181, 237, 248
stress test, 51, 93, 116, 204, 238, 243
Stress Test, 50, 51, 52, 145, 174, 175, 209, 234, 243, 247, 248, 249, 250
students, 115, 121, 122, 123, 124, 125, 128, 141, 145, 146, 147, 148, 149, 150, 151, 152, 153, 156, 178, 209, 210, 231
Sudan, 29, 86
suffering, 33, 45, 61, 63, 87, 107, 108, 109, 117, 121, 125, 136, 138, 146, 151, 161, 164, 165, 167, 169, 174, 183, 186, 187, 196, 209, 210, 214, 215, 219, 221, 229, 230, 231, 238, 239, 244, 248

Sukkot, 148
Sumud, 202
survivors, 15, 57, 85, 100, 125, 127, 166, 168, 169, 209, 210, 211, 212, 214, 226
Swidler, Leonard, 165
Swords of Iron War, 30
Syria, 18, 23, 29, 34, 47, 48, 49, 86, 102, 135, 184

T

teaching of contempt, 86
Tekumah, 168
Tel Aviv, 16, 23, 28, 34, 39, 42, 44, 45, 59, 81, 107
territorial sovereignty, 69, 71, 73, 79
terrorism/terrorists, 23, 31, 42, 44, 49, 103, 116, 122, 145, 173, 181, 211, 244
The Hague, 39, 47, 61, 62
theodicy, 209, 211, 212, 214, 215, 216, 217, 220, 221
Tito, Josip Broz, 56
Torah, 30, 75, 79, 196
trauma, 91, 162, 163, 166, 210, 219
Traverso, Enzo, 136
Tree of Life Synagogue, 165
Trinity University (Texas), 209
Turkey, 77, 136
two-state solution, 25, 29, 33, 34, 43, 55, 56, 74, 80, 87, 92, 109, 141, 146, 193, 218, 226, 236, 237, 243, 246, 249

U

U.S. Presidents
  Biden, Joe, 31, 33, 35, 36, 37, 39, 43, 44, 47, 50, 59, 60, 139, 211, 213, 230, 244
  Carter, Jimmy, 19
  Clinton, Bill, 24
  Truman, Harry, 16
  Trump, Donald, 28, 29, 33, 39, 47, 48, 107, 216, 217

Ukraine, 86, 135
UN High Commissioner for Human Rights, 169
Union Theological Seminary, 116, 121, 122, 124, 125
United Arab Emirates (UAE), 29
United Nations (UN), 15, 16, 17, 18, 21, 22, 25, 27, 34, 35, 36, 38, 39, 41, 43, 44, 46, 50, 55, 56, 57, 59, 61, 105, 126, 150, 169, 181, 183, 194, 197, 203, 213, 216, 227, 235, 236, 237
United Nations Educational, Scientific and Cultural Organization (UNESCO), 183
United Nations mandate, 105
United Nations Partition Plan, 194
University of Haifa, 231, 232
University of Pennsylvania, 115, 153
Urbi et Orbi, 139
US Capitol, 36, 40
US Congress, 37, 40
US Holocaust Memorial Museum, 15, 36, 211, 230
USC Shoah Foundation, 166

V

Vatican, 16, 18, 19, 20, 23, 48, 62, 63, 71, 72, 73, 80, 89, 92, 133, 134, 135, 136, 137, 139, 141, 152, 184, 185, 219, 235
Vatican Commission for Religious Relations with the Jews (CRRJ), 18, 23, 89, 90

W

Walzer, Michael, 75, 79
war crimes, 36, 38, 40, 47, 48, 51, 58, 61, 62, 81, 105, 126, 214, 235, 237
Washington, DC, 19, 22, 23, 24, 29, 146, 212, 216
Waxman, Dov, 228

West Bank, 17, 20, 22, 23, 24, 25, 27, 28, 29, 30, 33, 34, 39, 41, 45, 81, 104, 105, 107, 108, 120, 121, 125, 126, 127, 141, 166, 178, 179, 180, 181, 183, 198, 213, 217, 218, 226, 231, 236, 237, 243, 246, 247
Wiesel, Elie, 85, 231
Wilken, Robert, 70
Wilkinson, Jeffrey, 162
Williamson, Richard, 60
Wilzig, Ivan, 211
Wilzig, Siggi, 211
World Council of Churches (WCC), 31, 33, 71, 77, 203
World War I, 194
World War II, 15, 85, 88, 102, 134, 135, 136, 140, 226, 227, 230

Wye River Memorandum, 24

Y

Yad Vashem, 24, 100, 101, 168, 212, 219
Yemen, 39, 44
Yom Kippur War, 18, 48, 109
Yugoslavia, 56

Z

Zen Peacemakers, 219
Zionism/Zionists, 18, 22, 71, 104, 106, 116, 122, 126, 128, 133, 137, 164, 196, 197, 199, 216, 217, 226, 228, 236, 238, 239

iPub Cloud International

iPub Cloud International is a 501(c)(3) nonprofit publishing house dedicated to elevating the voices of the disenfranchised, marginalized, and those unable to afford the high costs of traditional publishing. As a women-owned and women-led organization, we also take immense pride in having individuals with disabilities in senior leadership roles, reflecting our mission of inclusivity and empowerment.

We are not just a publisher; we are a champion for change, seeking to amplify stories that matter. By fostering a culture of enlightenment and progress, we empower voices that inspire action, provoke thought, and pave the way for a more compassionate and understanding world. Our work touches lives—not only through the authors, contributors, and team members who make it possible but also through the readers and communities who engage with the transformative ideas we bring to light. At iPub Cloud International, every book, story, and idea we publish is a step toward building a brighter, more inclusive future.

iPub Cloud International
Poughkeepsie, NY 12603
Visit our website to stay up to date on your favorite writers and subscribe for news on new releases, events, and promotions:
www.iPubCloud.org
Join the conversation at Facebook.com/iPubCloud
Join our community at iPubForum.com

READ MORE FROM iPUB CLOUD iPub

SCAN ME!
TO REQUEST YOUR FREE COPY

THE DIALOGUE DECALOGUE
Ground Rules for Interreligious, Interideological Dialogue

WWW.iPUBCLOUD.ORG